Microsoft Azure Architect Technologies: Exam Guide AZ-300

A guide to preparing for the AZ-300 Microsoft Azure Architect Technologies certification exam

Sjoukje Zaal

BIRMINGHAM - MUMBAI

Microsoft Azure Architect Technologies: Exam Guide AZ-300

Commissioning Editor: Vijin Boricha
Acquisition Editor: Rahul Nair
Content Development Editor: Ronn Kurien
Senior Editor: Richard Brookes-Bland
Technical Editor: Mohd Riyan Khan
Copy Editor: Safis Editing
Project Coordinator: Anish Daniel
Proofreader: Safis Editing
Indexer: Pratik Shirodkar
Production Designer: Jyoti Chauhan

First published: January 2020

Production reference: 2170221

Published by Packt Publishing Ltd.
Livery Place
35 Livery Street
Birmingham
B3 2PB, UK.

ISBN 978-1-83855-353-1

www.packt.com

Packt.com

Subscribe to our online digital library for full access to over 7,000 books and videos, as well as industry leading tools to help you plan your personal development and advance your career. For more information, please visit our website.

Why subscribe?

- Spend less time learning and more time coding with practical eBooks and Videos from over 4,000 industry professionals

- Improve your learning with Skill Plans built especially for you

- Get a free eBook or video every month

- Fully searchable for easy access to vital information

- Copy and paste, print, and bookmark content

Did you know that Packt offers eBook versions of every book published, with PDF and ePub files available? You can upgrade to the eBook version at www.packt.com and as a print book customer, you are entitled to a discount on the eBook copy. Get in touch with us at customercare@packtpub.com for more details.

At www.packt.com, you can also read a collection of free technical articles, sign up for a range of free newsletters, and receive exclusive discounts and offers on Packt books and eBooks.

Contributors

About the author

Sjoukje Zaal is a management consultant, Microsoft cloud architect, and Microsoft Azure MVP with over 15 years' experience of providing architecture, development, consultancy, and design expertise. She works at Capgemini, a global leader in consulting, technology services, and digital transformation.

She loves to share her knowledge and is active in the Microsoft community as a co-founder of the Dutch user groups SP&C NL, MixUG, and the Global Mixed Reality Bootcamp. She is also a board member of the Global Azure Bootcamp and Azure Thursdays. She is a public speaker and is involved in organizing events. She has written several books, writes blogs, and is active in the Microsoft Tech Community. She is also part of the Diversity and Inclusion Advisory Board.

About the reviewers

Sander Rossel is a Microsoft-certified professional developer and author with experience and expertise in .NET and .NET Core, Azure, Azure DevOps, SQL Server, JavaScript, and other technologies. With his company, JUUN Software, he builds cloud-native applications and brings companies to the cloud. You can always reach Sander Rossel on LinkedIn (`/in/sanderrossel/`).

Stephane Eyskens is a cloud and cloud-native architect and digital transformation activist. He is a blogger, author, and speaker, and has a particular interest in hybrid architectures, modern authentication, and security in general, as well as artificial intelligence.

Packt is searching for authors like you

If you're interested in becoming an author for Packt, please visit `authors.packtpub.com` and apply today. We have worked with thousands of developers and tech professionals, just like you, to help them share their insight with the global tech community. You can make a general application, apply for a specific hot topic that we are recruiting an author for, or submit your own idea.

Table of Contents

Preface

This book is the successor of *Architecting Microsoft Azure Solutions – Exam Guide 70-535*, the book that I wrote only 2 years ago. I've noticed while writing this book that not only have most Azure resources got more functionalities, many more features have also been added to the Azure platform. This indicates how fast Azure is changing and how extremely difficult it is for professionals to keep up to date with this ever-evolving platform.

This book will prepare you for the AZ-300 exam, which is the most practical exam of the Azure Architect Expert series. By reading it, you will get updated with all those new functionalities, features, and resources. This book will cover all the exam objectives, giving you a complete overview of the objectives that are covered in the exam.

This book will start with deploying and configuring an infrastructure in Azure. You will learn how to analyze resource utilization and consumption. You will learn about storage accounts, Azure Virtual Networks, and Azure **Active Directory** (**AD**). Next, you will learn about implementing workloads and security in Azure, and how to create and deploy apps. Then, the focus in this book will switch to implementing authentication and securing data, and finally, how to develop for the cloud and for Azure storage.

Each chapter concludes with a *Further reading* section, which is a very important part of the book, because it will give you extra and sometimes crucial information for passing the AZ-300 exam. As the questions of the exam will change slightly over time and this book will eventually become outdated, the *Further reading* sections will be the place that provides access to all the updates.

Who this book is for

This book targets Azure solution architects who advise stakeholders and translate business requirements into secure, scalable, and reliable solutions. They should have advanced experience and knowledge of various aspects of IT operations, including networking, virtualization, identity, security, business continuity, disaster recovery, data management, budgeting, and governance. This role requires managing how decisions in each area affect an overall solution.

What this book covers

Chapter 1, *Analyzing Resource Utilization and Consumption*, covers how to use Azure Monitor, how to create and analyze metrics and alerts, how to create a baseline for resources, how to configure diagnostic settings on resources, how to view alerts in Log Analytics, and how to utilize Log Search Query functions.

Chapter 2, *Creating and Configuring Storage Accounts*, covers Azure storage accounts, creating and configuring a storage account, installing and using Azure Storage Explorer, configuring network access to the storage account, generating and managing SAS, and how to implement Azure storage replication.

Chapter 3, *Implementing and Managing Virtual Machines*, covers virtual machines, availability sets, provisioning VMs, VM scale sets, modifying and deploying ARM templates, and how to configure Azure Disk Encryption for VMs.

Chapter 4, *Implementing and Managing Virtual Networking*, covers Azure VNet, IP addresses, how to configure subnets and VNets, configuring private and public IP addresses, and user-defined routes.

Chapter 5, *Creating Connectivity between Virtual Networks*, covers VNet peering, how to create and configure VNet peering, VNet-to-VNet, how to create and configure VNet-to-VNet, verifying virtual network connectivity, and compares VNet peering with VNet-to-VNet.

Chapter 6, *Managing Azure Active Directory (Azure AD)*, covers how to create and manage users and groups, adding and managing guest accounts, performing bulk user updates, configuring self-service password reset, working with Azure AD join, and how to add custom domains.

Chapter 7, *Implementing and Managing Hybrid Identities*, covers Azure AD Connect, how to install Azure AD Connect, managing Azure AD Connect, and how to manage password sync and password writeback.

Chapter 8, *Migrating Servers to Azure*, covers Azure Migrate, the different Azure Migrate tools, and migrating on-premises machines to Azure.

Chapter 9, *Configuring Serverless Computing*, covers how to create and manage objects, managing a logic app resource, Azure Event Grid, and Azure Service Bus.

Chapter 10, *Implementing Application Load Balancing*, covers Azure Application Gateway, how to configure an application gateway, implementing frontend IP configurations, configuring load balancing rules, managing application load balancing, and Azure Front Door.

Chapter 11, *Integrating On-Premises Networks with Azure Virtual Network*, covers Azure VPN gateway, how to create and configure an Azure VPN gateway, creating and configuring an S2S VPN, verifying on-premises connectivity, managing on-premises connectivity with Azure, and VNet-to-VNet.

Chapter 12, *Managing Role-Based Access Control (RBAC)*, covers how to configure access to Azure resources by assigning roles, configuring management access to Azure, creating a custom role, Azure Policy, and how to implement and assign Azure policies.

Chapter 13, *Implementing Multi-Factor Authentication (MFA)*, covers Azure MFA, how to configure user accounts for MFA, how to configure verification methods, how to configure fraud alerts, configuring bypass options, and how to configure trusted IPs.

Chapter 14, *Creating Web Apps by Using PaaS*, covers App Services, App Service plans, web apps for containers, WebJobs, and how to enable diagnostics logging.

Chapter 15, *Designing and Developing Apps That Run in Containers*, covers Azure Container Instances, how to implement an application that runs on an Azure Container Instance, creating a container image by using a Docker file, publishing an image to the Azure Container Registry, Azure Kubernetes Service, and how to create an Azure Kubernetes Service.

Chapter 16, *Implementing Authentication*, covers App Services authentication, how to implement Windows-integrated authentication, implementing authentication by using certificates, OAuth2 authentication in Azure AD, how to implement OAuth2 authentication, implementing tokens, managed identities, and how to implement managed identities for Azure resources' Service Principal authentication.

Chapter 17, *Implementing Secure Data Solutions*, covers data security in Azure, how to encrypt and decrypt data at rest, encrypting and decrypting data in transit, encrypting data with Always Encrypted, Azure Confidential Compute, and how to create, read, update, and delete keys, secrets, and certificates by using the Key Vault API.

Chapter 18, *Developing Solutions that Use Cosmos DB Storage*, covers how to create, read, update, and delete data by using the appropriate APIs, partitioning schemes, and how to set the appropriate consistency level for operations.

Chapter 19, *Developing Solutions that Use a Relational Database*, covers Azure SQL Database, how to provision and configure an Azure SQL Database, create, read, update, and delete data tables by using code, how to configure elastic pools for Azure SQL Database, and Azure SQL Database Managed Instances.

Chapter 20, *Message-Based Integration Architecture and Autoscaling*, covers different Azure integration services, how to route events with Azure Event Grid, designing an effective messaging architecture, implementing autoscaling rules and patterns, and how to implement code that addresses the transient state.

Chapter 21, *Mock Questions*, consists of mock questions for the readers to test their knowledge. It tries to cover all the topics under the scope of the exam and challenges the reader's understanding of the topics.

Chapter 22, *Mock Answers*, contains the answers to the questions in the previous chapter.

To get the most out of this book

An Azure subscription is required to get through this book. Any other software and hardware requirements are mentioned in detail in the *Technical requirements* section of the respective chapters.

Download the example code files

You can download the example code files for this book from your account at www.packt.com. If you purchased this book elsewhere, you can visit www.packtpub.com/support and register to have the files emailed directly to you.

You can download the code files by following these steps:

1. Log in or register at www.packt.com.
2. Select the **Support** tab.
3. Click on **Code Downloads**.
4. Enter the name of the book in the **Search** box and follow the onscreen instructions.

Once the file is downloaded, please make sure that you unzip or extract the folder using the latest version of:

- WinRAR/7-Zip for Windows
- Zipeg/iZip/UnRarX for Mac
- 7-Zip/PeaZip for Linux

The code bundle for the book is also hosted on GitHub at `https://github.com/PacktPublishing/Microsoft-Azure-Architect-Technologies-Exam-Guide-AZ-300`. In case there's an update to the code, it will be updated on the existing GitHub repository.

We also have other code bundles from our rich catalog of books and videos available at `https://github.com/PacktPublishing/`. Check them out!

Download the color images

We also provide a PDF file that has color images of the screenshots/diagrams used in this book. You can download it here: `https://static.packt-cdn.com/downloads/9781838553531_ColorImages.pdf`.

Conventions used

There are a number of text conventions used throughout this book.

`CodeInText`: Indicates code words in text, database table names, folder names, filenames, file extensions, pathnames, dummy URLs, user input, and Twitter handles. Here is an example: "Create a new one and call it `PacktVMGroup`."

A block of code is set as follows:

```
"policyRule": {
            "if": {
                "allOf": [
                    {
                        "field": "type",
                        "equals": "Microsoft.Storage/storageAccounts"
                    },
```

When we wish to draw your attention to a particular part of a code block, the relevant lines or items are set in bold:

```
"policyRule": {
            "if": {
            "allOf": [
                {
                    "field": "type",
                    "equals": "Microsoft.Storage/storageAccounts"
                },
```

Any command-line input or output is written as follows:

```
Connect-AzAccount
Select-AzSubscription -SubscriptionId "********-****-****-****-***********"
```

Bold: Indicates a new term, an important word, or words that you see onscreen. For example, words in menus or dialog boxes appear in the text like this. Here is an example: "In the **Overview** blade of Azure AD, in the left menu, select **Groups** | **All groups**. Select + **New group** from the top menu."

Warnings or important notes appear like this.

Tips and tricks appear like this.

Get in touch

Feedback from our readers is always welcome.

General feedback: If you have questions about any aspect of this book, mention the book title in the subject of your message and email us at customercare@packtpub.com.

Errata: Although we have taken every care to ensure the accuracy of our content, mistakes do happen. If you have found a mistake in this book, we would be grateful if you would report this to us. Please visit www.packtpub.com/support/errata, selecting your book, clicking on the Errata Submission Form link, and entering the details.

Piracy: If you come across any illegal copies of our works in any form on the Internet, we would be grateful if you would provide us with the location address or website name. Please contact us at copyright@packt.com with a link to the material.

If you are interested in becoming an author: If there is a topic that you have expertise in and you are interested in either writing or contributing to a book, please visit authors.packtpub.com.

Reviews

Please leave a review. Once you have read and used this book, why not leave a review on the site that you purchased it from? Potential readers can then see and use your unbiased opinion to make purchase decisions, we at Packt can understand what you think about our products, and our authors can see your feedback on their book. Thank you!

For more information about Packt, please visit packt.com.

Section 1: Deploying and Configuring Infrastructure

As this section's objective, you will learn how to deploy and configure an infrastructure in Azure.

This section will contain the following chapters:

- Chapter 1, *Analyzing Resource Utilization and Consumption*
- Chapter 2, *Creating and Configuring Storage Accounts*
- Chapter 3, *Implementing and Managing Virtual Machines*
- Chapter 4, *Implementing and Managing Virtual Networking*
- Chapter 5, *Creating Connectivity between Virtual Networks*
- Chapter 6, *Managing Azure Active Directory (Azure AD)*
- Chapter 7, *Implementing and Managing Hybrid Identities*

Analyzing Resource Utilization and Consumption

1

This book will cover all of the exam objectives for the AZ-300 exam. When relevant, we will provide you with extra information and further reading guidance about the different topics of this book.

This chapter introduces the first objective, which is going to cover the *Deploy and Configure Infrastructure*. It will cover Azure Monitor and the various aspects of it. You will learn how to create and analyze metrics and alerts and how to create a baseline for resources. We are going to look at how to create action groups and how to configure diagnostic settings on resources. Finally, we are going to cover Azure Log Analytics and how to utilize log search query functions.

The following topics will be covered in this chapter:

- Understanding Azure Monitor
- Creating and analyzing metrics and alerts
- Creating a baseline for resources
- Configuring diagnostic settings on resources
- Viewing alerts in Log Analytics
- Utilizing log search query functions

 The demos in this chapter use an Azure Windows VM. To create a Windows VM in Azure, you can refer to the following walk-through: `https://docs.microsoft.com/en-us/azure/virtual-machines/windows/quick-create-powershell`.

Understanding Azure Monitor

Azure Monitor is a monitoring solution in the Azure portal that delivers a comprehensive solution for collecting, analyzing, and acting on telemetry from the cloud and on-premises environments. It can be used to monitor various aspects (for instance, the performance of applications) and identify issues affecting those applications and other resources that depend on them.

The data that is collected by Azure Monitor fits into two fundamental types: metrics and logs. Metrics describe an aspect of a system at a particular point in time and are displayed in numerical values. They are capable of supporting near real-time scenarios. Logs are different from metrics. They contain data that is organized into records, with different sets of properties for each type. Data such as events, traces, and performance data are stored as logs. They can then be combined for analysis purposes.

Azure Monitor supports data collection from a variety of Azure resources, which are all displayed on the overview page in the Azure portal. Azure Monitor provides the following metrics and logs:

- **Application monitoring data**: This will consist of data about the functionality and performance of the application and the code that is written, regardless of its platform.
- **Guest OS monitoring data**: This will consist of data about the operating system on which your application is running. This could be running in any cloud or on-premises environment.
- **Azure resource monitoring data**: This will consist of data about the operation of an Azure resource.
- **Azure subscription monitoring data**: This will consist of data about the operation and management of an Azure subscription, as well as data about the health and operation of Azure itself.
- **Azure tenant monitoring data**: This will consist of data about the operation of tenant-level Azure services, such as Azure Active Directory.

 Azure Monitor now integrates the capabilities of Log Analytics and Application Insights together. You can also keep using Log Analytics and Application Insights on their own.

The following diagram gives a high-level view of Azure Monitor. On the left, there are the sources of monitoring data, in the center are the data stores, and on the right are the different functions that Azure Monitor performs with this collected data, such as analysis, alerting, and streaming to external systems:

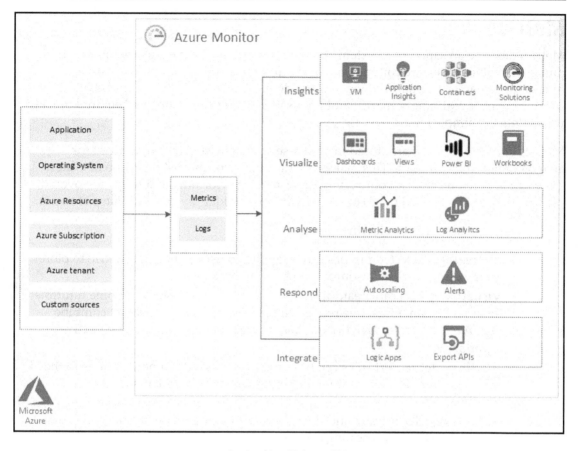

Overview of Azure Monitor capabilities

Now that we have some basic knowledge about Azure Monitor, we are going to look at how to analyze alerts and metrics across subscriptions.

Creating and analyzing metrics and alerts

To analyze alerts and metrics across Azure Monitor, we need to go to the monitoring resource inside the Azure portal. In the upcoming sections, we will set up metrics and alerts and show you how to analyze them.

Metrics

Metrics describe an aspect of a system at a particular point in time and are displayed in numerical values. They are collected at regular intervals and are identified with a timestamp, a name, a value, and one or more defining labels. They are capable of supporting near real-time scenarios and are useful for alerting. Alerts can be fired quickly with relatively simple logic.

Metrics in Azure Monitor are stored in a time-series database that is optimized for analyzing timestamped data. This makes metrics suited for the fast detection of issues. They can help to detect how your service or system is performing, but to get the overall picture, they typically need to be combined with logs to identify the root cause of issues.

You can use metrics for the following scenarios:

- **Analyzing**: Collected metrics can be analyzed using a chart in Metric Explorer. Metrics from various resources can be compared as well.
- **Visualizing**: You can create an Azure Monitor workbook to combine multiple datasets into an interactive report. Azure Monitor workbooks can combine text, Azure metrics, analytics queries, and parameters into rich interactive reports.
- **Alerting**: Metric alert rules can be configured to send out notifications to the user. They can also take automatic action when the metric value crosses a threshold.
- **Automating**: To increase and decrease resources based on metric values that cross a threshold, autoscaling can be used.
- **Exporting**: Metrics can be streamed to an Event Hub to route them to external systems. Metrics can also be routed to logs in the Log Analytics workspace, to be analyzed together with the Azure Monitor logs and to store the metric values for more than 93 days.
- **Retrieving**: Metric values can be retrieved from a command line using PowerShell cmdlets and the CLI, and from custom applications using the Azure Monitoring REST API.
- **Archiving**: Metric data can be archived in Azure Storage. It can store the performance or health history of your resource for compliance, auditing, or offline reporting purposes.

There are four main sources of metrics that are collected by Azure Monitor. Once they are collected and stored in the Azure Monitor Metric database, they can be evaluated together regardless of their source:

- **Platform metrics**: These metrics give you visibility of the health and performance of your Azure resources. Without any configuration required, a distinct set of metrics is created for each type of Azure resource. By default, they are collected at a one-minute frequency. However, you can configure them to run on a different frequency as well.
- **Guest OS metrics**: These metrics are collected from the guest operating system of a virtual machine. To enable guest OS metrics for Windows machines, the Windows Diagnostic Extension agent needs to be installed. For Linux machines, the InfluxData Telegraf Agent needs to be installed.
- **Application metrics**: These metrics are created by Application Insights. They can help to detect performance issues for your custom applications and track trends in how the application is being used.
- **Custom metrics**: These are metrics that you define manually. You can define them in your custom applications that are monitored by Application Insights or you can define custom metrics for an Azure service using the custom metrics API.

Multi-dimensional metrics

Metric data often has limited information to provide context for collected values. This challenge is addressed by Azure Monitor using multi-dimensional metrics. The dimensions of the metrics are name-value pairs that store additional data that describe the metric value. For example, a metric called **available disk space** could have a dimension called *Drive* with the values *C:, D,* stored inside. This value would allow the viewing of available disk space across all drives, or for each drive individually.

In the next section, we are going to create a metric in the Azure portal.

Creating a metric

To display the metrics for the various Azure resources in Azure Monitor, perform the following steps:

1. Navigate to the Azure portal by opening `https://portal.azure.com`.
2. In the left-hand menu, select **Monitor** to open the **Azure Monitor** overview blade.
3. First, we're going to look at metrics. Therefore, in the left-hand menu, select **Metrics** or select the **Explore Metrics** button from the overview blade.
4. In the **Metrics** overview blade, click on the **+ Select a scope** button. A new blade will open up where you can select the subscription, the resource group, and the resource type. Select the subscription that is used for the Linux VM, select the resource group, and then select the VM. You can filter by other resource types, as well:

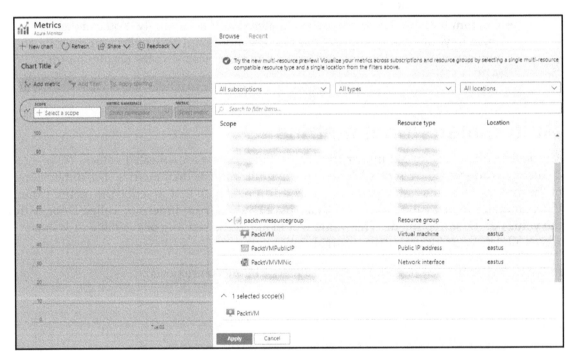

Selecting the resources

5. Click on **Apply**.

6. Then, you can select the metric type. Select **CPU Credits Consumed**, for instance:

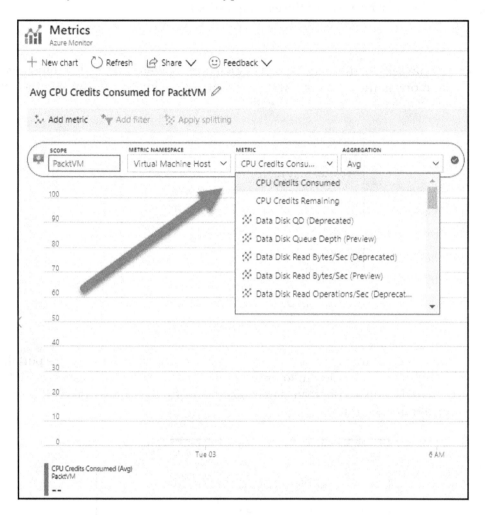

Metric type

Take some time to look at the different metrics that you can choose from. This may be a part of the exam questions.

7. You can select a different type of aggregation as well, such as the count, average, and more, in the filter box. At the top-right of the blade, you can select a different time range for your metric as well:

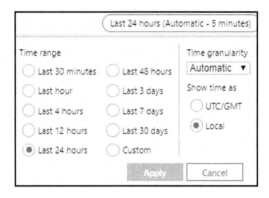

Time ranges

8. You can also pin this metric to the overview dashboard in the Azure portal. Therefore, click on the **Pin to dashboard** button, and then choose to pin it to the current dashboard or create a new dashboard for it. For now, select **Pin to current dashboard**:

Pin metric to dashboard

9. If you now select **Dashboard** from the left-hand menu, you'll see that this metric is added to it. This way, you can easily analyze this metric without the need to open Azure Monitor.

 Metrics are also available directly from the Azure resource blades. So, for instance, if you have a VM, go to the VM resource by selecting it. Then, in the left-hand menu, under **Monitoring**, you can select **Metrics**.

In the next section, we're going to look at how to set up and analyze alerts in Azure Monitor.

Alerts

With alerts, Azure can proactively notify you when critical conditions occur in the Azure or on-premises environment. Alerts can also attempt to take corrective actions automatically. Alert rules that are based on metrics will provide near real-time alerting, based on the metric. Alerts that are created based on logs can merge data from different resources together.

The alerts in Azure Monitor use action groups, which are unique sets of recipients and actions that can be shared across multiple rules. These action groups can use Webhooks to start external actions, based on the requirements that are set up for this alert. These external actions can then be picked up by different Azure resources, such as Runbooks, Functions, or Logic Apps. Webhooks can also be used for adding these alerts to external **IT Service Management (ITSM)** tools.

You can also set alerts for all of the different Azure resources. In the following sections, we are going to create an alert.

Creating an alert and an action group

To create an alert, perform the following steps:

1. From the **Azure Monitor** overview blade, in the left-hand menu, select **Alerts**. You can also go to the alerts settings by clicking on **Create alert** to create an alert directly.

2. In the **Alerts** blade, click on **+ New alert rule** in the top menu:

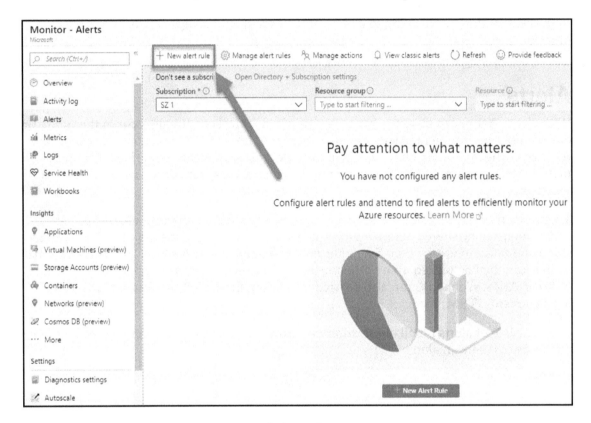

Creating a new alert

3. The **Create rule** blade is displayed. Here, you can create the rule and action groups. To create a new rule, you need to first select the resource. Click on the **Select** button under the **RESOURCE** section:

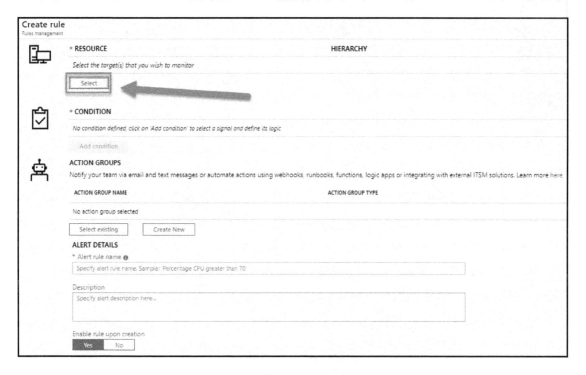

Creating a new rule

4. In the next blade, you can filter by the subscription and resource type. Select **Virtual machines**:

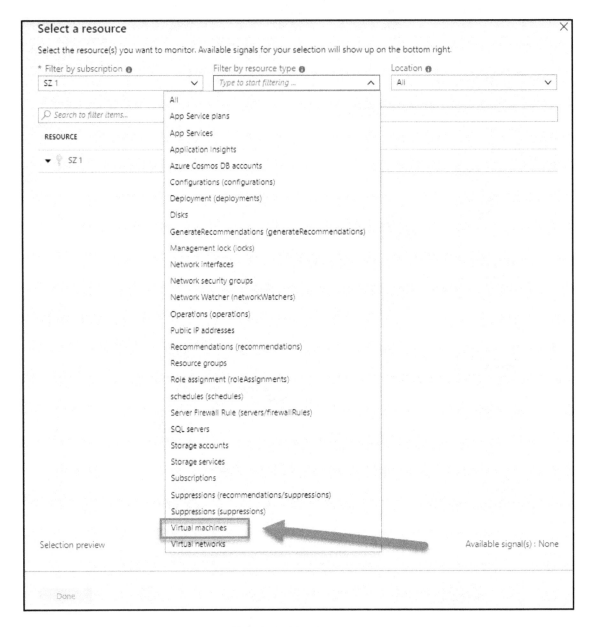

Filtering by subscription and resource type

5. Select the VM from the list and click **Done**.
6. Now that we have a resource selected, we're going to set up the condition. Click on **Add condition**.
7. The condition blade is open, and so we can filter by a certain signal. Select **Percentage CPU** and click **Done**:

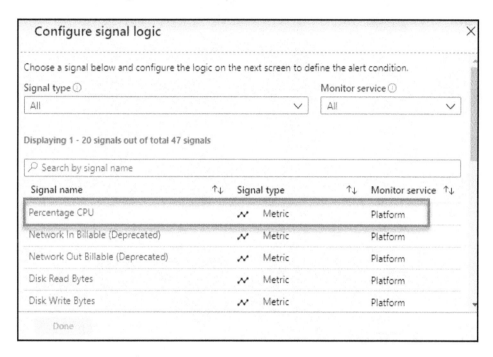

Filtering on a signal

8. Next, you can set the alert logic for this alert. You can choose multiple operators, set the aggregation type, and set the threshold value for this alert. Set the following:
   - **Threshold: Static** (in the next section, we are going to cover the difference between static and dynamic thresholds)
   - **Operator: Greater than**
   - **Aggregation type: Average**
   - **Threshold Value: 90%**
9. Leave **Evaluated based on** with its default settings.

10. This alert will notify you when the CPU of the virtual machines is greater than 90% over a 5-minute period. Azure Monitor will check this every minute:

Setting condition values

11. Click on **Done** to create this condition.

12. Now, we have to create an action group to send the alert to. This is then responsible for handling the alert and taking further action on it. The action group that you create here can be reused across other alerts as well. So, in our case, we will create an email action group that will send out an email to a certain email address. After its creation, you can add this existing action group to other alerts. Under **Action group**, select the **Create new** button.

13. In the **Action Group** blade, add the following settings:
    - **Action group name**: Type `Send email`.
    - **Short name**: Type `email`.
    - **Subscription**: Select the subscription where the VM is created.
    - **Resource group**: Select **Default-ActivityLogAlerts** (to be created).

14. Then, we have to provide the actual action. Add the following values:
    - **Action name**: `email`
    - **Action type**: **Email/SMS/Push/Voice**

15. Then, select **Edit details** and select the **Email** checkbox. Provide an email address and click on the **OK** button:

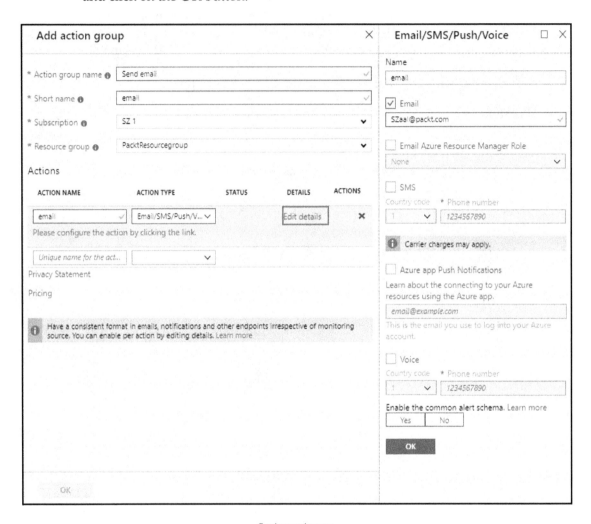

Creating an action group

16. Click on **OK** again.

17. Finally, you have to specify an alert name, set the severity level of the alert, and click on **Create alert rule**:

Alert settings

We have now created an alert and an action group that will alert a user via email when the CPU goes over 90%. In the next section, we're going to create a baseline for resources.

Creating a baseline for resources

To create a baseline for your resources, Azure offers Metric Alerts with Dynamic Thresholds. Using Dynamic Thresholds, you don't have to manually identify and set thresholds for alerts, which is an enhancement to Azure Monitor Metric Alerts. Advanced machine learning capabilities are used by the alert rule to learn the historical behavior of the metrics while identifying patterns and anomalies that indicate possible service issues. With Dynamic Thresholds, you can create an alert rule once and apply it automatically to different Azure resources during the creation of the resources.

In the following overview, you will find some scenarios when Dynamic Thresholds to metrics alerts are recommended:

- **Scalable alerting**: Dynamic Thresholds are capable of creating tailored thresholds for hundreds of metric series at a time. However, this is as easy as creating an alert rule for one single metric. They can be created using the Azure portal or **Azure Resource Manager (ARM)** templates and the ARM API. This scalable approach is useful when applying multiple resources or dealing with metric dimensions. This will translate to a significant time-saving on the creation of alert rules and management.
- **Intuitive Configuration**: You can set up metric alerts using high-level concepts with Dynamic Thresholds, so you don't need to have extensive domain knowledge about the metric.
- **Smart Metric Pattern Recognition**: By using a unique machine learning technology, Azure can automatically detect metric patterns and adapt to metric changes over time. The algorithm used in Dynamic Thresholds is designed to prevent wide (low recall) or noisy (low precision) thresholds that don't have an expected pattern.

In the next section, we're going to configure diagnostic settings on resources.

Configuring diagnostic settings on resources

You can also configure diagnostic settings on different Azure resources. There are two types of diagnostic logs available in Azure Monitor:

- **Tenant logs**: These logs consist of all of the tenant-level services that exist outside of an Azure subscription. An example of this is the Azure Active Directory logs.
- **Resource logs**: These logs consist of all of the data from the resources that are deployed inside an Azure subscription, for example, virtual machines, storage accounts, and network security groups.

The contents of the resource logs are different for every Azure resource. These logs differ from guest OS-level diagnostic logs. To collect OS-level logs, an agent needs to be installed on the virtual machine. The diagnostic logs don't require an agent to be installed; they can be accessed directly from the Azure portal.

The logs that can be accessed are stored inside a storage account and can be used for auditing or manual inspection purposes. You can specify the retention time in days by using the resource diagnostic settings. You can also stream the logs to event hubs to analyze them in Power BI or insert them into a third-party service. These logs can also be analyzed with Azure Monitor. Then, there will be no need to store them in a storage account first.

Enabling diagnostic settings

To enable the diagnostic settings for resources, perform the following steps:

1. Navigate to the Azure portal by opening `https://portal.azure.com`.
2. Go to the VM again. Make sure that the VM is running, and in the left-hand menu, under **Monitoring**, select **Diagnostic settings**.
3. The **Diagnostic Settings** blade will open up. You will need to select a storage account where the metrics can be stored.

4. Click on the **Enable guest-level monitoring** button to update the diagnostic settings for the virtual machine:

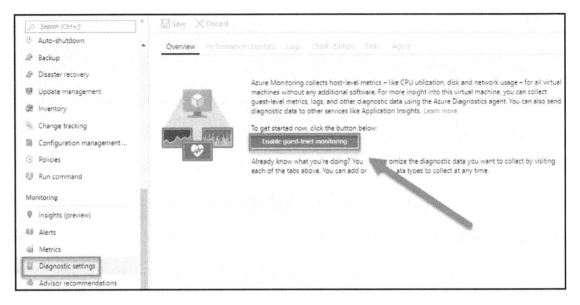

Enabling diagnostic settings for a virtual machine

5. When the settings are updated, you can go to **Metrics** in the top menu to set the metrics that are collected. The **syslog** blade is used for setting the minimum log level.

6. New metrics will be available from the metrics blade after enabling diagnostic logging in Azure Monitor. You can analyze them in the same way that we did earlier in this chapter, in the *Metrics* section.

In the next section, we're going to look at the Azure Log Analytics service, which is now a part of Azure Monitor as well.

Viewing alerts in Log Analytics

Azure Log Analytics is a service that collects telemetry data from various Azure resources and on-premises resources. All of that data is stored inside a Log Analytics workspace, which is based on Azure Data Explorer. It uses the Kusto query language, which is also used by Azure Data Explorer to retrieve and analyze the data.

Analyzing this data can be done from Azure Monitor. All of the analysis functionalities are integrated there. The term **Log Analytics** now primarily applies to the blade in the Azure portal where you can analyze metric data.

Before we can display, monitor, and query the logs from Azure Monitor, we need to create a Log Analytics workspace. For that, we have to perform the following steps:

1. Navigate to the Azure portal by opening `https://portal.azure.com`.
2. Click on **Create a resource**.
3. Type `Log Analytics` in the search box and create a new workspace.
4. Add the following values:
   - **Log Analytics workspace**: Type `PacktWorkspace` (the name for this Log Analytics workspace needs to be unique; if the name is already taken, specify another name).
   - **Subscription**: Select a subscription.
   - **Resource group**: Create a new one and call it `PacktWorkspace`.
   - **Location**: Select **West US**.
   - **Pricing tier**: Keep the default one, which is **per GB**.
5. Click on the **OK** button to create the workspace.

 You can also create this workspace from Azure Monitor. Go to the **Azure Monitor** blade, and under **Insights** in the left-hand menu, select **More**. When no workspace has been created, Azure will ask to create one.

Now that we have created a Log Analytics workspace, we can use it inside Azure Monitor to create some queries to retrieve data. We will do this in the next section.

Utilizing log search query functions

Azure Monitor is now integrated with the features and capabilities that Log Analytics was offering. This also includes creating search queries across the different logs and metrics by using the Kusto query language.

To retrieve any type of data from Azure Monitor, a query is required. Whether you are configuring an alert rule, analyzing data in the Azure portal, retrieving data using the Azure Monitor Logs API, or being notified of a particular condition, a query is used.

The following list provides an overview of all of the different ways queries are used by Azure Monitor:

- **Portal**: From the Azure portal, interactive analysis of log data can be performed. In there, you can create and edit queries and analyze the results in a variety of formats and visualizations.
- **Dashboards**: The results of a query can be pinned to a dashboard. This way, results can be visualized and shared with other users.
- **Views**: By using the View Designer in Azure Monitor, you can create custom views of your data. This data is provided by queries as well.
- **Alert rules**: Alert rules are also made up of queries.
- **Export**: Exports of data to Excel or Power BI are created with queries. The query defines the data to export.
- **Azure Monitor Logs API**: The Azure Monitor Logs API allows any REST API client to retrieve log data from the workspace. The API request includes a query to retrieve the data.
- **PowerShell**: You can run a PowerShell script from a command line or an Azure Automation runbook that uses `Get-AzOperationalInsightsSearchResults` to retrieve log data from Azure Monitor. You need to create a query for this cmdlet to retrieve the data.

In the following section, we are going to create some queries to retrieve data from the logs in Azure Monitor.

Querying logs in Azure Monitor

To query logs in Azure Monitor, perform the following steps:

1. Navigate to the Azure portal by opening `https://portal.azure.com`.
2. In the left-hand menu, select **Monitor** to open the **Azure Monitor** overview blade. Under **Insights**, select **More**. This will open the Log Analytics workspace that we created in the previous step.

3. On the overview page, click on **Logs** in the top menu. This will open the Azure Monitor query editor:

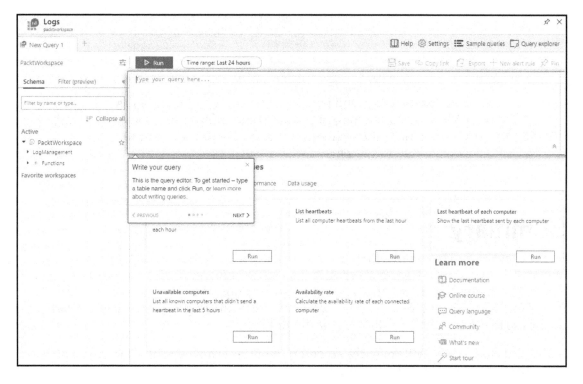

Azure Monitor query editor

4. Here, you can select some default queries. They are displayed at the bottom part of the screen. There are queries for retrieving unavailable computers, the last heartbeat of a computer, and much more. Add the following queries to the query editor window to retrieve data:

- This query will retrieve the top 10 computers with the most error events over the last day:

```
Event | where (EventLevelName == "Error") | where
(TimeGenerated > ago(1days)) | summarize ErrorCount =
count() by Computer | top 10 by ErrorCount desc
```

- This query will create a line chart with the processor utilization for each computer from the last week:

```
Perf | where ObjectName == "Processor" and CounterName
== "% Processor Time" | where TimeGenerated between
(startofweek(ago(7d)) .. endofweek(ago(7d)) ) |
summarize avg(CounterValue) by Computer,
bin(TimeGenerated, 5min) | render timechart
```

 A detailed overview and tutorial on how to get started with the Kusto query language are beyond the scope of this book. If you want to find out more about this query language, you can refer to `https://docs.microsoft.com/en-us/azure/azure-monitor/log-query/get-started-queries`.

Summary

In this chapter, we covered the first objective of the *Deploy and Configure Infrastructure* objective. We covered the various aspects of Azure Monitor and how you can use metrics to monitor all of your Azure resources and alerts to get notified when certain things are happening with your Azure resources. We also used Azure Log Analytics and created queries so that we could get valuable data out of the logs.

In the next chapter, we will cover the second part of this exam objective. In that chapter, we will cover how to create and configure storage accounts.

Questions

Answer the following questions to test your knowledge of the information in this chapter. You can find the answers in the *Assessments* section at the end of this book:

1. Is Azure Log Analytics now a part of Azure Monitor?
   - Yes
   - No

2. Suppose that you want to create a query to retrieve specific log data from a virtual machine. Do you need to write a SQL statement to retrieve this?
   - Yes
   - No

3. Are action groups used to enable metrics for Azure Monitor?
   - Yes
   - No

Further reading

You can check out the following links for more information about the topics that were covered in this chapter:

- **Azure Monitor overview**: https://docs.microsoft.com/en-us/azure/azure-monitor/overview
- **Azure Resource logs overview**: https://docs.microsoft.com/en-us/azure/azure-monitor/platform/diagnostic-logs-overview
- **Overview of log queries in Azure Monitor**: https://docs.microsoft.com/en-us/azure/azure-monitor/log-query/log-query-overview
- **Create custom views by using View Designer in Azure Monitor**: https://docs.microsoft.com/en-us/azure/azure-monitor/platform/view-designer

2
Creating and Configuring Storage Accounts

In the previous chapter, we covered the first part of this book's objective by covering how to analyze resource utilization and consumption in Azure. We covered how to monitor different Azure resources using Azure Monitor, and how to use Azure Log Analytics to query logs.

This chapter will introduce a new objective in terms of implementing and managing storage. In this chapter, we are going to cover the different types of storage accounts, and you will learn which types are available for storing your data in Azure. We will also cover how to install Azure Storage Explorer, which can be used to manage data inside Azure Storage accounts. We are going to look at how to secure data using **Shared Access Signatures** (**SAS**) and how to implement storage replication to keep data safe.

The following topics will be covered in this chapter:

- Understanding Azure Storage accounts
- Creating and configuring a storage account
- Installing and using Azure Storage Explorer
- Configuring network access to the storage account
- SAS and access keys
- Implementing Azure Storage replication

Technical requirements

This chapter will use Azure PowerShell (`https://docs.microsoft.com/en-us/powershell/azure/install-az-ps?view=azps-1.8.0`) for examples.

The source code for our sample application can be downloaded from `https://github.com/PacktPublishing/Microsoft-Azure-Architect-Technologies-Exam-Guide-AZ-300/tree/master/Chapter02`.

Understanding Azure Storage accounts

Azure offers a variety of types of storage accounts that can be used to store all sorts of files in Azure. You can store files, documents, and datasets, but also blobs and **Virtual Hard Disks** (**VHDs**). There is even a type of storage account for archiving, specifically. In the next section, we are going to look at the different types of storage accounts, and storage account replication types, that Azure has to offer.

Storage account types

Azure Storage offers three different account types, which can be used for blob, table, file, and queue storage.

General-purpose v1 (GPv1)

The **General-Purpose v1** (**GPv1**) storage account is the oldest type of storage account. It offers storage for page blobs, block blobs, files, queues, and tables, but it is not the most cost-effective storage account type. It is the only storage account type that can be used for the classic deployment model. It doesn't support the latest features, such as access tiers.

Blob storage

The blob storage account offers all of the features of `StorageV2` accounts, except that it only supports block blobs (and append blobs). Page blobs are not supported. It offers access tiers, which consist of hot, cool, and archive storage, and which will be covered later in this chapter, in the *Access tiers* section.

General-purpose v2 (GPv2)

StorageV2 is the newest type of storage account, and it combines V1 storage with blob storage. It offers all of the latest features, such as access tiers for blob storage, with a reduction in costs. Microsoft recommends using this account type over the V1 and blob storage account types.

V1 storage accounts can easily be upgraded to V2.

> For more information on pricing and billing for these different account types, you can refer to the following pricing page: https://azure.microsoft.com/en-us/pricing/details/storage/.

Storage replication types

Data that is stored in Azure is always replicated to ensure durability and high availability. This way, it is protected from unplanned and planned events, such as network or power outages, natural disasters, and terrorism. It also ensures that, during these types of events, your storage account still meets the SLA. Data can be replicated within the same data center, across zonal data centers within the same region, and across different regions. These replication types are named **Locally Redundant Storage (LRS)**, **Zone-Redundant Storage (ZRS)**, **Geo-Redundant Storage (GRS)**, **Geo-Zone-Redundant Storage (GZRS)**, and **Read-Access Geo-Redundant Storage (RA-GRS)**, and they will be covered in more detail in the upcoming sections.

> You choose a replication type when you create a new storage account. Storage accounts can be created inside the Azure portal, as well as from PowerShell or the CLI.

Locally redundant storage

LRS is the cheapest option and replicates the data three times within the same data center. When you make a write request to your storage account, it will be synchronously written during this request to all three replicas. The request is committed when the data is completely replicated. With LRS, the data will be replicated across multiple update domains and fault domains within one storage scale unit.

Zone-redundant storage

ZRS replicates three copies across two or three data centers. The data is written synchronously to all three replicas, in one or two regions. It also replicates the data three times inside the same data center where the data resided, just like LRS. ZRS provides high availability with synchronous replication across three Azure availability zones.

Geo-redundant storage

GRS replicates the data three times within the same region, like ZRS, and replicates three copies to other regions asynchronously. Using GRS, the replica isn't available for read or write access unless Microsoft initiates a failover to the secondary region. In the case of a failover, you'll have read and write access to that data after the failover has completed.

Geo-zone-redundant storage

At the time of writing this book, GZRS is in preview. Together with maximum durability, it provides high availability. Data is replicated synchronously across three Azure availability zones. Then, the data is replicated asynchronously to the secondary region. Read access to the secondary region can be enabled as well. GZRS is specially designed to provide at least 99.99999999999999% (16 9s) durability of objects over a given year.

Read-access geo-redundant storage

RA-GRS provides geo-replication across two regions, with read-only access to the data in the secondary location. This will maximize the availability of your storage account. When you enable RA-GRS, your data will be available on a primary and a secondary endpoint for your storage account as well. The secondary endpoint will be similar to the primary endpoint, but it appends the **secondary** suffix to it. The access keys that are generated for your storage account can be used for both endpoints.

Now that we have covered the different storage replication types that are set when you create a storage account, we can look at the different storage accounts that Azure has to offer.

Azure Blob Storage

Azure Blob Storage offers unstructured data storage in the cloud. It can store all kinds of data, such as documents, VHDs, images, and audio files. There are two types of blobs that you can create. One type is page blobs, which are used for the storage of disks. So, when you have a VHD that needs to be stored and attached to your Virtual **Machine** (**VM**), you will have to create a page blob. The maximum size of a page blob is 1 TB.

The other type is block blobs, which basically covers all of the other types of data that you can store in Azure, such as files and documents. The maximum size of a block blob is 200 GB. However, there is also a third blob type named append blob, but this one is used internally by Azure and can't be used to store actual files. There are a couple of ways that you can copy blobs to your blob storage account. You can use the Azure portal (only one at a time) or Azure Storage Explorer, or you can copy your files programmatically using .NET, PowerShell, or the CLI or by calling the REST API.

Access tiers

Blob storage accounts use access tiers to determine how frequently the data is accessed. Based on this access tier, you will get billed. Azure offers three storage access tiers: hot, cool, and archive.

Hot access tier

The hot access tier is most suitable for storing data that's accessed frequently and data that is in active use. For instance, you would store images and style sheets for a website inside the hot access tier. The storage costs for this tier are higher than for the other access tiers, but you pay less for accessing the files.

Cool access tier

The cool access tier is the most suitable for storing data that is not accessed frequently (less than once in 30 days). Compared with the hot access tier, the cool tier has lower storage costs, but you pay more for accessing the files. This tier is suitable for storing backups and older content that is not viewed often.

Archive

The archive storage tier is set on the blob level and not on the storage level. It has the lowest costs for storing data and the highest cost for accessing data compared to the hot and cool access tiers. This tier is for data that will remain in the archive for at least 180 days, and it will take a couple of hours of latency before it can be accessed. This tier is most suitable for long-term backups or compliance and archive data. A blob in the archive tier is offline and cannot be read (except for the metadata), copied, overwritten, or modified.

Azure file storage

With Azure Files, you can create file shares in the cloud. You can access your files using the **Server Message Block** (**SMB**) protocol, which is an industry standard and can be used on Linux, Windows, and macOS devices. Azure Files can also be mounted as if it is a local drive on these same devices, and they can be cached for fast access on Windows Server using Azure File Sync.

File shares can be used across multiple machines, which makes them suitable for storing files or data that are accessed from multiple machines, such as tools for development machines, configuration files, or log data. Azure File Share is part of the Azure Storage client libraries and offers an Azure Storage REST API, which can be leveraged by developers in their solutions.

Azure disk storage

The disks that are used for virtual machines are stored in Azure Blob Storage as page blobs. Azure stores two disks for each VM: the actual operating system (VHD) of the VM and a temporary disk that is used for short-term storage. This data is erased when the VM is turned off or rebooted.

There are two different performance tiers that Azure offers: standard disk storage and premium disk storage.

Standard disk storage

Standard disk storage offers HDD and SSD drives to store the data on, and it is the most cost-effective storage tier that you can choose. It can only use LRS or GRS to support high availability for your data and applications.

Premium disk storage

With premium disk storage, your data is stored on SSDs. Not all Azure virtual machines series can use this type of storage. It can only be used with DS, DSv2, GS, LS, or FS series Azure VMs. It offers high-performance and low-latency disk support.

Ultra disk storage

For high IOPS, high throughput, and consistent low-latency disk storage for Azure IaaS VMs, Azure offers Azure Ultra Disks. This type of disk offers some additional benefits, such as the ability to dynamically change the performance of the disk, along with your workloads, without the need to restart your VMs. Ultra disks are well suited for data-intensive workloads such as top-tier databases, SAP HANA, and transaction-heavy workloads. Ultra disks can only be used as data disks, and premium SSDs as OSes are then recommended.

Unmanaged versus managed disks

Managed disks automatically handle storage account creation for you. With unmanaged disks, which are the traditional disks used for VMs, you need to create a storage account manually, and then select that storage account when you create the VM. With managed disks, this burden is handled for you by Azure. You select the disk type and the performance tier (standard or premium), and the managed disk is created. It also handles scaling automatically for you.

Managed disks are recommended by Microsoft over unmanaged disks.

Now that we have covered all of the background information that you need to know about the different storage accounts, we are going to create a new storage account.

Creating and configuring a storage account

Before you can upload any data or files to Azure Storage, a storage account needs to be created. This can be done using the Azure portal, PowerShell, the CLI, ARM templates, or Visual Studio.

In this demonstration, we are going to create a storage account with PowerShell:

1. First, we need to log in to the Azure account:

   ```
   Connect-AzAccount
   ```

2. If necessary, select the right subscription:

   ```
   Select-AzSubscription -SubscriptionId "********-****-****-****-
   ***********"
   ```

3. Create a resource group:

   ```
   New-AzResourceGroup -Name PacktPubStorageAccount -Location EastUS
   ```

4. Create a storage account. The account name should be unique, so replace this with your own account name:

   ```
   New-AzStorageAccount -ResourceGroupName PacktPubStorageAccount -
   AccountName packtpubstorage -Location "East US" -SkuName
   Standard_GRS -Kind StorageV2 -AccessTier Hot
   ```

   In this demonstration, we created a new storage account using PowerShell. If you are new to storage accounts, I highly recommend creating a storage account from the Azure portal as well. That way, you will see all of the available storage account types, storage replication types, and access tiers that you can choose from and the different performance tiers (standard or premium), and how these are all connected. You can refer to the following tutorial on creating a storage account from the Azure portal: https://docs.microsoft.com/en-us/azure/storage/common/storage-quickstart-create-account?tabs=azure-portal.

Now that we have created a new storage account, we can install the Azure Storage Explorer tool.

Installing and using Azure Storage Explorer

Azure Storage Explorer is a standalone application that can be used to easily work with the different types of data that are stored in an Azure Storage account. You can upload, download, and manage Files, Queues, Tables, Blobs, Data Lake Storage, and Cosmos DB entities using Azure Storage Explorer. Aside from that, you can also use the application to configure and manage **Cross-Origin Resource Sharing** (**CORS**) rules for your storage accounts. This application can be used on Windows, Linux, and macOS devices.

To install the application, you have to perform the following steps:

1. Navigate to `https://azure.microsoft.com/en-us/features/storage-explorer/` to download the application.
2. Once it has been downloaded, install the application.
3. When it is installed, open the application. You will be prompted to connect to your Azure environment. There are a couple of options to choose from. You can add an Azure account by connecting to your Azure environment using your administrator credentials, use a shared access signature (which will be covered later in this chapter), and use a storage account name and key, and you can select the **Attach to a local emulator** option if you so desire. For this demonstration, keep the default option selected and click on **Sign in...**:

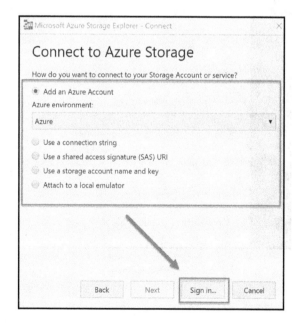

Connecting to Azure Storage

4. Provide your credentials and log in.
5. All of your subscriptions will be added to the left-hand pane. Once this is done, click on **Apply**:

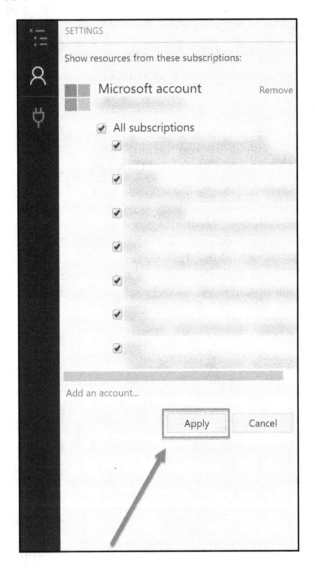

Applying the subscriptions

6. You can now drill down to the subscription and the storage account that we created in the first demonstration from the left-hand pane. Select the storage account. From there, you can access the blob containers, file shares, queues, and tables:

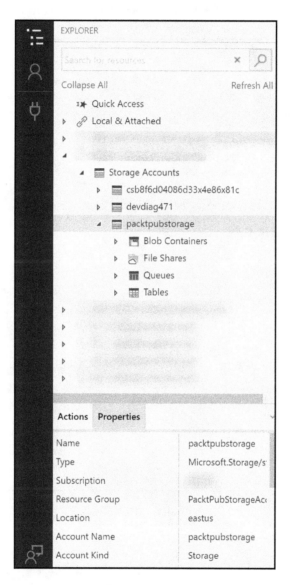

Storage account settings

7. To add some files to a blob container, we need to create a blob container in the storage account. Therefore, right-click on **Blob Containers** in the left-hand menu and select **Create Blob Container.** Call the `packtblobcontainer` container; now, you can upload files to that container. Click on the **Upload** button in the top menu, click on **Upload files**, and select some files from your local computer:

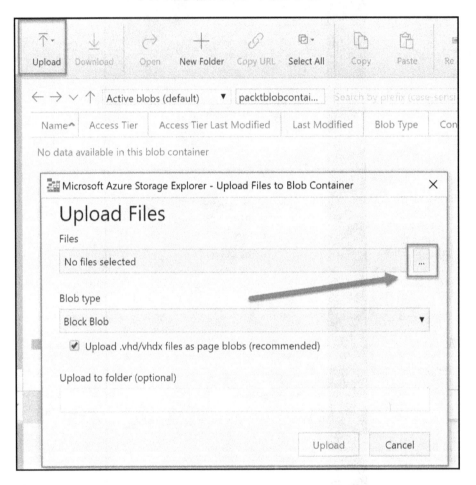

Uploading files to the blob container

You will see that the files will be uploaded to the blob container.

 If you navigate to the overview blade of the storage account in the Azure portal, you will see a button on the top menu that says **Open in explorer**. This will open Azure Storage Explorer, which can then be used to easily manage all of the data that resides in the storage account.

Now that we have installed the Azure Storage Explorer tool and uploaded some files to a blob container, we can configure network access to the storage account.

Configuring network access to the storage account

You can secure your storage account to a specific set of supported networks. For this, you have to configure network rules so that only applications that request data over the specific set of networks can access the storage account. When these network rules are effective, the application needs to use proper authorization on the request. This authorization can be provided by Azure Active Directory credentials for blobs and queues, with an SAS token or a valid account access key.

In the following demonstration, we are going to configure network access to the storage account that we created in the previous step. You can manage storage accounts through the Azure portal, PowerShell, or CLIv2. We are going to set this configuration from the Azure portal. Therefore, we have to perform the following steps:

1. Navigate to the Azure portal by opening `https://portal.azure.com`.
2. Go to the storage account that we created in the previous step.
3. From the overview blade, in the left-hand menu, select **Firewalls and virtual networks**.

4. To grant access to a virtual network with a new network rule, under **Virtual Networks**, there are two options to choose from: **All networks**, which allows traffic from all networks (both virtual and on-premises) and the internet to access the data, and **Selected networks**. If you select this option, you can configure which networks are allowed to access the data from the storage account. Select **Selected networks**. Then, you can select whether you want to add an existing virtual network or create a new one. For this demonstration, click on + **Add new virtual network**:

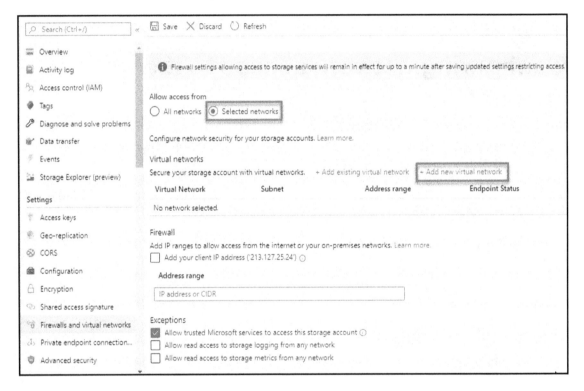

Creating a new network

5. A new blade will open, where you will have to specify the network configuration. Specify the configuration that's shown in the following screenshot and click on **Create**:

Network configuration settings

6. The virtual network will be added to the overview blade. This storage account is now secure and can be accessed only from applications and other resources that use this virtual network. In this same blade, you can also configure the firewall and only allow certain IP ranges from the internet or your on-premises environment:

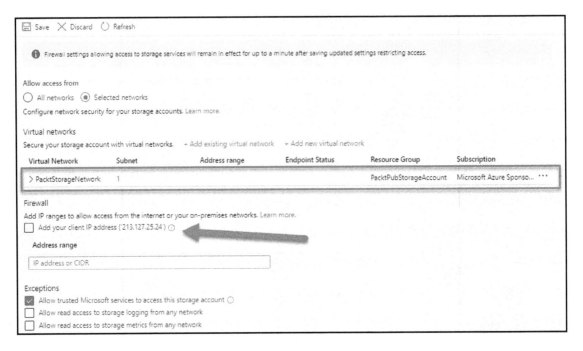

IP ranges

This concludes this demonstration. In the next demonstration, we are going to generate and manage SAS.

SAS and access keys

By using an SAS, you can provide a way to grant limited access to objects and data that are stored inside your storage account to the clients that connect to it. Using an SAS, you don't have to expose your access keys to the clients.

When you create a storage account, primary and secondary access keys are created. Both of these keys can grant administrative access to your account and all of the resources within it. Exposing these keys can also open your storage account to negligent or malicious use. SAS provides a safe alternative to this that will allow clients to read, write, and delete data in your storage account according to the permissions you've explicitly granted, without the need for an account key.

In the next section, we're going to look at how to manage our access keys and how to generate an SAS for our storage account.

Managing access keys

To manage access keys, perform the following steps:

1. Navigate to the Azure portal by opening `https://portal.azure.com`.
2. Again, go to the storage account that we created in the previous step.
3. Once the overview blade is open, under **Settings**, select **Access keys**.

4. Here, you can see both of the access keys that were generated for you when the storage account was created. The reason that Azure created two access keys for you is that if you regenerate a new key, all of the SAS that you created for this key will no longer work. You can then let applications access that data using the secondary key, and once the key is regenerated, you can share the new key with your clients. You can generate new keys by clicking on the buttons next to both keys:

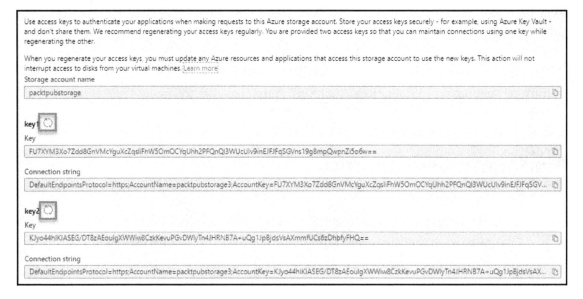

Use access keys to authenticate your applications when making requests to this Azure storage account. Store your access keys securely - for example, using Azure Key Vault - and don't share them. We recommend regenerating your access keys regularly. You are provided two access keys so that you can maintain connections using one key while regenerating the other.

When you regenerate your access keys, you must update any Azure resources and applications that access this storage account to use the new keys. This action will not interrupt access to disks from your virtual machines. Learn more

Storage account name

packtpubstorage

key1

Key

FU7XYM3Xo7Zdd8GnVMcYguXcZqsliFhW5OmOCYqUhh2PFQnQI3WUcUlv9inEJFJFqSGVns19g8mpQwpnZi5o6w==

Connection string

DefaultEndpointsProtocol=https;AccountName=packtpubstorage3;AccountKey=FU7XYM3Xo7Zdd8GnVMcYguXcZqsliFhW5OmOCYqUhh2PFQnQI3WUcUlv9inEJFJFqSGV...

key2

Key

KJyo44hIKJASEG/DT8zAEoulgXWWiw8CzkKevuPGvDWIyTn4JHRNB7A+uQg1JpBjdsVsAXmmfUCs6zDhbfyFHQ==

Connection string

DefaultEndpointsProtocol=https;AccountName=packtpubstorage3;AccountKey=KJyo44hIKJASEG/DT8zAEoulgXWWiw8CzkKevuPGvDWIyTn4JHRNB7A+uQg1JpBjdsVsAX...

Access keys

5. There is also a connection string provided for each key, which can be used by client applications to access the storage account.

In the next section, we're going to generate an SAS for the access keys.

Generating an SAS

In this demonstration, we are going to generate an SAS for our blob store. To generate an SAS, perform the following steps:

1. Navigate to the Azure portal by opening `https://portal.azure.com`.
2. Again, go to the storage account that we created in the previous step.
3. Once the overview blade is open, under **Settings**, select **Shared access signature**:

A shared access signature (SAS) is a URI that grants restricted access rights to Azure Storage resources. You can provide a shared access signature to clients who should not be trusted with your storage account key but whom you wish to delegate access to certain storage account resources. By distributing a shared access signature URI to these clients, you grant them access to a resource for a specified period of time.

An account-level SAS can delegate access to multiple storage services (i.e. blob, file, queue, table). Note that stored access policies are currently not supported for an account-level SAS.

Learn more

Allowed services ⓘ
☑ Blob ☑ File ☑ Queue ☑ Table

Allowed resource types ⓘ
☑ Service ☑ Container ☑ Object

Allowed permissions ⓘ
☑ Read ☑ Write ☑ Delete ☑ List ☑ Add ☑ Create ☑ Update ☑ Process

Start and expiry date/time ⓘ
Start
| 12/17/2019 | | 5:21:28 PM |

End
| 12/18/2019 | | 1:21:28 AM |

| (UTC+01:00) Sarajevo, Skopje, Warsaw, Zagreb | ⌄ |

Allowed IP addresses ⓘ
for example, 168.1.5.65 or 168.1.5.65-168.1.5.70

Allowed protocols ⓘ
◉ HTTPS only ○ HTTPS and HTTP

Signing key ⓘ
key1 ⌄

Generate SAS and connection string

Selecting Shared access signature

4. To only allow the blob storage to be accessed, disable the file, queue, and table. Keep the default permissions, and then select an expiration date and time. You can also set the allowed protocols here. At the bottom of the screen, you can apply these permissions to the different keys. Keep **key1** selected and click on **Generate SAS and connection string**:

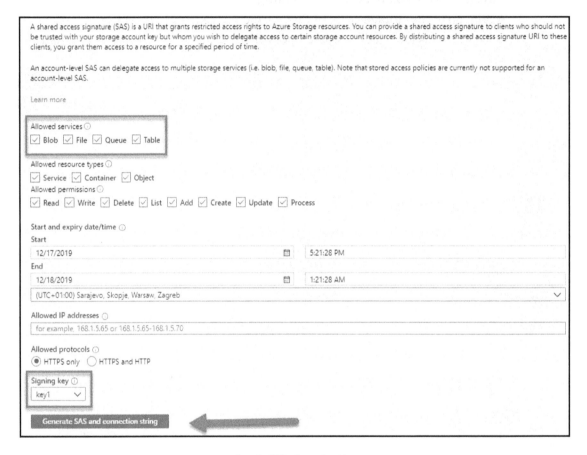

Generating SAS and connection string

5. You can now use this token to request the data from the blob storage.

This concludes this demonstration. In the next section, we are going to look at how to implement Azure Storage replication.

Implementing Azure Storage replication

The data in Azure is always replicated to ensure durability and high availability. Azure Storage copies your data so that it is protected from planned and unplanned events, including transient hardware failures, network or power outages, and massive natural disasters. We have already covered the different replication types that Azure offers for your storage accounts.

Storage replication can be set during the creation of the storage account. You can change the type of replication later as well by using the Azure portal, PowerShell, or the CLI. To change this in the Azure portal, you have to perform the following steps:

1. Navigate to the Azure portal by opening `https://portal.azure.com`.
2. Go to the storage account that we created in the previous step.
3. Under **Settings**, select **Configuration**. In this blade, under **Replication**, you can change the type of replication:

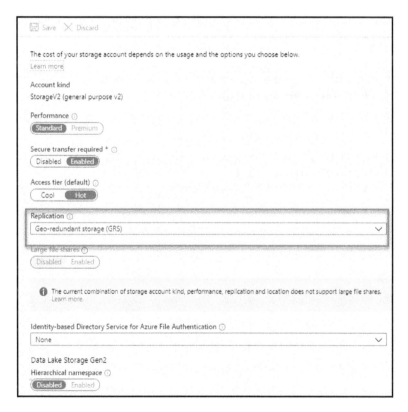

Changing the type of replication

Summary

In this chapter, we covered the second part of the *Deploy and Configure Infrastructure* objective. We covered the different types of storage that are available to us in Azure and when we should use them. We also covered how we can manage our data using Azure Storage Explorer and how we can secure our data using SAS. Finally, we covered how to replicate data from storage accounts.

In the next chapter, we'll cover the third part of this exam objective. In that chapter, we will cover how to implement and manage VMs.

Questions

Answer the following questions to test your knowledge of the information in this chapter. You can find the answers in the *Assessments* section at the end of this book:

1. Can the Azure Storage Explorer application only be used on Windows devices?
   - Yes
   - No

2. Can you configure storage accounts to be accessed from specific virtual networks and not from on-premises networks?
   - Yes
   - No

3. Can you only set the type of replication for your storage accounts during the creation of the storage account?
   - Yes
   - No

Further reading

You can check out the following links for more information about the topics that were covered in this chapter:

- **Azure Storage documentation**: `https://docs.microsoft.com/en-us/azure/storage/`
- **Get started with Storage Explorer**: `https://docs.microsoft.com/en-us/azure/vs-azure-tools-storage-manage-with-storage-explorer?tabs=windows`
- **Configure Azure Storage firewalls and virtual networks**: `https://docs.microsoft.com/en-us/azure/storage/common/storage-network-security`
- **Azure Storage redundancy**: `https://docs.microsoft.com/en-us/azure/storage/common/storage-redundancy`

Implementing and Managing Virtual Machines

3

In the previous chapter, we covered the different types of storage that are available in Azure and when you should use them. We also covered how to install and use Azure Storage Explorer to manage your data.

This chapter proceeds with the third part of the *Deploy and Configure Infrastructure* objective. In this chapter, we are going to cover **Virtual Machines** (**VMs**) in Azure, and the different VM sizes that are available for both Azure and Linux. You will learn how you can create and configure VMs for Windows and Linux. We will also cover high availability and what actions you can take to configure your VMs for high availability. You will also learn how to how to automate your deployment using scale sets, how to deploy and modify **Azure Resource Manager** (**ARM**) templates, and how to configure Azure Disk Encryption for VMs.

The following topics will be covered in this chapter:

- Understanding VMs
- Understanding Availability Sets
- Provisioning VMs
- Understanding VM scale sets
- Modifying and deploying ARM templates
- Configuring Azure Disk Encryption for VMs

Technical requirements

This chapter will use Azure PowerShell (`https://docs.microsoft.com/en-us/ powershell/azure/install-az-ps?view=azps-1.8.0`) and Visual Studio Code (`https:// code.visualstudio.com/download`) for examples.

The source code for this chapter can be downloaded from `https://github.com/ PacktPublishing/Microsoft-Azure-Architect-Technologies-Exam-Guide-AZ-300/tree/ master/Chapter03`.

Understanding VMs

You can run both Windows VMs as well as Linux VMs in Azure. VMs come in all sorts of sizes and a variety of prices, ranging from VMs with a small amount of memory and processing power for general purposes, to large VMs that can be used for **Graphics Processing Unit** (**GPU**)-intensive and high-performance computing workloads.

To create a VM, you can choose from several predefined images. There are images available for operating systems such as Windows Server or Linux, as well as predefined applications, such as SQL Server images, and complete farms, which consist of multiple VMs that can be deployed at once. An example of a farm is a three-tier SharePoint farm.

VMs can be created and managed either from the Azure portal, PowerShell, or the CLI, and they come in the following series and sizes.

VM series and sizes

At the time of writing this book, the following VM series and sizes are available:

Series	Type	Description
B, Dsv3, Dv3, Dasv3, Dav3, DSv2, Dv2, Av2, DC	General-purpose	These VMs have a balanced CPU-to-memory ratio and are ideal for testing and development scenarios. They are also suitable for small and medium databases and web servers with low-to-medium traffic.
Fsv2	Compute-optimized	These VMs have a high CPU-to-memory ratio and are suitable for web servers with medium traffic, application servers, and network appliances for nodes in batch processing.
Esv3, Ev3, Easv3, Eav3, Mv2, M, DSv2, Dv2	Memory-optimized	These VMs have a high memory-to-CPU ratio and are suitable for relational database servers, medium-to-large caches, and in-memory analytics.
Lsv2	Storage-optimized	These VMs have high disk throughput and IO and are suitable for big data, SQL, and NoSQL databases.
NC, NCv2, NCv3, ND, NDv2 (Preview), NV, NVv3	GPU	These VMs are targeted for heavy graphic rendering and video editing, deep learning applications, and machine learning model training. These VMs are available with single or multiple GPUs.
HB, HC, H	High-performance compute	These are the fastest VMs available. They offer the most powerful CPU with optional high-throughput network interfaces (**Remote Direct Memory Access (RDMA)**).

VM series are updated constantly. New series, types, and sizes are added and removed frequently. To stay up to date with these changes, you can refer to the following site for Windows VM sizes: `https://docs.microsoft.com/en-us/azure/virtual-machines/windows/sizes`. For Linux VM sizes, you can refer to `https://docs.microsoft.com/en-us/azure/virtual-machines/linux/sizes?toc=%2fazure%2fvirtualmachines%2flinux%2ftoc.json`.

Managed disks

Azure managed disks are the default disks selected when you create a VM in the Azure portal. They handle storage for your VMs completely. Previously, you would have had to manually create storage accounts to store VM hard disks, and when your VM needed to scale up, you had to add additional storage accounts to make sure you didn't exceed the limit of 20,000 **Input/Output Operations Per Second** (**IOPS**) per account.

With managed disks, this burden is now handled for you by Azure. You can now create 10,000 VM disks inside a subscription, which can result in thousands of VMs inside a subscription, without the need to copy disks between storage accounts.

Understanding Availability Sets

To create a reliable infrastructure, adding your VMs to an Availability Set is key. Several scenarios can have an impact on the availability of your Azure VMs. These are as follows:

- **Unplanned hardware maintenance event**: When hardware is about to fail, Azure fires an unplanned hardware maintenance event. Live migration technology is used, which predicts the failure and then moves the VM, the network connections, memory, and storage to different physical machines, without disconnecting the client. When your VM is moved, the performance is reduced for a short time because the VM is paused for 30 seconds. Network connections, memory, and open files are still preserved.
- **Unexpected downtime**: The VM is down when this event occurs because Azure needs to heal your VM inside the same data center. A hardware or physical infrastructure failure often causes this event to happen.
- **Planned hardware maintenance event**: This type of event is a periodic update from Microsoft in Azure to improve the platform. Most of these updates don't have a significant impact on the uptime of VMs, but some of them may require a reboot or restart.

To provide redundancy during these types of events, you can group two or more VMs in an Availability Set. By leveraging Availability Sets, VMs are distributed across multiple isolated hardware nodes in a cluster. This way, Azure can ensure that, during an event or failure, only a subset of your VMs is impacted and your overall solution will remain operational and available. This way, the 99.95% Azure **Service Level Agreement** (**SLA**) can still be met during outages and other failures.

> VMs can only be assigned to an Availability Set during initial deployment.

Fault domains and update domains

When you place your VMs in an Availability Set, Azure guarantees to spread them across fault and update domains. By default, Azure will assign three fault domains and five update domains (which can be increased to a maximum of 20) to the Availability Set.

When spreading your VMs over fault domains, your VMs sit over three different racks in the Azure data center. So, in the case of an event or failure of the underlying platform, only one rack gets affected and the other VMs remain accessible, as depicted in the following diagram:

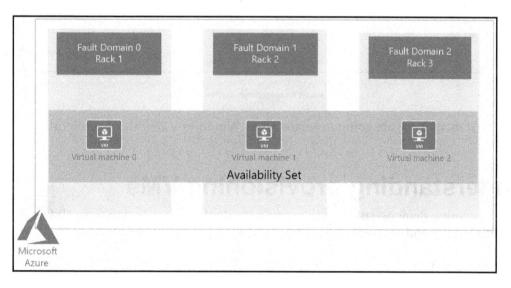

VMs spread over three fault domains

Update domains are useful in the case of an OS or host update. When you spread your VMs across multiple update domains, one domain will be updated and rebooted while the others remain accessible, as depicted in the following diagram:

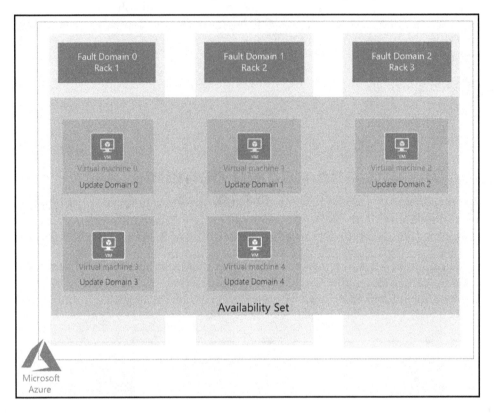

VMs spread over five update domains and three fault domains

In the next section, we are going to create a new Windows VM in the Azure portal.

Understanding provisioning VMs

In the upcoming demonstrations, we are going to deploy a Windows Server VM from both the Azure portal and PowerShell.

Deploying Linux machines is quite similar to deploying Windows machines. We are not going to cover how to deploy Linux machines. For more information about how to deploy Linux machines in Azure, you can refer to the *Further reading* section at the end of this chapter.

Deploying a Windows VM from the Azure portal

In this demonstration, we are going to deploy a Windows VM from the Azure portal. We are going to set up networking and storage and select a VM size for this VM. We are also going to configure high availability for this VM, by placing it in an **Availability Set**. To do so, perform the following steps:

1. Navigate to the Azure portal by opening `https://portal.azure.com`.
2. In the left menu, click **Virtual machines**, and then, in the top menu, click **+ Add** as follows:

Creating a new VM

3. We are going to create a Windows VM, so in the **Basics** blade, add the following values:
   - **Subscription**: Choose a subscription.
   - **Resource group**: Type `PacktVMGroup`.
   - **Virtual machine name**: Type `PacktWindowsVM`.
   - **Region**: Choose a region.
   - **Availability options**: Here, select **Availability set**.
   - **Availability set**: Create new, and call it `PacktWindowsAS`. Keep the default fault domains and update the domains for this VM.

- **Image**: Choose **Windows Server Datacenter 2016**.
- **Azure Spot instance**: Select **No.Size**: Here, you can choose between the different sizes. Click **Change size** and select **Standard DS1 v2**.
- **Administrator account**: Provide a username and a password.
- **Inbound port rules**: Select **Allow selected ports** and enable **Remote Desktop Protocol (RDP)**. You will need this to log in to the server after creation.
- **Save money**: If you already have a valid Windows Server Datacenter license, you get a discount on this VM.

4. Click **Next: Disks**.
5. Here, you can select the disk type. Keep the default as follows, which is **Premium SSD**:

Create a virtual machine

Basics   Disks   Networking   Management   Advanced   Tags   Review + create

Azure VMs have one operating system disk and a temporary disk for short-term storage. You can attach additional data disks. The size of the VM determines the type of storage you can use and the number of data disks allowed. Learn more

Disk options

OS disk type * ○ | Premium SSD   ⌄ |

Enable Ultra Disk compatibility ○   ○ Yes ◉ No

Data disks   Ultra Disk compatibility is not available for this VM size and location.

You can add and configure additional data disks for your virtual machine or attach existing disks. This VM also comes with a temporary disk.

| LUN | Name | Size (GiB) | Disk type | Host caching |

Create and attach a new disk   Attach an existing disk

⌄ Advanced

Select disk type

6. Click **Next: Networking**.
7. In the **Networking** blade, you can configure the virtual network. You can keep the default values for this machine as follows:

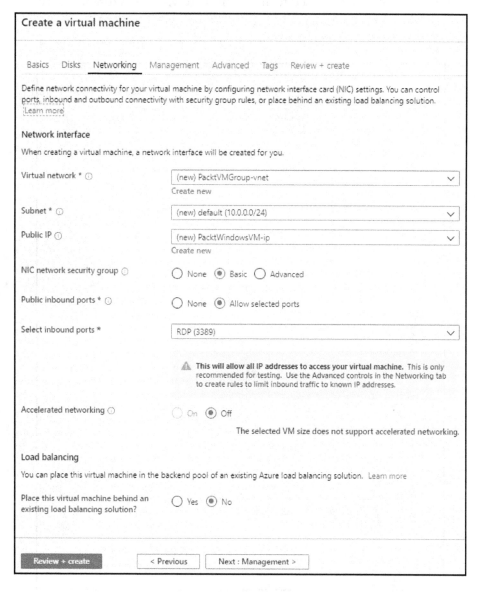

Set networking for VM

8. Click **Next: Management**.
9. In the **Management** blade, you can configure monitoring, and create and select a storage account for monitoring. You can also assign a system-assigned managed identity, which can be used to authenticate to various Azure resources, such as Azure Key Vault, without storing any credentials in code. You can also enable auto shutdown here, as follows:

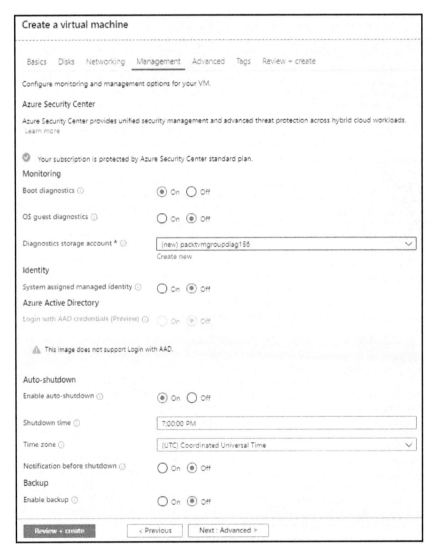

Set management features

10. We can now create the VM. Click **Review + create** and the settings will be validated. After that, click **Create** to actually deploy the VM.

We have now deployed a Windows VM, placed it in an Availability Set, and looked at the networking, storage, and monitoring features and capabilities for this VM. In the next section, we are going to deploy a Windows Server VM from PowerShell.

Deploying a Windows VM from PowerShell

In the next demonstration, we are going to create two Windows Server VMs from PowerShell and place them in an Availability Set. To do so, you have to perform the following steps:

1. First, we need to log in to the Azure account, as follows:

```
Connect-AzAccount
```

2. If necessary, select the right subscription, as follows:

```
Select-AzSubscription -SubscriptionId "********-****-****-****-
***********"
```

3. Create a resource group for the Availability Set, as follows:

```
New-AzResourceGroup -Name PacktVMResourceGroup -Location EastUS
```

4. Then, we can create an Availability Set for the VMs, as follows:

```
New-AzAvailabilitySet `
    -Location "EastUS" `
    -Name "PacktVMAvailabilitySet" `
    -ResourceGroupName PacktVMResourceGroup `
    -Sku aligned `
    -PlatformFaultDomainCount 2 `
    -PlatformUpdateDomainCount 2
```

5. We have to set the administrator credentials for the VMs, as follows:

```
$cred = Get-Credential
```

6. We can now create the two VMs inside the Availability Set, as follows:

```
for ($i=1; $i -le 2; $i++)
{
    New-AzVm `
        -ResourceGroupName PacktVMResourceGroup `
        -Name "PacktVM$i" `
        -Location "East US" `
        -VirtualNetworkName "PacktVnet" `
        -SubnetName "PacktSubnet" `
        -SecurityGroupName "PacktNetworkSecurityGroup" `
        -PublicIpAddressName "PacktPublicIpAddress$i" `
        -AvailabilitySetName "PacktVMAvailabilitySet" `
        -Credential $cred
}
```

In the last two demonstrations, we created VMs inside an Availability Set from the Azure portal and PowerShell. In the next section, we are going to cover scale sets.

Understanding VM scale sets

VM scale sets are used for deploying multiple VMs at once without the need for manual actions or using scripts. You can then manage them all at once from a single place. VM scale sets are typically used to build large-scale infrastructures, where keeping all of your VMs in sync is key. The maintenance of VMs, including keeping them in sync, is handled by Azure. VM scale sets use Availability Sets under the hood. VMs inside a scale set are automatically spread over the fault and update domains by the underlying platform. VM scale sets use Azure autoscale by default. You can, however, add or remove instances yourself instead of using autoscale.

When creating a scale set, a couple of artifacts are created for you automatically. As well as the number of VMs you have specified being added to the set, Azure Load Balancer and Azure autoscale are added, along with a virtual network and a public IP address, as shown in the following screenshot:

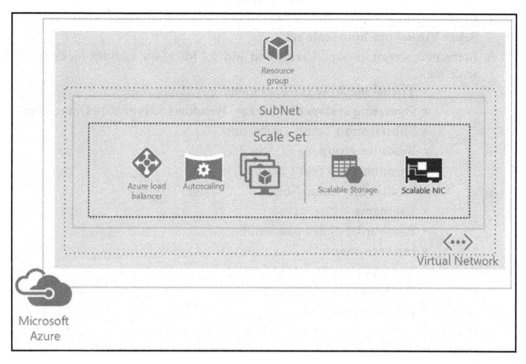

Azure VM scale set

In the next section, we are going to deploy and configure scale sets.

Deploying and configuring scale sets

To create a VM scale set from the Azure portal, take the following steps:

1. Navigate to the Azure portal by opening `https://portal.azure.com`.
2. Click on **Create a resource** and type in `Scale Set` in the search bar. Select **Virtual machine scale set**.
3. In the next screen, click on **Create** and add the following settings for creating the scale set:
   - **Virtual machine scale set name**: `PacktScaleSet`
   - **Operating system disk image: Windows Server 2016 Datacenter**
   - **Subscription**: Select a subscription
   - **Resource group**: `PacktVMGroup`
   - **Location: (US) East US**
   - **Availability zone: None**
   - **Username**: `SCPacktUser`
   - **Password**: Fill in a password
   - **Instance count**: 2
   - **Instance size: Standard DS1 v2**
   - **Deploy as low priority:** No
   - **Use managed disks: Yes**
4. If you scroll down, you can configure the autoscale settings, choose between the different load balancing settings, and configure networking and monitoring capabilities, as follows:

Scale set configuration settings

5. Scroll down again and keep the default settings for network security ports and so on.

6. Click **Create**. The scale set with the number of provided VMs in it is now deployed.

In the next section of this chapter, we are going to cover how to automate the deployment of VMs using ARM templates.

Modifying and deploying ARM templates

ARM templates define the infrastructure and configuration of your Azure solution. Azure is managed by an API, which is called the Resource Manager or ARM API. You can use this API to deploy infrastructure as code and configure your Azure environment. This API can be called from various tooling and resources; you can do it using the Azure portal, PowerShell, or the CLI, or by calling the API directly, or creating ARM templates.

You can create an ARM template in JSON format and use this to repeatedly deploy your solution across your Azure environment in a consistent state. The template is processed by Resource Manager like any other request, and it will parse the template and convert the syntax into REST API operations for the appropriate resource providers. The REST API uses the resources section inside the template to call the resource-specific APIs. An example of a resource provider is `Microsoft.Storage/storageAccounts`.

 Microsoft offers various predefined ARM templates that can be downloaded and deployed. You can download the quick start templates from GitHub and deploy them directly from GitHub, or download them and make the necessary adjustments: `https://github.com/Azure/azure-quickstart-templates`.

In the next section, we are going to modify an ARM template in the Azure portal.

Modifying an ARM template

In this demonstration, we are going to create an ARM template of a storage account in the Azure portal. We are going to modify this template so that it will generate a storage account name automatically. We will then deploy this template again and use it to create a new storage account from the Azure portal. Therefore, you have to take the following steps:

1. Navigate to the Azure portal by opening `https://portal.azure.com`.
2. Select **Create a resource**, then **Storage** and then select **Storage account**. Create a new storage account.
3. Add the following values:
    - **Subscription**: Pick a subscription.
    - **Resource group**: Create a new one and call it `PacktARMResourceGroup`.
    - **Storage account name**: Type `packtarm`.
    - **Location**: Select **(US) East US**.
    - **Performance**: Select **Standard**.

- **Account kind**: Select **StorageV2 (general purpose v2)**.
- **Replication**: Select **Read-access geo-redundant storage (RA-GRS)**.
- **Access tier:** Select **Hot**.

4. Click **Review + create**. Do not select **Create**.
5. But, in the next step, select **Download a template for automation**:

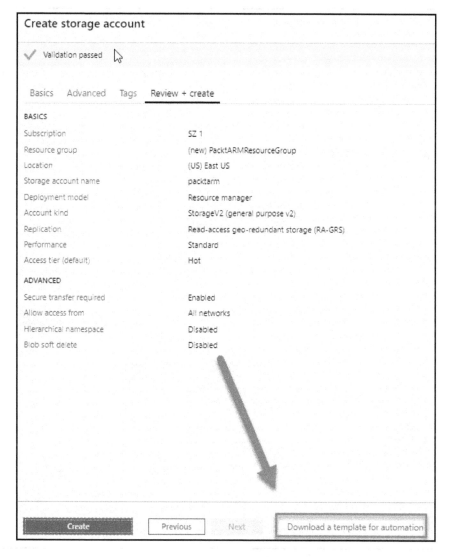

Download template for automation

6. The editor will be opened and the generated template will be displayed. The main pane shows the template. It has six top-level elements: `schema`, `contentVersion`, `parameters`, `variables`, `resources`, and `output`. There are also six parameters. `storageAccountName` is highlighted in the following screenshot. In the template, one Azure resource is defined. The type is `Microsoft.Storage/storageAccounts`. Select **Download** from the top menu:

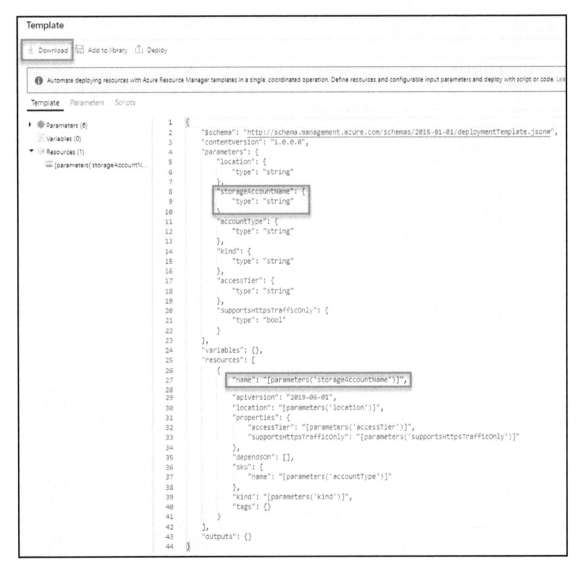

Main ARM template

7. Open the downloaded ZIP file and then save `template.json` to your computer. In the next section, you will use a template deployment tool to edit the template.

8. Select **Parameters** in the top menu and look at the values. We will need this later during the deployment:

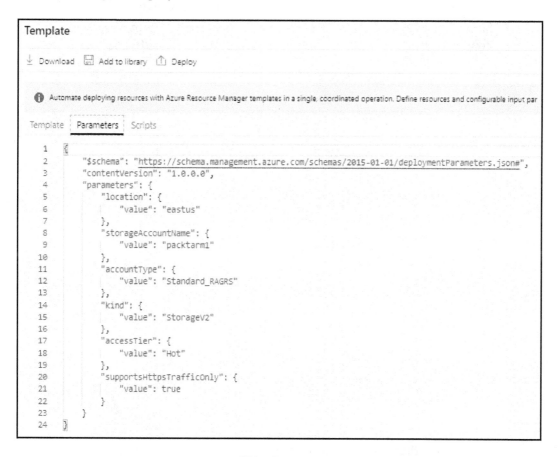

ARM template parameters

9. The Azure portal can be used for the basic editing of ARM templates. More complex ARM templates can be edited using Visual Studio Code, for instance. We are going to use the Azure portal for this demonstration. Therefore, select **+ Create a resource**; then, in the search box, type `Template Deployment (deploy using custom templates)`. Then select **Create**.

10. In the next blade, you have different options for loading templates. For this demonstration, select **Build your own template in the editor**:

Template options

11. Select **Load file**, and then follow the instructions to load `template.json`, which we downloaded in the last section. Make the following changes:
    1. Remove the `storageAccountName` parameter.
    2. Add a new variable:

       ```
       "storageAccountName":
       "[concat(uniqueString(subscription().subscriptionId),
       'storage')]",
       ```

    3. Replace `"name": "[parameters('storageAccountName')]",` with `"name": "[variables('storageAccountName')]":`

Make changes to the highlighted sections

4. The code of the template will look as follows:

The schema and parameters sections are as follows:

```
{
    "$schema":
"http://schema.management.azure.com/schemas/2015-01-01
/deploymentTemplate.json#",
    "contentVersion": "1.0.0.0",
    "parameters": {
        "location": {
            "type": "string"
```

```
        },
        "accountType": {
            "type": "string"
        },
        "kind": {
            "type": "string"
        },
        "accessTier": {
            "type": "string"
        },
        "supportsHttpsTrafficOnly": {
            "type": "bool"
        }
    },
```

The `variable` and `resources` section is as follows:

```
    "variables": {
        "storageAccountName":
"[concat(uniqueString(subscription().subscriptionId),
'storage')]"
    },
    "resources": [
        {
            "name":
"[variables('storageAccountName')]",
            "type":
"Microsoft.Storage/storageAccounts",
            "apiVersion": "2018-07-01",
            "location": "[parameters('location')]",
            "properties": {
                "accessTier":
"[parameters('accessTier')]",
                "supportsHttpsTrafficOnly":
"[parameters('supportsHttpsTrafficOnly')]"
            },
            "dependsOn": [],
            "sku": {
                "name": "[parameters('accountType')]"
            },
            "kind": "[parameters('kind')]"
        }
    ],
    "outputs": {}
}
```

5. Then select **Save.**

12. In the next screen, fill in the values for creating the storage account. You will see that the parameter for filling in the storage account name is removed. This will be generated automatically. Fill in the following values:

    - **Resource group**: Select the resource group name you created in the previous section.
    - **Location**: Select **East US**.
    - **Account type**: Select **Standard_LRS**.
    - **Kind**: Select **StorageV2**.
    - **Access Tier**: Select **Hot**.
    - **Https Traffic Only Enabled**: Select **true**.
    - **I agree to the terms and conditions stated above**: Select this checkbox.

13. Select **Purchase**.

14. The ARM template will now be deployed. After deployment, go to the **Overview** blade of the resource group. You will see that the storage account name is automatically generated for you:

Storage account name

For more information about the syntax and structure of ARM templates, you can refer to the following website: `https://docs.microsoft.com/en-us/azure/azure-resource-manager/resource-group-authoring-templates`.

We have now modified an ARM template in the Azure portal and created a new storage account using the modified ARM templates. In the next demonstration, we are going to save a deployment as an ARM template.

Saving a deployment as an ARM template

For this demonstration, we are going to save a deployment as an ARM template from the Azure portal. We are going to export the template of the two VMs that we created in an Availability Set using PowerShell.

Once downloaded, you can then make changes to it, and redeploy it in Azure using PowerShell or code. The generated ARM template consists of a large amount of code, which makes it very difficult to make changes to it. For saving a deployment as an ARM template, take the following steps:

1. Navigate to the Azure portal by opening `https://portal.azure.com`.
2. Open the resource group that we created in the previous demonstration and, under **Settings**, select the **Export template** as follows:

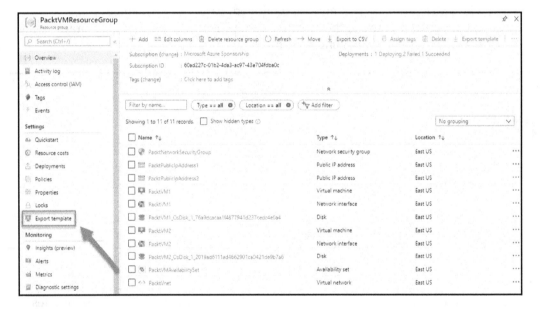

Export template

3. The template is generated for you based on the settings that we made during the creation of the different resources. You can download the template and redeploy it from here. You can also download the scripts for the CLI, PowerShell, .NET, and Ruby, and create different resources using these programming languages. Select **Download** from the top menu, as follows:

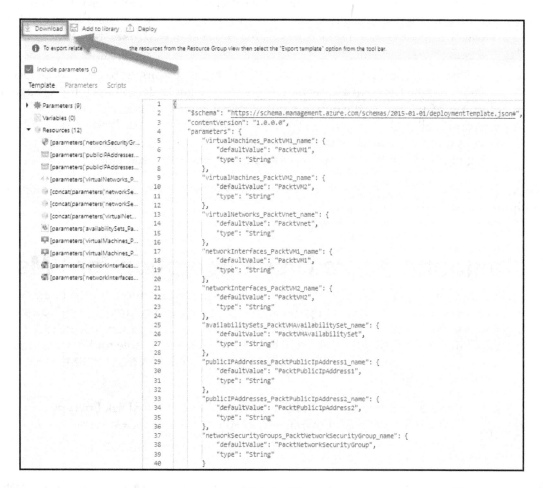

Download template

The template is downloaded as a ZIP file to your local filesystem.

4. You can now extract the template files from the ZIP file and open them in Visual Studio Code. If you don't have this installed, you can use the download link provided at the beginning of this chapter or use Notepad or some other text editing tool. The ZIP file contains three different deployment files, created in different languages. There is one each for PowerShell, the CLI, and Ruby. It also consists of a `DeploymentHelper.cs` file, a `parameters.json` file, and a `template.json` file.

5. In Visual Studio Code, you can make all of the modifications to the parameters and template files that are needed. If you then want to deploy the template again to Azure, use one of the deployment files inside the container. In the case of PowerShell, right-click on `deploy.ps1` and select **Run with PowerShell**. Fill in the subscription ID, provide the resource group name and deployment name and log in using your Azure credentials. This will start the deployment.

We have now saved a deployment as an ARM template. In the next section, we are going to configure Azure Disk Encryption for VMs.

Configuring Azure Disk Encryption for VMs

Azure Disk Encryption for VMs can help you to meet your organizational security and compliance commitments by encrypting the disks of your VMs in Azure. For Windows VMs, it uses the BitLocker feature and, for Linux VMs, it uses the DM-Crypt feature for encryption of the OS and data disks. Azure Disk Encryption is available for Windows and Linux VMs with a minimum of 2 GB of memory, and for Standard VMs and VMs with Azure Premium Storage.

 For more information about the prerequisites of Azure Disk Encryption, you can refer to the following site: `https://docs.microsoft.com/en-us/azure/security/azure-security-disk-encryption-prerequisites`.

It uses Azure Key Vault to help to control and manage the disk encryption keys and secrets. Azure Disk Encryption also ensures that disks that are stored in Azure Storage are encrypted at rest.

You will get a High Severity alert in Azure Security Center if you have VMs that are not encrypted. From there, you will get the recommendation to encrypt these VMs, and you can take action to encrypt the VMs from the Azure Security Center directly.

In the next demonstration, we are going to encrypt the data disk of one of the VMs that we created in the *Deploying a Windows VM from PowerShell* demo. However, before we can encrypt the disk, we first need to create an Azure Key Vault. We are going to create this from the Azure portal.

Creating an Azure Key Vault

To create the Key Vault from the Azure portal, take the following steps:

1. Navigate to the Azure portal by opening `https://portal.azure.com`.
2. From the left menu, click **Create a resource.** In the search box, type **Key Vault** and create a new Key Vault.
3. Fill in the following values:
    - **Subscription:** Select the same subscription that you used for the *Deploying a Windows VM from PowerShell* demo.
    - **Resource group**: Select the resource group name you created in the previous demo, which is `PacktVMResourceGroup`.
    - **Key Vault Name**: Type `PacktEncryptionVault`.
    - **Region**: Select **East US**.
    - **Pricing Tier**: Select **Standard**.
4. Click **Review + create** and **Create**.

Now that the Key Vault is in place, we can encrypt the disk.

Encrypting the disk

Disks can only be encrypted using PowerShell and CLI. In the next demonstration, we are going to encrypt the disk of `PacktVM1` using PowerShell.

To encrypt the disk, take the following steps:

1. First, we need to log in to the Azure account, as follows:

```
Connect-AzAccount
```

2. If necessary, select the right subscription, as follows:

```
Select-AzSubscription -SubscriptionId "********-****-****-****-
***********"
```

3. Set some parameters, as follows:

```
$ResourceGroupName = 'PacktVMResourceGroup'
$vmName = 'PacktVM1'
$KeyVaultName = 'PacktEncryptionVault'
```

4. Then, retrieve the Key Vault, as follows:

```
$KeyVault = Get-AzKeyVault -VaultName $KeyVaultName -
ResourceGroupName $ResourceGroupName
$diskEncryptionKeyVaultUrl = $KeyVault.VaultUri
$KeyVaultResourceId = $KeyVault.ResourceId
```

5. Then, encrypt the disk, as follows:

```
Set-AzVMDiskEncryptionExtension `
 -ResourceGroupName $ResourceGroupName `
 -VMName $vmName `
 -DiskEncryptionKeyVaultUrl $diskEncryptionKeyVaultUrl `
 -DiskEncryptionKeyVaultId $KeyVaultResourceId
```

It will take approximately 10 minutes before the disk is encrypted. This concludes this demonstration and this chapter.

Summary

In this chapter, we covered the third part of the *Deploy and Configure Infrastructure* objective by covering how to provision and configure VMs for Windows and Linux. You learned about the various aspects and parts that are created when you deploy a VM in Azure. We also covered how to automate the deployment of VMs using scale sets and ARM templates. Finally, we covered how to configure Azure Disk Encryption for VMs.

In the next chapter, we will continue with this objective by covering how to implement and manage virtual networking.

Questions

Answer the following questions to test your knowledge of the information in this chapter. You can find the answers in the *Assessments* section at the end of this book:

1. Can you use VM scale sets to automate the deployment of multiple VMs?
   - Yes
   - No

2. Can you use Availability Sets for spreading VMs across update and fault domains?
   - Yes
   - No

3. Do you have to define resource providers in your ARM templates to deploy the various resources in Azure?
   - Yes
   - No

Further reading

You can check out the following links for more information about the topics that were covered in this chapter:

- **Quickstart: Create a Linux virtual machine in the Azure portal**: https://docs.microsoft.com/en-us/azure/virtual-machines/linux/quick-create-portal
- **Virtual Machine Scale Sets Documentation**: https://docs.microsoft.com/en-us/azure/virtual-machine-scale-sets/
- **Manage the availability of Windows virtual machines in Azure**: https://docs.microsoft.com/en-us/azure/virtual-machines/windows/manage-availability
- **Understand the structure and syntax of Azure Resource Manager templates**: https://docs.microsoft.com/en-us/azure/azure-resource-manager/resource-group-authoring-templates
- **Deploy resources with Resource Manager templates and Azure PowerShell**: https://docs.microsoft.com/en-us/azure/azure-resource-manager/resource-group-template-deploy
- **Define resources in Azure Resource Manager templates**: https://docs.microsoft.com/en-us/azure/templates/

4
Implementing and Managing Virtual Networking

In the previous chapter, we covered the third part of the *Deploy and Configure Infrastructure* objective. We covered **virtual machines** (**VMs**) in Azure, as well as the different VM sizes that are available for both Azure and Linux. We also learned how to provision VMs and how to create and deploy **Azure Resource Manager** (**ARM**) templates.

This chapter introduces the fourth part of this objective. In this chapter, we are going to focus on virtual networking in Azure and how you can implement and manage this. You will learn about the basics of Azure virtual networking, including private and public IP addresses, and learn how to configure subnets, **Virtual Networks** (**VNets**), and public and private IP addresses.

The following topics will be covered in this chapter:

- Understanding Azure VNet
- Understanding IP addresses
- Configuring subnets and VNets
- Configuring private and public IP addresses
- User-defined routes

Technical requirements

The code example for this chapter uses Azure PowerShell. For more details, visit https://docs.microsoft.com/en-us/powershell/azure/install-az-ps?view=azps-1.8.0.

The source code for our sample application can be downloaded from https://github.com/PacktPublishing/Microsoft-Azure-Architect-Technologies-Exam-Guide-AZ-300/tree/master/Chapter04.

Understanding Azure VNet

An Azure VNet is a virtual representation of a traditional network that's hosted in the cloud. It is totally software-based, whereas traditional networks use cables, routers, and more. VNets provide a secure and isolated environment and they connect Azure resources to each other. By default, the different resources can't be reached from outside of the VNet. However, you can connect multiple VNets to each other or connect a VNet to your on-premises network. All the Azure resources that are connected to each other inside the same VNet must reside in the same region and subscription.

When you create a VNet, one subnet is automatically created for you. You can create multiple subnets inside the same VNet (with a maximum of 1,000 subnets per VNet). Connecting multiple VNets together is called VNet peering. A maximum of 10 peering is allowed per Azure subscription.

The smallest subnet that can be used in Azure is the /29 subnet, which consists of eight addresses. The largest is /8, which consists of 16 million addresses.

> For more information on subnetting, please refer to the *Subnet Mask Cheat Sheet*: https://www.aelius.com/njh/subnet_sheet.html.

Understanding IP addresses

A VNet in Azure can have private and public IP addresses. Private IP addresses are only accessible from within the VNet, though public IP addresses can be accessed from the internet as well. You can access private IP addresses from a VPN gateway or an ExpressRoute connection. Both private and public IP addresses can be static or dynamic, but when you create a new VNet, the IP address is static by default. You can change the IP address to *static* from the Azure portal, PowerShell, or **command-line interface (CLI)**. The following are the two states of an IP address:

- **Dynamic**: Dynamic IP addresses are assigned by Azure automatically and are selected from the configured subnet's address range from the virtual network where the Azure resource resides. The IP address is assigned to the Azure resource upon creation or start. The IP address will be released when the resource is stopped and deallocated (when you stop the VM from the Azure portal, the VM is deallocated automatically) and added back to the pool of available addresses inside the subnet by Azure.

- **Static**: Static IP addresses (private and public) are preassigned and will remain the same until you delete the assignment. You can select a static private IP address manually. They can only be assigned to non-internet-facing connections, such as an internal load balancer. You can assign a private static IP address to a connection on your on-premises network or to an ExpressRoute circuit. Public static IP addresses are created by Azure automatically and can be assigned to internet-facing connections such as an external load balancer.

Public IP address

Public IP addresses can be used for internal communication between Azure services and external communication over the internet. You can use IPv4 and IPv6 for public IP addresses, but support for IPv6 is limited. At the time of writing, you can only assign IPv6 addresses to external load balancers.

When an Azure resource is started or created, Azure will assign the public IP address to the network interface of the VNet. When an outbound connection is initiated, Azure will map the private IP address to the public IP addresses, which is also known as **source network address translation (SNAT)**.

Azure assigns the public IP address to the network interface when the Azure resource is started or created. When an outbound connection is initiated, Azure will map the private IP address to the public IP address (SNAT). Returning traffic to the resource is allowed as well. Public IP addresses are typically used for VMs, internet-facing load balancers, VPN gateways, and application gateways. A maximum of 60 dynamic public IP addresses and 20 static public IP addresses is allowed per subscription. The first five static IP addresses are free to use.

Private IP addresses

Private IP addresses support IPv4 and IPv6 as well, but support for IPv6 is limited. They can only be assigned dynamically, and IPv6 addresses cannot communicate with each other inside a VNet. The only way to use IPv6 addresses is by assigning them to an internet-facing load balancer, where the frontend IP address is an IPv4 address and the backend is an IPV6 address.

Private IP addresses are typically used for VMs, internal load balancers, and application gateways. Because of the fact that a VPN is always internet-facing, it cannot have a private IP address. You can have a maximum of 4,096 private IP addresses per VNet. However, you can create multiple VNets (with a maximum amount of 50 VNets per subscription).

 These limits are based on the default limits from the following page: https://docs.microsoft.com/en-us/azure/azure-subscription-service-limits?toc=%2fazure%2fvirtual-network%2ftoc.json#networking-limits. You can open a support request to raise these limits.

Now that we have some background information about the various networking aspects in Azure, we can configure a virtual network with a subnet.

Configuring virtual networks and subnets

In this section, we are going to create and configure a virtual network and a subnet from the Azure portal. We created both of these in earlier demonstrations, for instance, when we created VMs. Now, we are going to cover this topic in more detail.

Here, we are going to configure a virtual network and a subnet using PowerShell. Therefore, we have to perform the following steps:

1. First, we need to log into our Azure account, as follows:

    ```
    Connect-AzAccount
    ```

2. If necessary, select the right subscription, as follows:

    ```
    Select-AzSubscription -SubscriptionId "********-****-****-****-
    ***********"
    ```

3. Create a resource group for the VNet as follows:

    ```
    New-AzResourceGroup -Name PacktVNetResourceGroup -Location
    EastUS
    ```

4. Next, we can create the VNet, as follows:

```
$virtualNetwork = New-AzVirtualNetwork `
  -ResourceGroupName PacktVNetResourceGroup `
  -Location EastUS `
  -Name PacktVirtualNetwork `
  -AddressPrefix 10.0.0.0/16
```

5. Then, we can create the subnet, as follows:

```
$subnetConfig = Add-AzVirtualNetworkSubnetConfig `
  -Name default `
  -AddressPrefix 10.0.0.0/24 `
  -VirtualNetwork $virtualNetwork
```

6. Finally, we can associate the subnet with the virtual network, as follows:

```
$virtualNetwork | Set-AzVirtualNetwork
```

Now, we have created a VNet and a subnet from PowerShell. We will use this for further demonstration purposes in this chapter. In the next section, we are going to configure both a private and a public IP address in PowerShell and associate them with this VNet.

Configuring private and public IP addresses

In this section, we are going to configure both a private and a public IP address. When we created the VNet, a private IP address was created for us automatically by Azure. However, we are going to create another in this demonstration and associate it, along with the public IP address, to a **network interface card** (**NIC**). To configure a private and public IP address from PowerShell, you have to perform the following steps:

1. In the same PowerShell window, add the following code to retrieve the VNet and subnet configuration:

```
$vnet = Get-AzVirtualNetwork -Name PacktVirtualNetwork -
ResourceGroupName PacktVNetResourceGroup
$subnet = Get-AzVirtualNetworkSubnetConfig -Name default -
VirtualNetwork $vnet
```

2. Next, create a private and a public IP address and assign them to the configuration, as follows:

```
$publicIP = New-AzPublicIpAddress `
    -Name PacktPublicIP `
    -ResourceGroupName PacktVNetResourceGroup `
    -AllocationMethod Dynamic `
    -Location EastUS

$IpConfig = New-AzNetworkInterfaceIpConfig `
  -Name PacktPrivateIP `
  -Subnet $subnet `
  -PrivateIpAddress 10.0.0.4 `
  -PublicIPAddress $publicIP `
  -Primary
```

3. Then, create a network interface and assign the configuration to it, as follows:

```
$NIC = New-AzNetworkInterface `
 -Name PacktNIC `
 -ResourceGroupName PacktVNetResourceGroup `
 -Location EastUS `
 -IpConfiguration $IpConfig
```

Now, we have configured an NIC, a public and a private IP address, and associated them with the VNet that we created in the previous section.

User-defined routes

When you create subnets, Azure creates system routes that enable all the resources in a subnet so that they can communicate with each other. Every subnet has a default system route table, which contains the following minimum routes:

- **Local VNet**: This is a route for resources that reside in the VNet. For these routes, there is no next hop address. If the destination IP address contains the local VNet prefix, traffic is routed there.
- **On-premises**: This is a route for defined on-premises address spaces. For this route, the next hop address will be the VNet gateway. If the destination IP address contains the on-premises address prefix, traffic is routed there.
- **Internet**: This route is for all the traffic that goes over the public internet, and the internet gateway is always the next hop address. If the destination IP address doesn't contain the VNet or on-premises prefixes, traffic is routed to the internet using **network address translation (NAT)**.

You can override these system routes by creating **user-defined routes** (**UDRs**). This way, you can force traffic to follow a particular route. For instance, you have a network that consists of two subnets and you want to add a VM that is used as a **demilitarized zone** (**DMZ**) and has a firewall installed on it. You only want traffic to go through the firewall and not between the two subnets. To create UDRs and enable IP forwarding, you have to create a routing table in Azure. When this table is created and there are custom routes in there, Azure prefers the custom routes over the default system routes.

Creating user-defined routes

To create **UDRs**, follow these steps:

1. Navigate to the Azure portal by going to `https://portal.azure.com/`.
2. Click **Create a resource**, type `Route Table` into the search bar, and create a new one.
3. Add the following values, as shown in the following screenshot:
    - **Name:** `PacktRoutingTable`.
    - **Subscription**: Select a subscription.
    - **Resource Group**: Create a new one and call it `PacktRoutingTable`.
    - **Location: (US) East US:**

Creating a new route table

4. Click **Create**.

5. A new and empty route table will be created. After creation, open the **Overview** blade of the route table. To add custom routes, click **Routes** from the left menu, as follows:

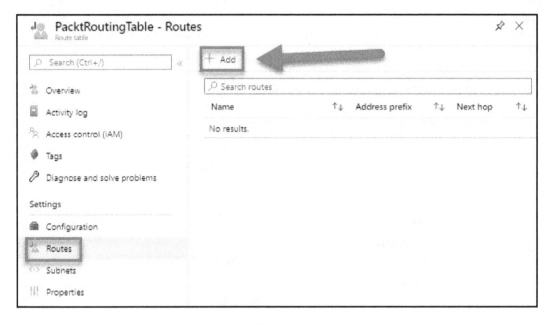

Adding a new route

6. In this example, we want all the internet traffic to go through the firewall. To do this, add the following values, as shown in the following screenshot:

- **Name**: DefaultRoute.

- **Address prefix**: 0.0.0.0/0.

- **Next hop type**: **Virtual appliance**; this is the firewall.

- **Next hop address**: 10.1.1.10. This will be the internal IP address of the firewall:

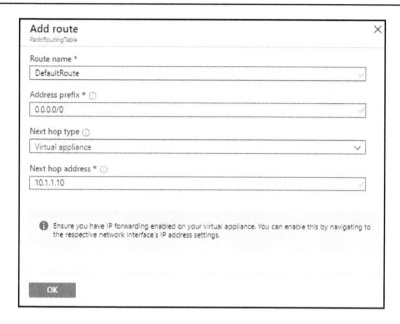

Adding a route to the table

7. Click **OK**. The route will be created for you.

For more detailed instructions on how to create UDRs and virtual appliances, you can refer to the following tutorial: `https://docs.microsoft.com/en-us/azure/virtual-network/tutorial-create-route-table-portal`.

In this section, we created a custom route table and added a route to it that routes all the traffic to a firewall. This concludes this chapter.

Summary

In this chapter, we completed the fourth part of the *Deploying and Managing Virtual Networks* objective by covering the basics of Azure virtual networking, including private and public IP addresses. We also covered how to configure subnets, VNets, and public and private IP addresses.

In the next chapter, we will continue with the fifth part of the *Deploy and Configure Infrastructure* objective by covering how to create connectivity between virtual networks.

Questions

1. There is a maximum of 120 dynamic public IP addresses and 10 static public IP addresses per subscription.
   - Yes
   - No

2. Can you create custom route tables to adjust the routing between the different resources inside your VNets?
   - Yes
   - No

3. Can you assign IPv6 addresses for all Azure resources?
   - Yes
   - No

Further reading

Check out the following links if you want to find out more about the topics that were covered in this chapter:

- **Azure Networking Limits**: `https://docs.microsoft.com/en-us/azure/azure-subscription-service-limits?toc=%2fazure%2fvirtual-network%2ftoc.json#networking-limits`
- **Quickstart: Creating a virtual network using the Azure portal**: `https://docs.microsoft.com/en-us/azure/virtual-network/quick-create-portal`
- **Tutorial: Routing network traffic with a Route table using the Azure portal**: `https://docs.microsoft.com/en-us/azure/virtual-network/tutorial-create-route-table-portal`

5
Creating Connectivity between Virtual Networks

In the previous chapter, we covered the fourth part of the *Deploy and Configure Infrastructure* objective. We have also previously covered virtual networking in Azure and how you can implement and manage it. You've learned about the basics of virtual networking, including private and public IP addresses, and more.

In this chapter, you will learn how to create connectivity between virtual networks. We are going to cover how to create and configure **Virtual Network** (**VNet**) peering, how to create and configure VNet-to-VNet, how to verify virtual network connectivity, and the differences between VNet peering, VNet-to-VNet connections, and when to use what type of connection.

The following topics will be covered in this chapter:

- Understanding VNet peering
- Creating and configuring VNet peering
- Understanding VNet-to-VNet
- Creating and configuring VNet-to-VNet
- Verifying virtual network connectivity
- VNet peering versus VNet-to-VNet

Technical requirements

This chapter will use Azure PowerShell (`https://docs.microsoft.com/en-us/ powershell/azure/install-az-ps?view=azps-1.8.0`) in the examples that it shows.

The source code for our sample application can be downloaded from `https://github.com/ PacktPublishing/Microsoft-Azure-Architect-Technologies-Exam-Guide-AZ-300/tree/ master/Chapter04`.

Understanding VNet peering

VNet peering is a mechanism that seamlessly connects two VNets in the same region through the Azure backbone infrastructure. Once peered, the VNets appear as one for connectivity purposes, just like routing traffic between **virtual machines** (**VMs**) that are created in the same VNet. The VMs that reside in the peered VNets communicate with each other using private IP addresses. VNet peering is the easiest and most effective way to connect two VNets together.

Azure supports the following two different types of peering:

- **VNet peering**: This is used for connecting VNets in the same Azure region.
- **Global VNet peering**: This is used for connecting VNets across different Azure regions.

The network traffic between peered VNets is private. The traffic is kept on the Microsoft backbone network completely, so there is no need to use any additional gateways or to route traffic over the public internet. There is also no encryption required in the communication between the peered VNets. It uses a low-latency, high-bandwidth connection between the resources in the different virtual networks.

You can use VNet peering to connect VNets that are created through the resource manager and the classic deployment model, and it gives you the ability to transfer data across Azure regions and subscriptions.

The other way to connect VNets is to set up VNet-to-VNet connections. This requires you to deploy gateways in each of the connected VNets, which are both connected by a tunnel. This limits the connection speeds to the bandwidth of the gateway.

Creating and configuring VNet peering

In the following demonstration, we are going to create and configure VNet peering from the Azure portal. We need two VNets for this. We are going to use the VNet that we created in the first demonstration, and with the resource group for which we created the VNet in the previous chapter, we are going to create an additional VNet, which has a different address space than the first VNet. Note that you can't use overlapping address spaces when you peer two VNets together.

To create the VNet and set up VNet peering from the Azure portal, go through the following steps:

1. Navigate to the Azure portal by opening `https://portal.azure.com/`.
2. Click **Create a resource** | **Networking** | **Virtual network**. Create a new VNet.
3. Add the following values:
   - **Name:** `PacktVNetPeering`
   - **Address space:** `10.2.0.0/16`
   - **Subscription:** Pick a subscription
   - **Resource group:** `PacktVNetResourceGroup`
   - **Location:** East US
   - **Subnet:** `default`
   - **Address range:** `10.2.0.0/24`
   - **DDoS protection:** Basic
   - **Service endpoints:** Disabled
   - **Firewall:** Disabled
4. Click **Create**.

5. The VNet is created for you. After its creation, open the **VNet Overview** blade of the VNet that we created in the first demonstration of this chapter, which is called `PacktVirtualNetwork`, as follows:

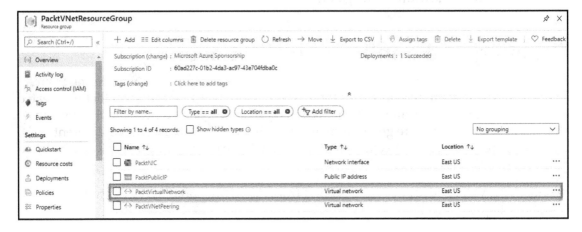

VNet overview blade

6. Then, under **Settings**, select **Peerings**. Click **Add** in the top menu, as shown in the following screenshot:

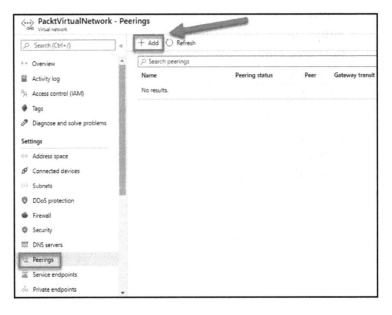

Adding a new VNet peering

7. In the **Add peering** blade, add the following values:
   - Name of the peering from `PacktVirtualNetwork` to `PacktVNetPeering`: `PacktPeering`.
   - **Virtual network deployment model**: **Resource manager**.
   - **Subscription**: Keep the default selected.
   - **Virtual network**: Select `PacktVNetPeering`.

8. There are a couple of other settings that you can set here as well. The first one is **Allow forwarded traffic from PacktVirtualNetwork to PacktVNetPeering**. This means that you allow traffic from outside the peered VNet. The second one is **Configure gateway transit settings**. This means that the peered network uses the gateway of this VNet to connect to resources outside the peered VNet, for instance, an on-premises environment. The last one is **Configure Remote Gateway Settings**. For this setting, you have to enable the previous one as well, but by enabling this one, you are using the other VNet gateway to connect resources outside the VNet.

9. Click **OK,** and the peering is created.

We have now configured VNet peering from the Azure portal. In the next section, we are going to look at VNet-to-VNet.

Understanding VNet-to-VNet

A VNet-to-VNet connection is a simple way to connect multiple VNets together. Connecting a virtual network to another virtual network is similar to creating a site-to-site IPSec connection to an on-premises environment. Both the connection types use the Azure **virtual private network** (**VPN**) gateway. The VPN gateway provides a secure IPSec/IKE tunnel, and each side of the connection communicates in the same way. The difference is in the way the local network gateway is configured.

 In this chapter, we are going to create a VPN gateway to connect two VNets together using PowerShell. The VPN gateway is covered in more detail in `Chapter 11`, *Integrating On-Premises Networks with Azure Virtual Network*.

The local network gateway address space is automatically created and populated when a VNet-to-VNet connection is created. When the address space of one VNet is updated, this will result in the other VNet automatically routing the traffic to the updated address space. This makes it more efficient and quicker to create a VNet-to-VNet connection instead of an S2S connection.

There are a couple of reasons why you might want to set up a VNet-to-VNet connection:

- **Cross-region geo-redundancy and geo-presence**: Using a VNet-to-VNet connection, you can set up your own geo-replication or synchronization without going over internet-facing endpoints. You can set up highly available workloads with geo-redundancy across multiple Azure regions using the Azure Load Balancer and Azure Traffic Manager.

- **Regional multi-tier applications with isolation or administrative boundaries**: In the case of isolation or administrative requirements, you can set up multitier applications with multiple networks in the same region. Those networks can then all be connected together.

You can combine VNet-to-VNet communication with multisite configurations. Network topologies that combine inter-virtual network connectivity with cross-premises connectivity can be established using these configurations, as shown in the following diagram:

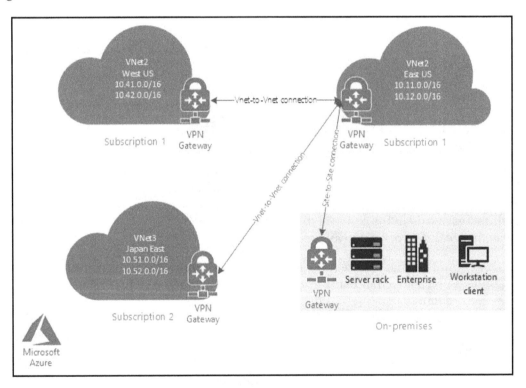

Combined VNet-to-VNet communication

To create a VNet-to-VNet connection, go through the steps shown in the following example.

Creating and configuring VNet-to-VNet

In this demonstration, we are going to create a VNet-to-VNet connection using PowerShell.

In the following steps, we will create two VNets together with the gateway configurations and subnets. We then create a VPN connection between the two VNets. We are going to set up a connection in the same Azure subscription. In the first step, we are going to plan the IP address ranges for the network configurations. We need to make sure that none of the VNet or local ranges overlap.

Planning IP ranges

We are going to use the following values for the IP ranges:

Values for PacktVNet1 are as follows:

- **VNet Name:** PacktVNet1
- **Resource Group:** PacktResourceGroup1
- **Location: East US**
- **PacktVNet1:** 10.11.0.0/16 and 10.12.0.0/16
- **Frontend:** 10.11.0.0/24
- **Backend:** 10.12.0.0/24
- **Gateway Subnet:** 10.12.255.0/27
- **Gateway Name:** PacktVNet1Gateway
- **Public IP:** PacktVNet1GWIP
- **VPN Type:** RouteBased
- **Connection:** VNet1toVNet2
- **Connection Type:** VNet2VNet

Values for TestVNet2 are as follows:

- **VNet Name:** PacktVNet2
- **Resource Group:** PacktResourceGroup2
- **Location: West US**
- **PacktVNet2:** 10.41.0.0/16 and 10.42.0.0/16

- **Frontend**: 10.41.0.0/24
- **Backend**: 10.42.0.0/24
- **Gateway Subnet**: 10.42.255.0/27
- **Gateway Name**: PacktVNet2Gateway
- **Public IP**: PacktVNet2GWIP
- **VPN Type**: RouteBased
- **Connection**: VNet2toVNet1
- **Connection Type**: VNet2VNet

Now that we have planned our IP configurations, we can create the VNets.

Creating PacktVNet1

To create PacktVNet1, we have to go through the following steps:

1. First, we need to log in to the Azure account:

   ```
   Connect-AzAccount
   ```

2. If necessary, select the right subscription:

   ```
   Select-AzSubscription -SubscriptionId "********-****-****-****-
   **********"
   ```

3. Define the variables for the first VNet:

   ```
   $RG1 = "PacktResourceGroup1"
   $Location1 = "East US"
   $VNetName1 = "PacktVNet1"
   $FESubName1 = "FrontEnd"
   $BESubName1 = "Backend"
   $VNetPrefix01 = "10.11.0.0/16"
   $VNetPrefix02 = "10.12.0.0/16"
   $FESubPrefix1 = "10.11.0.0/24"
   $BESubPrefix1 = "10.12.0.0/24"
   $GWSubPrefix1 = "10.12.255.0/27"
   $GWName1 = "PacktVNet1Gateway"
   $GWIPName1 = "PacktVNet1GWIP"
   $GWIPconfName1 = "gwipconf1"
   $Connection01 = "VNet1toVNet2"
   ```

4. Create a resource group:

   ```
   New-AzResourceGroup -Name $RG1 -Location $Location1
   ```

5. Create subnet configurations for `PacktVNet1`. In this demonstration, we are going to create a VNet, called `PacktVNet1`, and three subnets, called `FrontEnd`, `Backend`, and `GatewaySubnet`. It is important to name your gateway subnet `GatewaySubnet`; otherwise, the gateway creation will fail.

   It is recommended that you create a gateway subnet using a `/27`. This includes more addresses, which will accommodate possible additional configurations that you may want to make in the future:

```
$fesub1 = New-AzVirtualNetworkSubnetConfig -Name $FESubName1 -
AddressPrefix $FESubPrefix1
$besub1 = New-AzVirtualNetworkSubnetConfig -Name $BESubName1 -
AddressPrefix $BESubPrefix1
$gwsub1 = New-AzVirtualNetworkSubnetConfig -Name
"GatewaySubnet" -AddressPrefix $GWSubPrefix1
```

6. Create `PacktVNet1`:

```
New-AzVirtualNetwork -Name $VNetName1 `
    -ResourceGroupName $RG1 `
    -Location $Location1 `
    -AddressPrefix $VNetPrefix01,$VNetPrefix02 `
    -Subnet $fesub1,$besub1,$gwsub1
```

7. Request a public IP address to be allocated to the gateway that you will create for `PacktVNet1`. Here, you cannot specify the IP address that you want to use. It's dynamically allocated to your gateway:

```
$gwpip1 = New-AzPublicIpAddress `
    -Name $GWIPName1 `
    -ResourceGroupName $RG1 `
    -Location $Location1 `
    -AllocationMethod Dynamic
```

8. Create the gateway configuration. The gateway configuration defines the subnet and the public IP address to use:

```
$vnet1 = Get-AzVirtualNetwork `
    -Name $VNetName1 `
    -ResourceGroupName $RG1
$subnet1 = Get-AzVirtualNetworkSubnetConfig `
    -Name "GatewaySubnet" `
    -VirtualNetwork $vnet1
$gwipconf1 = New-AzVirtualNetworkGatewayIpConfig `
    -Name $GWIPconfName1 `
    -Subnet $subnet1 `
    -PublicIpAddress $gwpip1
```

9. Create the gateway for `PacktVNet1`. VNet-to-VNet configurations require a `RouteBased` setting for `VpnType`:

```
New-AzVirtualNetworkGateway `
    -Name $GWName1 `
    -ResourceGroupName $RG1 `
    -Location $Location1 `
    -IpConfigurations $gwipconf1 `
    -GatewayType Vpn `
    -VpnType RouteBased `
    -GatewaySku VpnGw1
```

 Creating a gateway can often take 45 minutes or more, depending on the selected gateway SKU. The different gateway SKUs are covered in more detail in `Chapter 11`, *Integrating On-Premises Networks with Azure Virtual Networks*.

We have now created the first VNet. In the next section, we are going to create `PacktVNet2`.

Creating PacktVNet2

To create `PacktVNet2`, we have to take the following steps:

1. Define the variables for the first VNet:

```
$RG2 = "PacktResourceGroup2"
$Location2 = "West US"
$VNetName2 = "PacktVNet2"
$FESubName2 = "FrontEnd"
$BESubName2 = "Backend"
$VnetPrefix11 = "10.41.0.0/16"
$VnetPrefix12 = "10.42.0.0/16"
$FESubPrefix2 = "10.41.0.0/24"
$BESubPrefix2 = "10.42.0.0/24"
$GWSubPrefix2 = "10.42.255.0/27"
$GWName2 = "PacktVNet2Gateway"
$GWIPName2 = "PacktVNet1GWIP"
$GWIPconfName2 = "gwipconf2"
$Connection2 = "VNet2toVNet1"
```

2. Create a resource group:

```
New-AzResourceGroup -Name $RG2 -Location $Location2
```

3. Create subnet configurations for `PacktVNet2`:

```
$fesub2 = New-AzVirtualNetworkSubnetConfig -Name $FESubName2 -
AddressPrefix $FESubPrefix2
$besub2 = New-AzVirtualNetworkSubnetConfig -Name $BESubName2 -
AddressPrefix $BESubPrefix2
$gwsub2 = New-AzVirtualNetworkSubnetConfig -Name
"GatewaySubnet" -AddressPrefix $GWSubPrefix2
```

4. Create `PacktVNet2`:

```
New-AzVirtualNetwork `
    -Name $VnetName2 `
    -ResourceGroupName $RG2 `
    -Location $Location2 `
    -AddressPrefix $VnetPrefix11,$VnetPrefix12 `
    -Subnet $fesub2,$besub2,$gwsub2
```

5. Request a public IP address:

```
$gwpip2 = New-AzPublicIpAddress `
    -Name $GWIPName2 `
    -ResourceGroupName $RG2 `
    -Location $Location2 `
    -AllocationMethod Dynamic
```

6. Create the gateway configuration:

```
$vnet2 = Get-AzVirtualNetwork `
    -Name $VnetName2 `
    -ResourceGroupName $RG2
$subnet2 = Get-AzVirtualNetworkSubnetConfig `
    -Name "GatewaySubnet" `
    -VirtualNetwork $vnet2
$gwipconf2 = New-AzVirtualNetworkGatewayIpConfig `
    -Name $GWIPconfName2 `
    -Subnet $subnet2 `
    -PublicIpAddress $gwpip2
```

7. Create the gateway:

```
New-AzVirtualNetworkGateway -Name $GWName2 `
    -ResourceGroupName $RG2 `
    -Location $Location2 `
    -IpConfigurations $gwipconf2 `
    -GatewayType Vpn `
    -VpnType RouteBased `
    -GatewaySku VpnGw1
```

Wait for the gateway to be created. After its creation, we can create connections between the VNets.

Creating connections

To create connections, we need to take the following steps:

1. First, get a reference to the two gateways:

    ```
    $vnet1gw = Get-AzVirtualNetworkGateway -Name $GWName1 -
    ResourceGroupName $RG1
    $vnet2gw = Get-AzVirtualNetworkGateway -Name $GWName2 -
    ResourceGroupName $RG2
    ```

2. Next, we can create a connection. Make sure that the keys match:

    ```
    New-AzVirtualNetworkGatewayConnection `
        -Name $Connection01 `
        -ResourceGroupName $RG1 `
        -VirtualNetworkGateway1 $vnet1gw `
        -VirtualNetworkGateway2 $vnet2gw `
        -Location $Location1 `
        -ConnectionType Vnet2Vnet `
        -SharedKey 'AzurePacktGateway'

    New-AzVirtualNetworkGatewayConnection `
        -Name $Connection02 `
        -ResourceGroupName $RG2 `
        -VirtualNetworkGateway1 $vnet2gw `
        -VirtualNetworkGateway2 $vnet1gw `
        -Location $Location2 `
        -ConnectionType Vnet2Vnet `
        -SharedKey 'AzurePacktGateway'
    ```

In this demo, we configured a VNet-to-VNet connection. To do this, we created two VNets, both with a virtual network gateway. We also set up the connections between the gateways. In the next section, we are going to cover how you can verify the network connectivity for your VNet-to-VNet connection after creation.

Verifying virtual network connectivity

To verify whether the VNet-to-VNet connection is successfully set up, you have to go through the following steps:

1. In PowerShell, use the following code to verify the network connection:

   ```
   Get-AzVirtualNetworkGatewayConnection -Name $Connection01 -
   ResourceGroupName $RG1
   Get-AzVirtualNetworkGatewayConnection -Name $Connection02 -
   ResourceGroupName $RG2
   ```

2. If the connection status shows `Connected`, then the connection is successful:

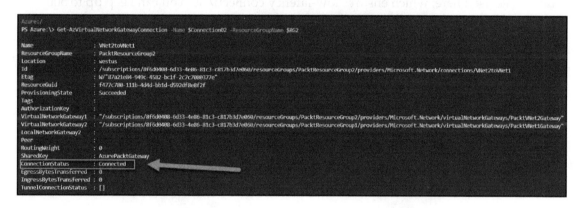

Verify the connection

In this demo, we verified the VNet-to-VNet connection. In the next section, we will look at the differences between VNet peering and VNet-to-VNet connections.

VNet peering versus VNet-to-VNet connections

VNet peering and VNet-to-VNet both offer ways to connect VNets together. But based on your specific scenario and needs, you might want to pick one over the other:

- **VNet peering**: This offers high-bandwidth, low-latency connections, which are useful in cross-region data replication and database failover scenarios. The traffic remains on the Microsoft backbone and is completely private; that's why customers with strict data security requirements prefer to use VNet peering, as public internet is not involved. There are also no extra hops because no gateway is used here, which ensures low-latency connections. You can keep up to 500 VNets with one VNet. The ingress and egress are charged using VNet peering. In region/cross-region scenarios, VNet peering is recommended.
- **VPN gateways**: These provide a limited bandwidth connection and are useful in scenarios where encryption is needed, but bandwidth restrictions are tolerable. The bandwidth limitations vary based on the type of gateway, from 100 MBps to 1.25 GBps. In these scenarios, customers are also not as latency-sensitive. Each VNet can only have one VPN gateway, and the gateway and egress are charged. There is a public IP address involved, which is bound to the gateway.

In this section, we've covered the scenarios in which VNet peering and VPN gateways are most suitable. This concludes this chapter.

Summary

In this chapter, we covered the fifth part of the *Deploying and Managing Virtual Networks* objective by covering how to create connectivity between virtual networks in Azure. We have covered how to create and configure VNet peering, how to create and configure VNet-to-VNet connections, how to verify virtual network connectivity, and the main differences between VNet peering and VNet-to-VNet connections.

In the next chapter, we will continue with this objective by covering how to manage Azure **Active Directory** (**AD**).

Questions

Answer the following questions to test your knowledge of the information in this chapter. You can find the answers in the *Assessments* section at the end of this book.

1. When you use VNet peering, do you have to create an Azure VPN gateway to connect both of the VNets to each other?
   - Yes
   - No

2. Is a VNet-to-VNet connection most suitable in scenarios where you don't want to use a public IP address?
   - Yes
   - No

3. VNet peering doesn't have any bandwidth limitations.
   - Yes
   - No

Further reading

You can check out the following links for more information about the topics that were covered in this chapter:

- **Virtual network peering**: https://docs.microsoft.com/en-us/azure/virtual-network/virtual-network-peering-overview
- **What is a VPN gateway?**: https://docs.microsoft.com/en-us/azure/vpn-gateway/vpn-gateway-about-vpngateways
- **Configuring a VNet-to-VNet VPN gateway connection by using the Azure portal**: https://docs.microsoft.com/en-us/azure/vpn-gateway/vpn-gateway-howto-vnet-vnet-resource-manager-portal

6
Managing Azure Active Directory (Azure AD)

In the previous chapter, we covered the fifth part of the *Deploy and Configure Infrastructure* objective. We covered how to create connectivity between virtual networks in Azure, as well as how to create and configure VNet peering, how to create and configure VNet-to-VNet, and how to verify network connectivity. Finally, we learned about the differences between VNet peering and VNet-to-VNet.

This chapter covers the sixth part of this objective. In this chapter, we are going to cover how to create and manage users and groups in **Azure Active Directory** (**Azure AD**). You will learn how to manage this from the Azure portal and how to perform bulk updates inside your Azure AD tenant. You will learn how to configure a self-service password reset for your users in order to reduce user management overhead. By doing so, we will cover conditional access policies. We are also going to cover Azure AD join and how you can manage devices that have been registered or joined in Azure AD. To conclude this chapter, we will add a custom domain to Azure AD.

The following topics will be covered in this chapter:

- Understanding Azure AD
- Creating and managing users and groups
- Adding and managing guest accounts
- Performing bulk user updates
- Configuring a self-service password reset
- Understanding conditional access policies
- Working with Azure AD join
- Adding custom domains

Understanding Azure AD

Azure AD offers a directory and identity management solution from the cloud. It offers traditional username and password identity management, as well as roles and permissions management. On top of that, it offers more enterprise-grade solutions, such as **Multi-Factor Authentication** (**MFA**) and application monitoring, solution monitoring, and alerting. Azure AD can easily be integrated with your on-premises Active Directory to create a hybrid infrastructure.

Azure AD offers the following pricing plans:

- **Free**: This offers the most basic features, such as support for up to 500,000 objects, **single sign-on** (**SSO**), Azure B2B for external users, support for Azure AD Connect synchronization, self-service password change, groups, and standard security reports.
- **Basic**: This offers no object limit, has an SLA of 99.9%, a self-service password reset, company branding features, and support for the application proxy.
- **Premium P1**: This offers advanced reporting, MFA, conditional access, MDM auto-enrollment, cloud app discovery, and Azure AD Connect Health.
- **Premium P2**: This offers identity protection and privileged identity management.

For a detailed overview of the different pricing plans and all the features that are offered for each plan, you can refer to the following pricing page: `https://azure.microsoft.com/en-us/pricing/details/active-directory/`.
Note that Azure AD Premium is part of the enterprise mobility and security suite.

In the next section, we are going to create and manage users and groups inside an Azure AD tenant.

Creating and managing users and groups

In this section, we are going to create and manage users and groups in the Azure portal. You can also use PowerShell and its CLI to create users.

We aren't going to create an Azure AD tenant in this section since it's assumed that you already have one. If you need to create an Azure AD tenant, you can refer to the following tutorial: `https://docs.microsoft.com/en-us/azure/active-directory/develop/quickstart-create-new-tenant`.

You can also create multiple Azure AD tenants in one subscription. These directories can be used for development and testing purposes, for instance.

Creating users in Azure AD

We will begin by creating a couple of users in our Azure AD tenant from the Azure portal. To do this, follow these steps:

1. Navigate to the Azure portal by going to `https://portal.azure.com`.
2. In the left menu, select **Azure Active Directory**.
3. In the **Overview** blade of Azure AD, in the left menu, select **Users** | **All users**. Select **+ New user** from the top menu, as follows:

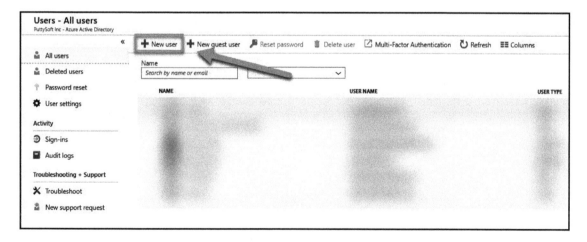

Creating a new user

4. Next, we are going to create three users. Add the following values, which can be seen in the following screenshot:
   - **Name**: `PacktUser1`.

- **Username**: The username is the identifier that the user enters to sign in to Azure AD. Use the domain name that has been configured for you and add this to the end of the username. In my case, this is `PacktUser1@sjoukjezaal.com`.

- **Profile**: Here, you can create a new profile for your user. Add the **First name**, **Last name**, **Job title**, and **Department** boxes. After that, click **Create**, as follows:

Creating a profile for your user

- **Group**: You can also add your user to a group from here. We are going to do this in the next section, so you can skip this part for now.
- **Roles**: Here, you can assign the user to an RBAC role. Select **Directory readers** from the list, as follows:

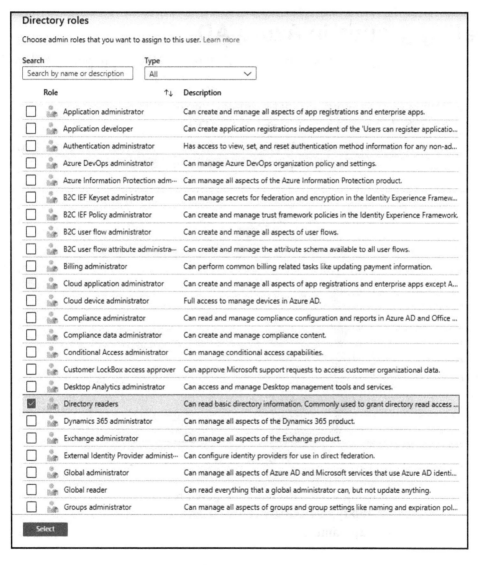

Selecting a directory role

5. Click **Select** and then **Create**.
6. Repeat these steps and create `PackUser2` and `PacktUser3`.

Now that we have created a couple of users in our Azure AD tenant, we can add them to a group in Azure AD.

Creating groups in Azure AD

To create and manage groups from the Azure AD tenant in the Azure portal, follow these steps:

1. Navigate to the Azure portal by going to `https://portal.azure.com`.
2. From the left menu, select **Azure Active Directory**.
3. In the **Overview** blade of Azure AD, in the left menu, select **Groups | All groups**. Select **+ New group** from the top menu, as follows:

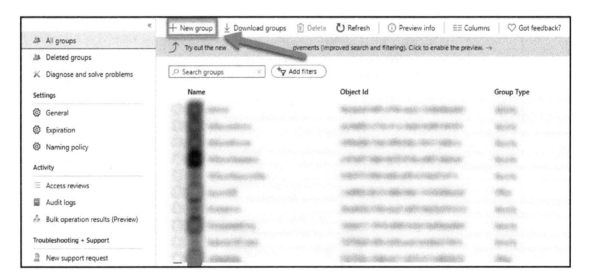

Creating a new group

4. Add the following values to create the new group:
   • **Group type**: **Security**.
   • **Group name**: `PacktGroup`.

- **Membership type**: Here, you can choose between three different values. The first is **Assigned** and is where you assign the members manually to the group; then, there's **Dynamic user**, which is where the group membership is determined based on certain user properties. Dynamic group membership eliminates the management overhead of adding and removing users. The last option is **Dynamic device**, which is where the group membership is determined based on certain device properties. Select the first option: **Assigned**.

5. Click the **Members** tab to add members to this group. Select the three user accounts that we created in the previous section, as follows:

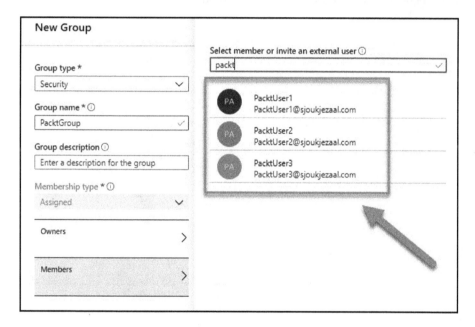

Adding users to a group

6. Click **Select** to add the members and then **Create** to create the group.

Now, we have created a new group inside Azure AD and added the user accounts to it that we created in the previous section. In the next section, we are going to learn how to add and manage guest accounts.

Adding and managing guest accounts

You can also add guest accounts in Azure AD using Azure AD B2B. Azure AD B2B is a feature on top of Azure AD that allows organizations to work safely with external users. To be added to Azure B2B, external users don't need to have a Microsoft work or personal account that has been added to an existing Azure AD tenant. All sorts of accounts can be added to Azure B2B.

You don't have to configure anything in the Azure portal to use B2B; this feature is enabled by default for all Azure AD tenants. Perform the following steps to do this:

1. Adding guest accounts to your Azure AD tenant is similar to adding internal users to your tenant. When you go to the user's overview blade, you can choose **+ New guest user** from the top menu, as follows:

Adding a guest user

2. Then, you can provide the same credentials as an internal user. You need to provide a name and an email address, as well as a personal message, which is sent to the user's inbox. This personal message includes a link so that you can log in to your tenant. You can also add the user to a group, as well as an RBAC role:

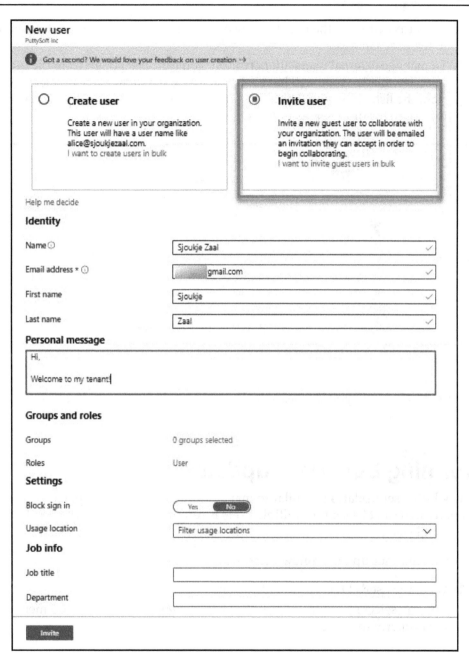

External user properties

3. Click **Invite** to add the user to your Azure AD tenant and send out the invitation to the user's inbox.

4. To manage external users after creation, you can select them from the user overview blade. They will have a **USER TYPE** of **Guest**. Simply select the user from the list. Now, you'll be able to manage the settings that are displayed in the top menu for this user, as follows:

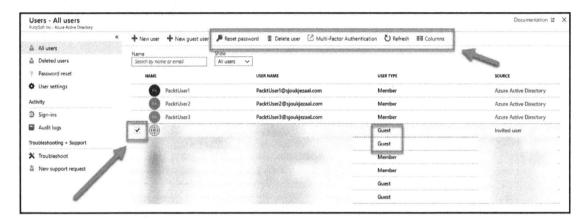

Managing external users

In the next section, we are going to learn how to perform bulk user updates from the Azure portal.

Performing bulk user updates

Performing bulk user updates is similar to managing single users (internal and guest). The only property that can't be set for multiple users is resetting their passwords. This has to be done for a single user.

To perform a bulk user update, follow these steps:

1. Go to the user's **Overview** blade again.

2. You can select multiple users in the **Overview** blade. From the top menu, select the property that you want to configure, as follows:

Performing a bulk user update

This concludes how to perform bulk user updates. In the next section, we are going to cover how you can configure a self-service password reset for your users.

Configuring a self-service password reset

By enabling a self-service password for your users, they are able to change their passwords automatically, without calling the help desk. This eliminates management overhead significantly.

A self-service password reset can easily be enabled from the Azure portal. To do so, follow these steps:

1. Navigate to the Azure portal by going to `https://portal.azure.com`.
2. From the left menu, select **Azure Active Directory**.
3. In the Azure AD **Overview** blade, in the left menu, under **Manage**, select **Password reset**.

4. In the password reset **Overview** blade, you can enable self-service password resets for all your users by selecting **All** or for selected users and groups by selecting **Selected**. For demonstration purposes, enable it for all users and click **Save**, as follows:

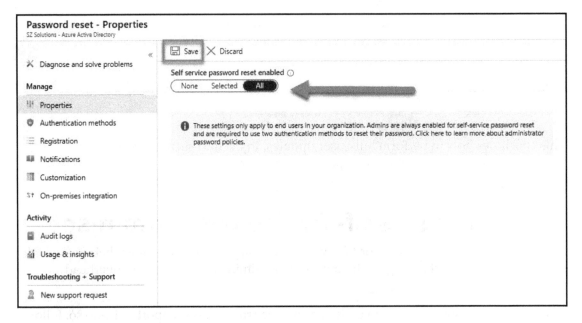

Enabling a self-service password reset for all users

5. Next, we need to set the different required authentication methods for your users. For this, under **Manage**, select **Authentication methods**.

6. In the next blade, we can set the number of authentication methods that are required to reset a password and what methods there are available for your users, as follows:

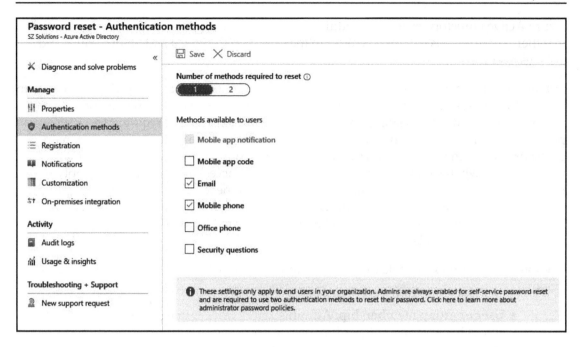

Different authentication methods

7. Make a selection and click **Save**.

> If you want to test the self-service password reset after it's been configured, make sure that you use a user account without administrator privileges.

Now, we have configured a self-service password reset for all our users inside our Azure AD tenant. In the next section, we are going to cover conditional access policies in Azure AD.

Understanding conditional access policies

Nowadays, modern security extends beyond the boundaries of an organization's network to include user and device identity. These identity signals can be used by organizations as part of their access control decisions.

Azure Active Directory provides conditional access to bring all those identity signals together. These signals can then be used to make certain decisions and enforce rules and policies over them.

In their most basic form, conditional access policies are if-then statements. If a user wants to access a certain resource, they must complete a certain action. For instance, a guest user wants access to data that is stored in an Azure SQL database and is required to perform multi-factor authentication to access it. This achieves administrators' two main goals: protecting the organization's assets and empowering users to be productive wherever and whenever. By implementing conditional access policies, you can apply the right access controls for all those different signals when needed to keep the organization's data and assets secure and enable different types of users and devices to easily get access to it. With conditional access policies, you have the choice to block access or grant access based on different signals.

The following common signals can be taken into account when policy decisions need to be made:

- **User or group membership**: Administrators can get fine-grained control over access by targeting policies for specific users and groups.
- **Device**: Policies and rules can be enforced for specific devices or platforms.
- **Application**: Different conditional access policies can be triggered when users are trying to access specific applications.
- **IP Location information**: Administrators can specify IP ranges and addresses to block or allow traffic from.
- **Microsoft Cloud App Security (MCAS)**: User applications and sessions can be monitored and controlled in real time. This increases control and visibility over access and activities inside the cloud environment.
- **Real-time and calculated risk detection**: The integration of signals with Azure AD Identity Protection allows conditional access policies to identify risky sign-in behavior. These risk levels can then be reduced, or access can be blocked by enforcing conditional access policies that perform **multi-factor authentication (MFA)** or password changes.

Implementing a conditional access policy could come up as an exam question. For a complete walkthrough on how to enable MFA for specific apps using a conditional access policy, you can refer to the following website: `https://docs.microsoft.com/en-us/azure/active-directory/conditional-access/app-based-mfa`.

In the next section, we are going to cover how we can join devices directly to Azure AD.

Working with Azure AD join

With Azure AD join, you are able to join devices directly to Azure AD without the need to join your on-premises Active Directory in a hybrid environment. While hybrid Azure AD Join with an on-premises AD may still be preferred for some scenarios, Azure AD join simplifies adding devices and modernizes device management for your organization. This can result in the reduction of device-related IT costs. Let's say your users are getting access to corporate assets through their devices. To protect these corporate assets, you want to control these devices. This allows your administrators to make sure that your users are accessing resources from devices that meet your standards for security and compliance.

Azure AD join is a good solution when you want to manage devices with a cloud device management solution, modernize your application infrastructure, simplify device provisioning for geographically distributed users, and when your company is adopting Microsoft 365 as the productivity suite for your users.

Managing device settings

Azure AD offers you the ability to ensure that users are accessing Azure resources from devices that meet corporate security and compliance standards. Device management is the foundation for device-based conditional access and is where you can ensure that access to the resources in your environment is only possible from managed devices.

Device settings can be managed from the Azure portal. To manage your device settings, your device needs to be registered or joined to Azure AD.

To manage your device settings from the Azure portal, follow these steps:

1. Navigate to the Azure portal by going to `https://portal.azure.com`.
2. From the left menu, select **Azure Active Directory**.
3. In the Azure AD **Overview** blade, under **Manage**, select **Devices**.
4. The **Device management** blade will open. Here, you can configure your device management settings, locate your devices, perform device management tasks, and review the device management-related audit logs.
5. To configure device settings, select **Device settings** from the left menu. Here, you can configure the following settings, which can be seen in the following screenshot:

   - **Users may join devices to Azure AD**: Here, you can set which users can join their devices to Azure AD. This setting is only applicable to Azure AD Join on Windows 10.

   - **Additional local administrators on Azure AD joined devices**: Here, you can select the users that are granted local administrator permissions on a device. The users that are selected here are automatically added to the device administrator's role in Azure AD. Global administrators in Azure AD and device owners are granted local administrator rights by default (this is an Azure AD Premium option).

   - **Users may register their devices with Azure AD**: This setting needs to be configured to allow devices to be registered with Azure AD. There are two options here: **None**, that is, devices are not allowed to register when they are not Azure AD joined or hybrid Azure AD joined, and **All**, that is, all devices are allowed to register. Enrollment with Microsoft Intune or **Mobile Device Management** (**MDM**) for Office 365 requires registration. If you have configured either of these services, **All** is selected and **None** is not available.

   - **Require multi-factor authentication to join devices**: Here, you can set that users are required to perform MFA when registering a device. Before you can enable this setting, MFA needs to be configured for the users that register their devices.

   - **Maximum number of devices**: This setting allows you to select the maximum number of devices that a user can have in Azure AD:

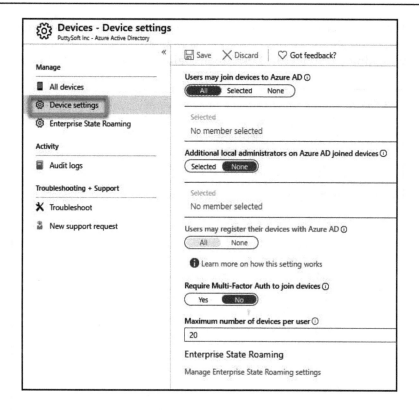

Device settings overview

6. To locate your devices, under **Manage**, select **All devices**. Here, you will see all the joined and registered devices, as follows:

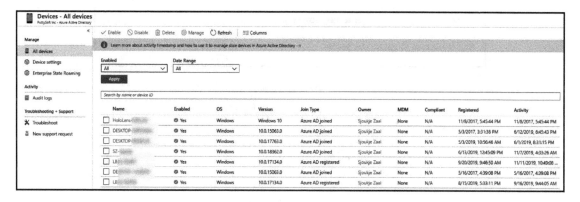

Located devices

7. You can also select the different devices from the list to get more detailed information about the device in question. Here, global administrators and cloud device administrators can **Disable** or **Delete** the device, as follows:

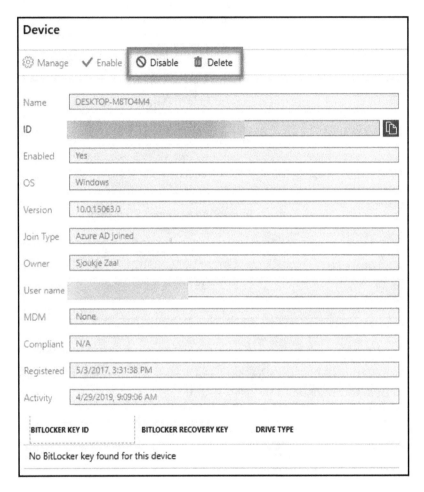

Device information

8. For audit logs, under **Activity**, select **Audit logs**. From here, you can view and download the different log files. You can also create filters to search through the logs, as follows:

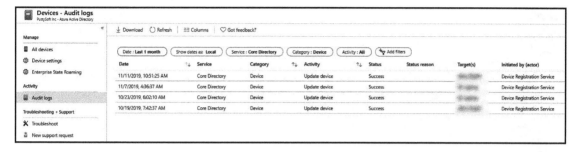

Audit logs

Now, we have looked at all the different management and configuration options for devices that are registered or joined to Azure AD. In the next section, we are going to learn how to add custom domains to Azure AD.

Adding custom domains

Azure creates an initial domain for every Azure AD tenant that is created in a subscription. This domain name consists of the tenant name, followed by `onmicrosoft.com` (`packtpub.onmicrosoft.com`). You cannot change or delete the initial domain name, but you can add custom domains to your Azure AD tenant.

This custom domain name can be registered at a third-party domain registrar and, after registration, can be added to the Azure AD tenant.

To add a custom domain to Azure AD from the Azure portal, follow these steps:

1. Navigate to the Azure portal by going to `https://portal.azure.com`.
2. From the left menu, select **Azure Active Directory**.

3. In the Azure AD **Overview** blade, under **Manage**, select **Custom domain names**. To add a custom domain, select the **+ Add custom domain** button from the top menu, as follows:

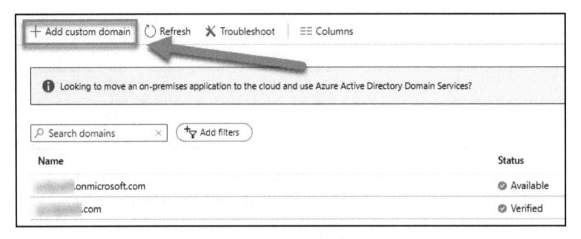

Adding a custom domain

4. Type the custom domain name into the **Custom domain name** field (for example, `packtpub.com`) and select **Add domain**, as follows:

Providing a custom domain name

5. After you've added your custom domain name to Azure AD, you need to create a **TXT** record inside the DNS settings of your domain registrar. Go to your domain registrar and add the Azure AD DNS information from your copied TXT file. Creating this TXT record for your domain *verifies* ownership of your domain name. After creating the TXT file, click **Verify**, as follows:

Verifying the ownership of the domain

6. After you've verified your custom domain name, you can delete your verification TXT or MX file.

Now, we have configured a custom domain for our Azure AD tenant. Your users can now use this domain name to log in to the various Azure resources they have access to.

Summary

In this chapter, we covered the sixth part of the *Deploy and Configure Infrastructure* objective. We covered the various aspects of Azure AD by learning how to add users and groups, how to add guest users, and how to manage devices in Azure AD. We also covered how to add custom domain names to our Azure AD tenant from the Azure portal.

In the next chapter, we will cover the last part of this exam objective and learn how to implement and manage hybrid identities.

Questions

Answer the following questions to test your knowledge of the information in this chapter. You can find the answers in the *Assessments* section at the end of this book:

1. If you want to create a guest user using PowerShell, you have to use the `New-AzureADMSInvitation` cmdlet.
   - Yes
   - No

2. If you want to use Azure AD join for your devices, you need to configure your on-premises AD environment in a hybrid environment, along with Azure AD.
   - Yes
   - No

3. When you add a custom domain to Azure AD, you need to verify it by adding a TXT record to the DNS settings of your domain registrar.
   - Yes
   - No

Further reading

Check out the following links if you want to find out more about the topics that were covered in this chapter:

- **Azure Active Directory Documentation**: https://docs.microsoft.com/en-us/azure/active-directory/

- **Adding or deleting users using Azure Active Directory**: https://docs.microsoft.com/en-us/azure/active-directory/fundamentals/add-users-azure-active-directory

- **Azure Active Directory version 2 cmdlets for group management**: https://docs.microsoft.com/en-us/azure/active-directory/users-groups-roles/groups-settings-v2-cmdlets

- **Quickstart: Adding a guest user with PowerShell**: https://docs.microsoft.com/en-us/azure/active-directory/b2b/b2b-quickstart-invite-powershell

- **Quickstart: Self-service password reset**: https://docs.microsoft.com/en-us/azure/active-directory/authentication/quickstart-sspr

- **How to: Planning your Azure Active Directory join implementation**: https://docs.microsoft.com/en-us/azure/active-directory/devices/azureadjoin-plan

- **What is device management in Azure Active Directory?**: https://docs.microsoft.com/en-us/azure/active-directory/devices/overview

- **Adding your custom domain name using the Azure Active Directory portal**: https://docs.microsoft.com/en-us/azure/active-directory/fundamentals/add-custom-domain

Implementing and Managing Hybrid Identities

In the previous chapter, we covered how to manage **Azure Active Directory** (**Azure AD**). We've learned how to manage this from the Azure portal and how to perform bulk updates inside your Azure AD tenant. We also covered how to configure self-service password reset for your users to reduce user management overhead, Azure AD Join, and how you can manage your devices that are registered or joined in Azure AD.

This chapter is the last part of the *Deploy and Configure Infrastructure* objective. In this chapter, we are going to cover how to implement and manage hybrid identities. We are going to install and configure Azure AD Connect to synchronize the identities from your on-premises Active Directory to Azure AD. Then, you will learn how to manage Azure AD Connect. In the last part of this chapter, we will dive into password synchronization and password writeback. You will learn how to enable password synchronization in Azure AD Connect and the Azure portal. Lastly, you will learn how to manage password synchronization.

The following topics will be covered in this chapter:

- Understanding Azure AD Connect
- Installing Azure AD Connect
- Managing Azure AD Connect
- Managing password synchronization and password writeback

Understanding Azure AD Connect

Azure AD Connect is a service that you can use to synchronize your on-premises Active Directory identities with Azure. This way, you can use the same identities for authentication on your on-premises environment as well as in the cloud and other **Software as a Service** (**SaaS**) applications.

The Azure AD Connect sync service consists of two parts: the Azure AD Connect sync component, which is a tool that is installed on a separate server inside your on-premises environment, and the Azure AD Connect sync service, which is part of Azure AD. The sync component can sync data from Active Directory and SQL Servers to Azure. There is also a third component named the **Active Directory Federation Services** (**ADFS**) component, which can be used in a scenario where ADFS is involved. To monitor the on-premises identity infrastructure and the different Azure AD components, you can use a tool named Azure AD Connect Health. The following diagram illustrates the architecture of Azure AD Connect:

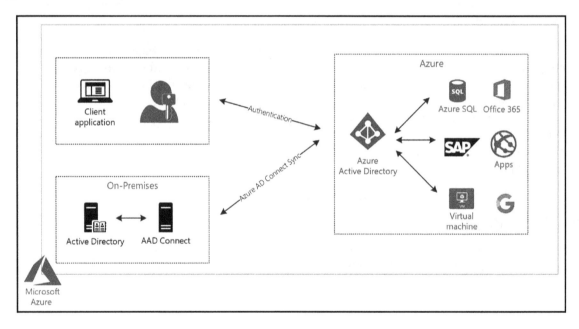

Azure AD Connect architecture

Azure AD Connect offers support for your users to sign in with the same passwords to both on-premises and cloud resources. It provides three different authentication methods for this: the password hash synchronization method, the pass-through authentication method, and the Federated SSO method (in conjunction with ADFS).

Azure AD password hash synchronization

Most organizations only have a requirement to enable users to sign in to Office 365, SaaS applications, and other Azure AD-based resources. The password hash synchronization method is well suited for those scenarios.

Using this method, hashes of the user's password are synced between the on-premises Active Directory and Azure AD. When there are any changes to the user's password, the password is synced immediately, so users can always log in with the same credentials on-premises as well as in Azure.

This authentication method also provides Azure AD Seamless **Single Sign-On** (**SSO**). This way, users are automatically signed in when they are using a domain-joined device on the corporate network. Users only have to enter their username when using Seamless SSO. To use Seamless SSO, you don't have to install additional software or components on the on-premises network. You can push this capability to your users using group policies.

Azure AD pass-through authentication

Azure AD pass-through authentication offers the same capability as Azure AD password hash synchronization. Users can log in to their Azure resources as well as on-premises resources using the same credentials. The difference is that the passwords don't sync with Azure AD using pass-through authentication. The passwords are validated using the on-premises Active Directory and are not stored in the Azure AD at all.

This method is suitable for organizations that have security and compliance restrictions and aren't allowed to send usernames and passwords outside the on-premises network. Pass-through authentication requires an agent to be installed on a domain-joined Windows server that resides inside the on-premises environment. This agent then listens for password validation requests and only makes an outbound connection from within your network. It also offers support for **multi-factor authentication** (**MFA**) and Azure AD Conditional Access policies.

Azure AD pass-through authentication offers Azure AD Seamless SSO as well.

In the next section, we are going to install Azure AD Connect and synchronize some on-premises users to Azure.

Installing Azure AD Connect

Azure AD Connect is installed on an on-premises server with Active Directory installed and configured on it. The first step is to download Azure AD Connect. After downloading, we can install it on a domain controller.

 For this demonstration, I have already deployed a Windows Server 2016 virtual machine in Azure and installed and configured Active Directory on it. Configuring Active Directory is beyond the scope of the exam and this book. Make sure that when you configure Active Directory Domain Services, the forest name matches one of the existing verified custom domains in Azure AD. Otherwise, you will receive a warning message when you install Azure AD Connect on your domain controller, which will state that SSO is not enabled for your users. For installing Active Directory on a Windows Server 2016 machine, you can refer to the following website: `https://blogs.technet.microsoft.com/canitpro/2017/02/22/step-by-step-setting-up-active-directory-in-windows-server-2016/`.

Therefore, perform the following steps:

1. Before downloading Azure AD Connect, add at least one user to your on-premises Active Directory.
2. To download Azure AD Connect, you can refer to the following website: `https://www.microsoft.com/en-us/download/details.aspx?id=47594`. Store it on a local drive on your domain controller and run `AzureADConnect.msi` after downloading.
3. The installation wizard starts with the welcome screen. Select the checkbox to agree with the license terms:

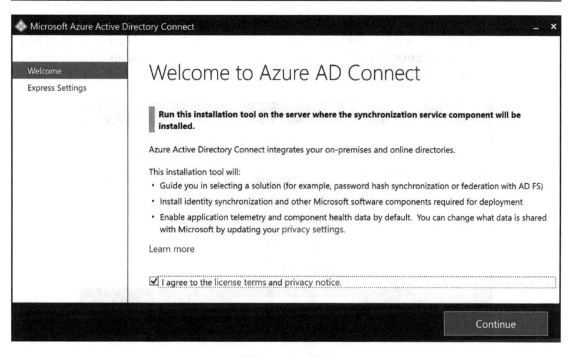

Azure AD Connect welcome screen

4. Select **Use express settings** in the next screen:

Installing Azure AD Connect using express settings

5. On the next screen, provide the username and password of a global administrator account for your Azure AD and click **Next** (this account must be a school or organization account and cannot be a Microsoft account or any other type of account):

Provide global administrator credentials

6. On the **Connect to AD DS** screen, enter the **USERNAME** and **PASSWORD** for an enterprise administrator account, and click **Next** as follows:

Enter enterprise administrator account

The last screen will give you an overview of what is going to be installed, as follows:

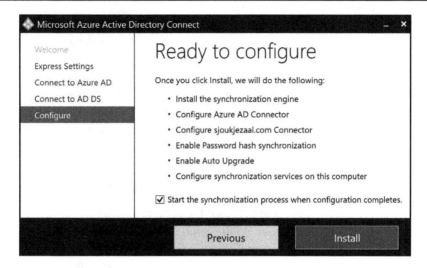

Ready to configure

7. Click **Install.**

8. This will install Azure AD Connect on your domain controller. The synchronization process of user accounts to Azure AD will automatically be started after configuration.

9. After successful configuration, you will see the following outcome:

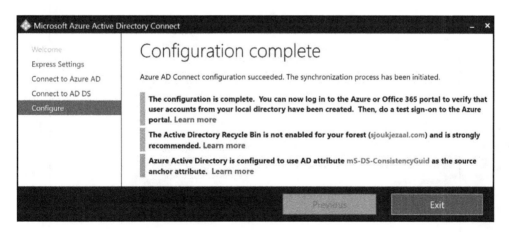

Configuration complete

10. Click **Exit** to close the installer.

In this demonstration, we installed Azure AD Connect on an on-premises domain controller. In the next section, we are going to manage it from the Azure portal.

Managing Azure AD Connect

Azure AD Connect can be managed from the Azure portal after installation and configuration on the on-premises domain controller. To manage it, you have to perform the following steps:

1. Navigate to the Azure portal by opening `https://portal.azure.com`.
2. In the left menu, select **Azure Active Directory**.
3. Under **Manage**, select **Azure AD Connect**. In the **Azure AD Connect** blade, as shown in the following screenshot, you can see that sync is enabled, that the last sync was more than a day ago, and that **Password Hash Sync** is enabled:

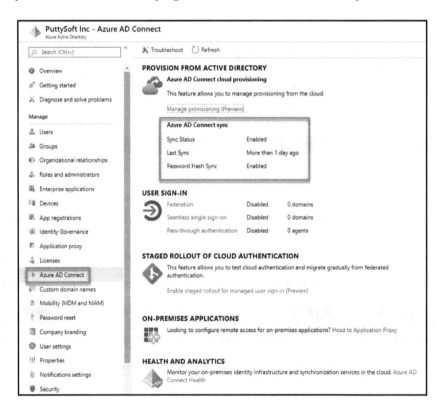

Azure AD Connect settings

4. You can also set the three authentication methods under **USER SIGN-IN**. Here, you can set the authentication method to **Federation, Seamless single sign-on**, or **Pass-through authentication**. You can monitor the health of your on-premises infrastructure and synchronization services under **HEALTH AND ANALYTICS**.

5. To check whether the users are synced, you can go to the **User overview** blade. Here, you will find your synced users, as shown in the following screenshot:

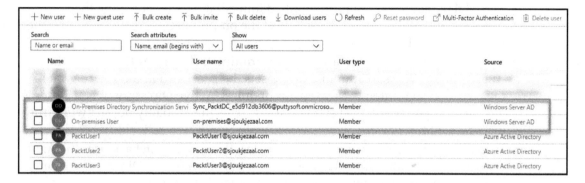

Synced users

Azure AD Connect sync synchronizes changes in your on-premises directory using a scheduler. There are two scheduler processes: one for password synchronization and another for object/attribute sync and maintenance tasks. For more information on how to configure this or how to create a custom scheduler using PowerShell, you can refer to the following tutorial: `https://docs.microsoft.com/en-us/azure/active-directory/hybrid/how-to-connect-sync-feature-scheduler`.

In this demonstration, we managed Azure AD Connect from the Azure portal. In the next section, we are going to cover how to manage password writeback in more detail.

Password writeback

Password writeback is used for synchronizing password changes in Azure AD back to your on-premises Active Directory environment. This setting is enabled as part of Azure AD Connect, and it provides a secure mechanism to send password changes from Azure AD back to an on-premises Active Directory.

It provides the following features and capabilities:

- **Enforcement of on-premises Active Directory password policies**: When a user resets their password, the on-premises Active Directory policy is checked to ensure it meets the password requirements before it gets committed to the directory. It checks the password complexity, history, password filters, age, and other password restrictions that are defined in the on-premises Active Directory.
- **Zero-delay feedback**: Users are notified immediately after changing their password if their password doesn't meet the on-premises Active Directory policy requirements. This is a synchronous operation.
- **Supports password writeback when an administrator resets them from the Azure portal**: When an administrator resets the password in the Azure portal, the password is written back to the on-premises Active Directory (when a user is federated or password hash synchronized). This functionality doesn't work from the Office admin portal.
- **Doesn't require any inbound firewall rules**: Password writeback uses the Azure Service Bus for communicating with the on-premises Active Directory, so there is no need to open the firewall. All communication is outbound and goes over port 443.
- **Supports password changes from the access panel and Office 365**: When federated or password hash synchronized users change their password, those passwords are written back to your on-premises Active Directory as well.

In the next demonstration, we are going to enable password writeback.

Managing password writeback

To enable password writeback, we need to make some changes to both the configuration of Azure AD Connect on the on-premises domain controller, and from the Azure portal.

Enabling password writeback in Azure AD Connect

To enable password writeback in Azure AD Connect, we have to take the following steps:

1. Log in to your on-premises domain controller using **Remote Desktop** (**RDP**) and start the Azure AD Connect wizard again.

2. On the **Welcome to Azure AD Connect** page, select **Configure** as follows:

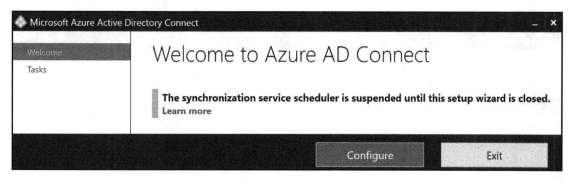

Welcome screen

3. In the **Additional tasks** screen, select **Customize synchronization options**, and then select **Next** as follows:

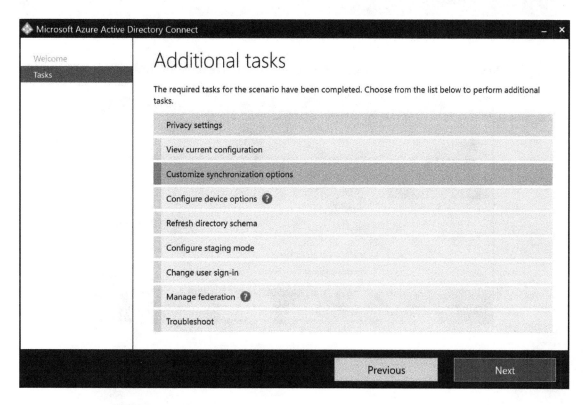

Additional tasks screen

4. Provide Azure AD global administrator credentials and then select **Next** as follows:

Providing administrator credentials

5. On the **Connect your directories** screen, select **Next** as follows:

Connecting your directories

6. On the **Domain/OU Filtering** screen, select **Next** again, as follows:

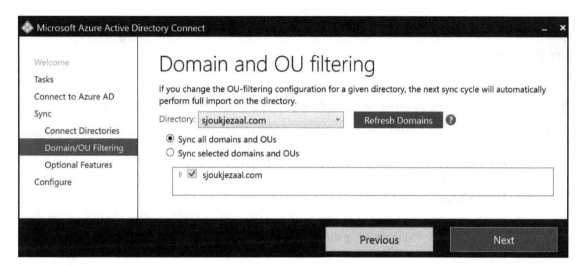

Domain and OU filtering screen

7. On the **Optional features** screen, select the box next to **Password writeback** and then select **Next** as follows:

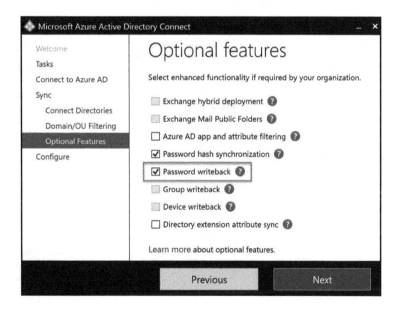

Enabling password writeback

8. On the **Ready to configure** page, select **Configure**.
9. When the configuration is finished, select **Exit**.

We have now enabled password writeback on the domain controller. In the next section, we are going to enable it in the Azure portal as well.

Enabling password writeback in the Azure portal

To enable password writeback in the Azure portal, we have to perform the following steps:

1. Navigate to the Azure portal by opening `https://portal.azure.com`.
2. In the left menu, select **Azure Active Directory**.
3. Under **Manage**, select **Password reset**.
4. In the **password reset** blade, under **Manage**, select **On-premises integration**. Set the option for **Write back passwords to your on-premises directory?** to **Yes** and set the option for **Allow users to unlock accounts without resetting their password?** to **Yes** as follows:

Enabling password writeback

5. Click **Save**.

We have now completely configured password writeback in Azure AD Connect and the Azure portal. In the next section, we are going to cover how to manage password synchronization.

Password synchronization

In this last section of this chapter, we are going to cover password synchronization. We installed Azure AD Connect using the **Express Settings** option. Password hash synchronization is automatically enabled if you use this option.

If you install Azure AD Connect using the custom settings, password hash synchronization is available on the **User Sign-in** screen and you can enable it there, as shown in the following screenshot:

Enabling password hash synchronization during installation

Summary

In this chapter, we covered the last part of the *Deploy and Configure Infrastructure* objective. We covered how to implement and manage hybrid identities by covering Azure AD Connect, and you've learned how to install and manage it after installation. We also covered how to enable password writeback and password hash synchronization.

In the next chapter, we will start with the *Implement Workloads and Security* objective by covering how to migrate servers to Azure.

Questions

Answer the following questions to test your knowledge of the information in this chapter. You can find the answers in the *Assessments* section at the end of this book:

1. If you use the **Express Settings** option when installing Azure AD Connect, password hash synchronization is disabled by default:
    - Yes
    - No

2. When you want to enable password synchronization, you only have to do this inside the Azure portal:
    - Yes
    - No

3. If the on-premises forest name doesn't match one of the Azure AD custom domain names, you cannot install Azure AD Connect:
    - Yes
    - No

Further reading

You can check out the following links for more information about the topics that were covered in this chapter:

- **What is hybrid identity with Azure Active Directory?**: https://docs. microsoft.com/en-us/azure/active-directory/hybrid/whatis-hybrid-identity
- **What is federation with Azure AD?**: https://docs.microsoft.com/en-us/ azure/active-directory/hybrid/whatis-fed
- **What is password hash synchronization with Azure AD?**: https://docs. microsoft.com/en-us/azure/active-directory/hybrid/whatis-phs
- **User sign-in with Azure Active Directory Pass-through Authentication**: https://docs.microsoft.com/en-us/azure/active-directory/hybrid/how-to-connect-pta
- **Azure AD Connect sync: Understand and customize synchronization**: https:// docs.microsoft.com/en-us/azure/active-directory/hybrid/how-to-connect-sync-whatis
- **Azure AD Connect user sign-in options**: https://docs.microsoft.com/en-us/ azure/active-directory/hybrid/plan-connect-user-signin
- **Tutorial: Enabling password writeback**: https://docs.microsoft.com/en-us/ azure/active-directory/authentication/tutorial-enable-writeback
- **Implement password hash synchronization with Azure AD Connect sync**: https://docs.microsoft.com/en-us/azure/active-directory/hybrid/how-to-connect-password-hash-synchronization

Section 2: Implementing Workloads and Security

2

As this section's objective, you will learn how to implement workloads and security in Azure.

This section will contain the following chapters:

- Chapter 8, *Migrating Servers to Azure*
- Chapter 9, *Configuring Serverless Computing*
- Chapter 10, *Implementing Application Load Balancing*
- Chapter 11, *Integrating On-Premises Networks with Azure Virtual Network*
- Chapter 12, *Managing Role-Based Access Control (RBAC)*
- Chapter 13, *Implementing Multi-Factor Authentication (MFA)*

Migrating Servers to Azure

8

In the previous chapter, we learned how to implement and manage hybrid identities, as well as how to install and configure Azure AD Connect. Then, we migrated some users.

This chapter is the first chapter of the *Implement Workloads and Security* objective. In this chapter, we will cover Azure Migrate and the different tooling that is integrated with Azure Migrate that's used to create assessments and migrate servers, databases, web applications, and data to Azure. We are also going to migrate some Hyper-V VMs to Azure using Azure Migrate.

In this chapter, we will cover the following topics:

- Understanding Azure Migrate
- Azure Migrate tools
- Migrating on-premises machines to Azure

Understanding Azure Migrate

You can use Azure Migrate to migrate your on-premises environment to Azure. It offers a centralized hub in the Azure portal, which can be used to track the discovery, assessment, and migration of your on-premises infrastructure, applications, and data. It offers the following features:

- **Unified Migration platform**: The migration journey can be started, executed, and tracked directly from the Azure portal.
- **Range of tools**: Assessments and migrations are offered from the hub in the Azure portal. This is integrated with other Azure services (such as Azure Site Recovery), other tools, and **independent software vendor (ISV)** offerings.

- **Different workloads**: Azure Migrate provides assessments and migration for the following:

  - **Servers**: You can use the Azure Migrate Assessment tool, Azure Migrate Server Migration tool, and more, for assessing and migrating your servers to Azure VMs.

  - **Databases**: You can use **Database Migration Assistant** (**DMA**) to assess databases and the **Database Migration Service** (**DMS**) for migrating on-premises databases to Azure SQL Database or Azure SQL Managed Instances.

  - **Web applications**: You can use the Azure App Service Assistant to assess and migrate on-premises web applications to Azure App Service.

  - **Virtual desktops**: You can use different ISV tools to assess and migrate on-premises **virtual desktop infrastructures** (**VDIs**) to Windows Virtual Desktop in Azure.

  - **Data**: Azure Data Box products can be used to quickly and cost-effectively migrate large amounts of data to Azure.

 Currently, Azure offers two different versions of the migrate service. First, there's the current version, which is described in this chapter and can be used to create Azure Migrate projects, discover on-premises machines, and orchestrate assessments and migrations. The previous version can no longer be used to create Azure Migrate projects. It can be used to perform new discoveries, but this is not recommended. However, you can still access existing projects in the Azure portal.

In the next section, we are going to look at the different tools that Azure Migrate has to offer.

Azure Migrate tools

Azure Migrate offers a variety of tools that can be used to assess and migrate on-premises environments, databases, applications, and more. These will be covered in more detail in the upcoming sections.

Azure Migrate Server Assessment tool

The Azure Migrate Server Assessment tool is used for assessing your on-premises infrastructure. It can assess Hyper-V VMs, VMware VMs, and physical servers. It can help you identify the following:

- **Azure readiness**: It can help you define whether your on-premises machines are ready for migration to Azure. It scans the OS of the VM to assess whether your on-premises machines are ready for migration to Azure. The VMs that are assessed can be added to the following categories:
    - **Ready for Azure**: The machine is up-to-date and can be migrated as-is to Azure without any changes. It will start in Azure with full Azure support.
    - **Conditionally ready for Azure**: Machines in this category might start in Azure but might not have full Azure support. This can be the case for machines that run an older version of Windows Server that isn't supported in Azure. It's recommended that you follow the remediation guidance that is suggested in the assessment to fix these issues.
    - **Not ready for Azure**: Machines in this category will not start in Azure. For instance, you might have a machine with a disk of more than 64 TB attached to it. These disks cannot be hosted in Azure. For these machines, it is also recommended to follow the remediation guidance and fix the issues that appear before they are migrated. Note that for the machines in this category, right-sizing and cost estimation is not done.
    - **Readiness unknown**: Azure Migrate wasn't able to determine the readiness of the machine because of insufficient metadata that was collected from the on-premises environment.
- **Azure sizing**: Based on historical data, such as the growth of the disks of the VM, Azure Migrate can estimate the size of Azure VMs after migration.
- **Azure cost estimation**: Azure Migrate can also estimate the costs for running your on-premises servers in Azure.
- **Dependency visualization**: When dependency visualization is enabled, Azure Migrate is capable of visualizing cross-server dependencies, and it will also provide you with optimal ways to move dependent servers to Azure.

Before you can execute a server assessment, a lightweight appliance needs to be installed on the on-premises environment. Then, the appliance needs to be registered with the server assessment tool in Azure. This appliance does the following:

- It discovers the on-premises machines in your current environment.
- It connects to the server assessment and sends machine metadata and performance data to Azure Migrate.
- The appliance discovery process is completely agentless; it doesn't require anything to be installed on the discovered machines.
- Discovered machines can be placed into groups. Typically, you place machines into groups that you want to migrate to the same batch.
- For each group, you can create an assessment. You can figure out your migration strategy by analyzing the different assessments.

Azure Migrate Server Migration tool

The Azure Migrate Server Migration tool can be used to migrate the machines to Azure. It supports the migration of physical and virtualized servers using agent-based replication. A wide range of machines can be migrated to Azure, such as Hyper-V or VMware VMs, on-premises physical servers, VMs running in private clouds, VMs running in public clouds such as **Amazon Web Services** (**AWS**) or **Google Cloud Platform** (**GCP**), and VMs virtualized by platforms such as Xen and KVM.

You can migrate machines after assessing them, or without an assessment.

Database Migration Assistant

You can assess your on-premises SQL Server databases from Azure Migrate using Microsoft's **Database Migration Assistant** (**DMA**). Your on-premises databases can be assessed for migration to Azure SQL DB, Azure SQL managed instances, or Azure VMs running SQL Server. DMA allows you to do the following:

- Assess on-premises SQL Server instances for migrating to Azure SQL databases. The assessment workflow helps you to detect migration blocking issues, as well as partially supported or unsupported features.
- Discover issues that can affect an upgrade to an on-premises SQL Server. These are organized into different categories: breaking changes, behavior changes, and deprecated features.

- Assess on-premises **SQL Server Integration Services** (**SSIS**) packages that can be migrated to an Azure SQL Database or Azure SQL Database managed instance.
- Discover new features in the target SQL Server platform that the database can benefit from after an upgrade.

Database Migration Service

To perform the actual migration of the databases, Azure Migrate integrates with the Azure **Database Migration Service** (**DMS**). This tool is used to migrate the on-premises databases to Azure VMs running SQL, Azure SQL DB, and Azure SQL managed instances.

Web App Migration Assistant

You can use the Azure App Service Migration Assistant directly from the Azure Migrate hub. This tool can help you assess and migrate your on-premises web apps to Azure.

It offers the following features:

- **Assess web apps online**: You can assess on-premises websites for migration to Azure App Services using the App Service Migration Assistant.
- **Migrate web apps**: Using the Azure App Service Migration Assistant, you can migrate .NET and PHP web apps to Azure.

The assessment process starts by providing a public endpoint that is scanned to provide a detailed list specifying the different technologies that are used. These technologies are then compared to other sites that are hosted on Azure App Service to generate an accurate assessment report for your site.

Offline data migration

Azure Migrate also supports offline data migration. You can use the different Azure Data Box products to move large amounts of data offline to Azure.

With the Azure Data Box solution, you can send terabytes of data into Azure quickly. You can order this Data Box solution from the Azure portal. By doing this, you will receive a Data Box storage device with storage capacity that can be used to transfer the data securely.

Azure offers the following three different types of storage devices:

- **Data Box**: This device, with 100 TB of capacity, uses standard **network-attached storage** (**NAS**) protocols and common copy tools. It features AES 256-bit encryption for safer transit.
- **Data Box Disk**: This device had a capacity of 8 TB with SSD storage (with packs of up to 5 for a total of 40 TB). It has a USB/SATA interface and has 128-bit encryption.
- **Data Box Heavy**: This is a self-contained device that is designed to lift 1 PB of data to the cloud.

You can copy this data from your servers to one of the devices and ship this back to Azure. Then, Microsoft will upload this data to the Azure Datacenter from the device. This entire process is tracked in the Azure Migrate hub in the Azure portal to deliver insights about all the steps of the data migration process.

The Data Box solution is well-suited for scenarios where there is no or limited network connectivity and where data sizes larger than 40 TB need to be migrated. It is also an ideal solution for one-time migrations and initial bulk transfers, followed by incremental transfers over the network.

For incremental transfers over the network, Azure offers the following services:

- **Azure Data Box Gateway**: Data Box Gateway is a virtual device based on a virtual machine that's been provisioned in your virtualized environment or hypervisor. The virtual device resides in your on-premises environment and you write data to it using the **Network File System** (**NFS**) and **Server Message Block** (**SMB**) protocols. The device then transfers your data to Azure block blobs, page blobs, or Azure Files.
- **Azure Data Box Edge**: Azure Data Box Edge is a physical device supplied by Microsoft for secure data transfer. This device resides in your on-premises environment, and you can write data to it using the NFS and SMB protocols. Data Box Edge has all the gateway capabilities of Data Box Gateway. Additionally, Data Box is equipped with AI-enabled edge computing capabilities that help analyze, process, or filter data as it moves to Azure block blobs, page blobs, or Azure Files.

The following diagram shows an overview of the steps that are taken to store the data onto the device and ship it back to Azure:

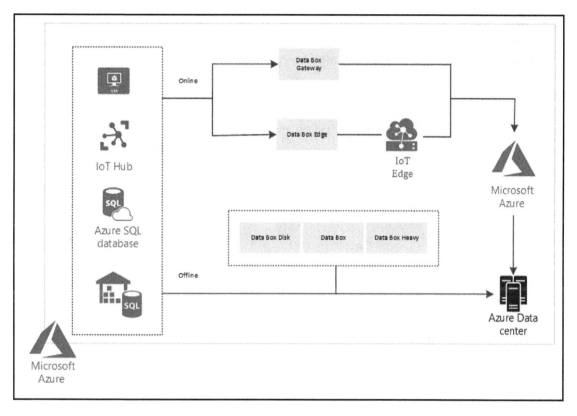

Azure Data Box

Azure Migrate also supports Movere. Movere is a SaaS platform that was acquired by Microsoft and increases business intelligence by accurately presenting entire IT environments within a single day. For more information, you can refer to the following website: `https://www.movere.io/`.

In this section, we covered the different migration tooling that's integrated into Azure Migrate. In the next section, we are going to migrate on-premises machines to Azure.

Migrating on-premises machines to Azure

In the upcoming demo, we are going to use Azure Migrate to assess a Hyper-V environment and migrate virtual machines that are deployed inside the Hyper-V environment to Azure. This demo is going to be divided into different steps. The first step is to create an assessment for the on-premises environment. Due to this, we need an Azure Migrate project in the Azure portal.

Create an Azure Migrate project

Before we can create an assessment in the Azure portal, we need to create an Azure Migrate project. Therefore, we have to perform the following steps:

1. Navigate to the Azure portal by opening `https://portal.azure.com`.
2. Click **Create a resource** and type `Azure Migrate` into the search bar.
3. Create a new Azure Migrate project.
4. In the overview blade, click **Assess and migrate servers**.
5. The first step is to add a tool to Azure Migrate. Select **Add tool(s)**.
6. The **Add a tool** blade will open. In the **Migrate Project** tab, add the following settings:
    1. **Subscription**: Pick a subscription.
    2. **Resource group**: `PacktMigrateProjectResourceGroup`.
    3. **Migrate project**: `PacktMigrateProject`.
    4. **Geography**: **United States**.
7. Click **Next**.
8. The **Select Assessment tool** blade will open. Here, select **Azure Migrate: Server Assessment** and click **Next**.
9. Then, we need to select a Migrate tool. Here, select **Azure Migrate: Server Migration** and click **Next**.
10. In the review blade, click **Add tool(s)**.
11. The Azure Migrate project will be deployed and the tools added to the project.
12. After creation, you'll see the tools that were added to the project, as shown in the following screenshot:

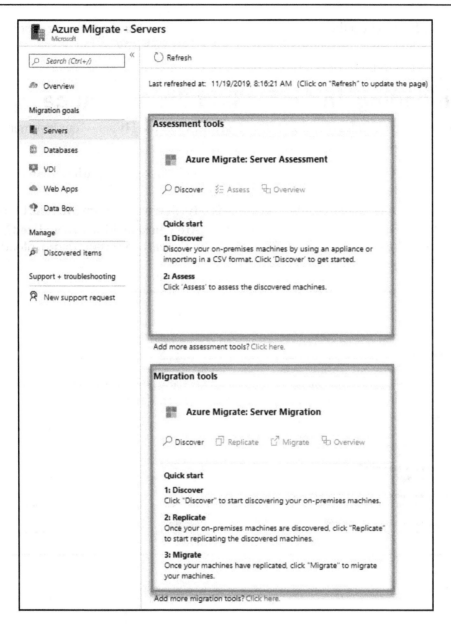

Azure Migrate project tools

Now that we have set up the Azure Migrate project and added the necessary tools, we are going to download and install the appliance in the Hyper-V environment.

Downloading and installing the appliance

The next step is to download and install the appliance in the Hyper-V environment. Therefore, we need to perform the following steps:

1. In the Azure Migrate project overview blade, under **Migration goals**, select **Servers**.
2. Under **Assessment tools** | **Azure Migrate: Server Assessment**, select **Discover**.
3. In the **Discover machines** blade, under **Are your machines virtualized?**, select **Yes, with Hyper-V**. Then, click the **Download** button to download the appliance to your local disk:

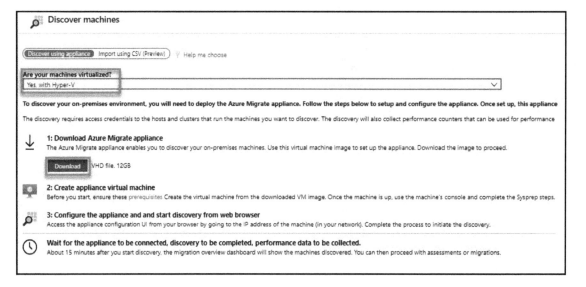

Downloading the Azure Migrate appliance

4. Once the appliance has been downloaded, we can import it to Hyper-V. First, extract the .zip file.

5. Open Hyper-V Manager and from the top menu, select **Action** | **Import Virtual Machine**:

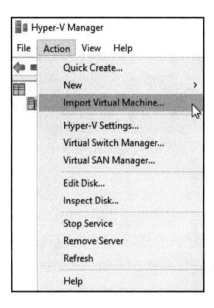

Import Virtual Machine

6. Follow the steps in the wizard to import the virtual machine into Hyper-V Manager.

7. In the **Import Virtual Machine Wizard** | **Before you begin** section, click **Next**.

8. In **Locate Folder**, navigate to the folder where you unzipped the appliance after downloading it.

9. In **Select Virtual Machine**, select the appliance VM.

10. From the **Choose Import Type** screen in the wizard, select **Copy the virtual machine (create a new unique ID)**:

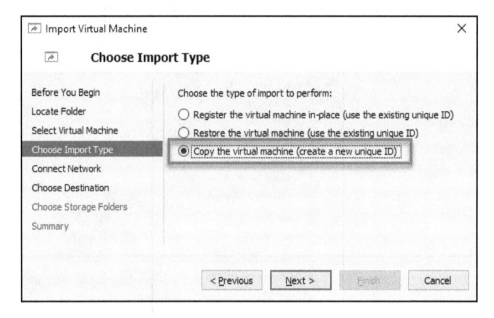

Copy the virtual machine

11. Click **Next**.
12. In **Choose Destination**, leave the default settings as-is and click **Next**.
13. In **Storage Folders**, leave the default setting as well and click **Next**.
14. In **Choose Network**, specify the virtual switch that the VM will use. Internet connectivity is required in order to send the data to Azure from the appliance.
15. In the **Summary** screen, review your settings and click **Finish**.
16. Now that you've imported the appliance into Hyper-V, you can start the VM.

 For this demonstration, I've created a couple of VMs inside the Hyper-V environment that can be used for the assessment and migration processes. You can create some VMs yourself as well.

Now, we have downloaded the appliance and imported and started the VM. In the next section, we are going to configure the appliance so that it can communicate with Azure Migrate.

Configuring the appliance and starting continuous discovery

The appliance needs to be configured before it can send data about your on-premises machines to Azure. Therefore, we have to perform the following steps:

1. Go back to Hyper-V Manager and select **Virtual Machines**. Then, right-click the appliance VM | **Connect**.
2. Accept the license terms and provide the password for the appliance. Click **Finish**.
3. Now, the configuration of Windows Server has been finalized. This means you can login to the appliance using the Administrator username and the password you provided in the previous step.
4. After logging into the VM, click the Microsoft Migrate icon on the desktop again or wait for Internet Explorer to open automatically, along with the wizard to set up the server as a configuration server. The first step is to set up the prerequisites. First, you need to accept the license terms:

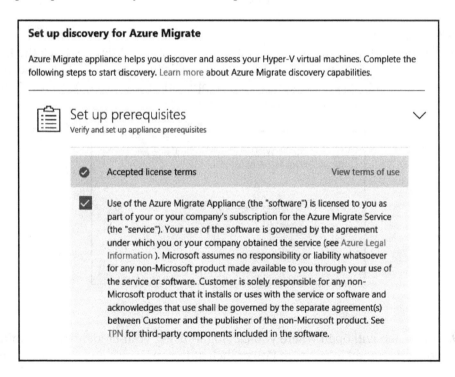

Accepting the license terms

5. Check the box to be automatically redirected to the next step.

6. After that, your network connectivity will be checked, a check will be performed to ensure that the time of the VM is in sync with the internet time server, and the latest Azure Migrate updates will be installed. Once you've done this, you will see the following output:

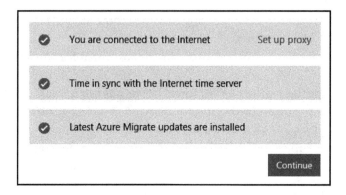

Checking the prerequisites

7. Click **Continue**.

8. The next step is to register the appliance with Azure Migrate. Click the **Login** button and log in with your Azure credentials (make sure that you use an account that has permission to create applications in Azure AD since Azure Migrate will create an application in there):

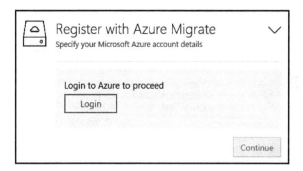

Logging in with your Azure account

9. A new tab will open where you can log in using your credentials. By doing so, you'll be signed into Azure PowerShell at the appliance and you can close the tab.

10. You will be taken back to the **Register with Azure Migrate** step in the configuration process. Now that you are signed into Azure Migrate, you can select the subscription where the Migrate project will be created. Then, select the project to migrate from the **Migrate project** dropdown and specify the appliance's name. You can obtain this value from the URL in Internet Explorer, as shown in the following screenshot:

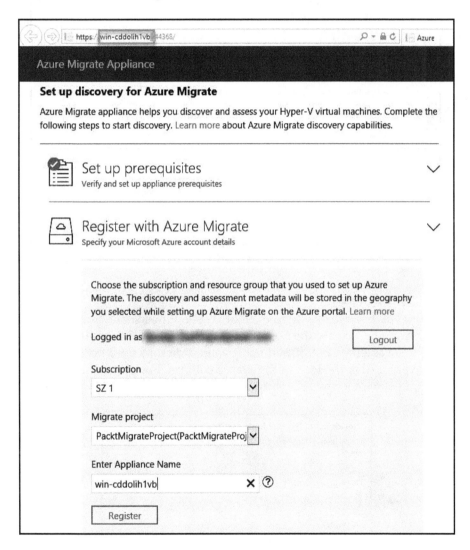

Registering the appliance

11. Click **Register**.

12. When the appliance has been successfully registered, you can click **Continue**.

13. In the next step, we are going to configure continuous discovery. To do so, we need to provide the Hyper-V hosts details. For this, use an account that has permissions on the VMs that need to be discovered and give it a friendly name:

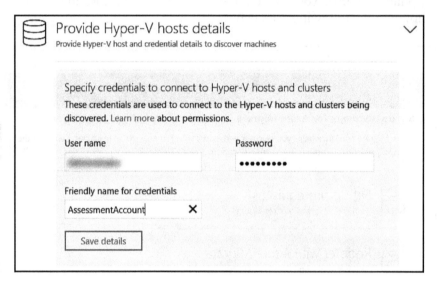

Adding an assessment account

14. Click **Save details**.

15. Finally, you have to specify the list of Hyper-V hosts and clusters to discover. Click **Add** and specify the host IP address or FQDN. Make sure that the VMs that need to be assessed are turned on. If validation fails for a host, review the error by hovering over the icon in the **Status** column. Fix the issues and then validate it again, as shown in the following screenshot:

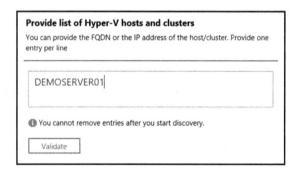

Validating the host IP address

16. Click **Validate**.
17. After validation, click **Save and start discovery** to start the discovery process. The appliance will start collecting and discovering the virtual machines. It will take around 15 minutes for the metadata of the discovered VMs to appear in the Azure portal. If you want to use performance data in your assessment, it is recommended that you create a performance-based assessment after 24 hours or more.
18. Now, if you go back to the Azure Migrate project in the Azure portal and select **Discovered items** under **Manage**, you can select the subscription where the project has been created, the project, and the appliance's name.

The discovered VMs will be displayed in the overview:

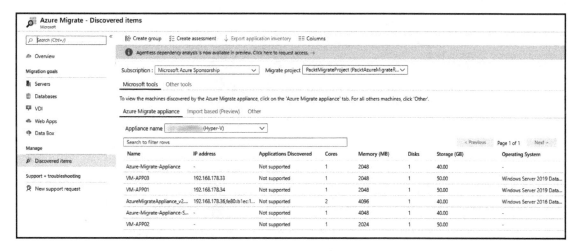

Discovered VMs

In this section, we have configured the appliance and configured continuous discovery. In the next section, we are going to create an assessment from the Azure portal.

Creating and viewing an assessment

In this section, we are going to create an assessment in the Azure portal. To do so, follow these steps:

1. Open the Azure Migrate project that we created earlier and under **Manage**, select **Discovered items** again.
2. From the top menu, select **Create assessment**.

3. Add the following values:

  1. **Discovery source**: Leave the default value as it is, which is **Machines discovered from Azure Migrate appliance**.

  2. **Assessment name**: `PacktAssessment1`.

  3. **Select or create a group**: Create a new one and call it `PacktVMGroup`.

  4. **Appliance name**: Leave the default as it is.

  5. Select the VMs that you want to add to the assessment:

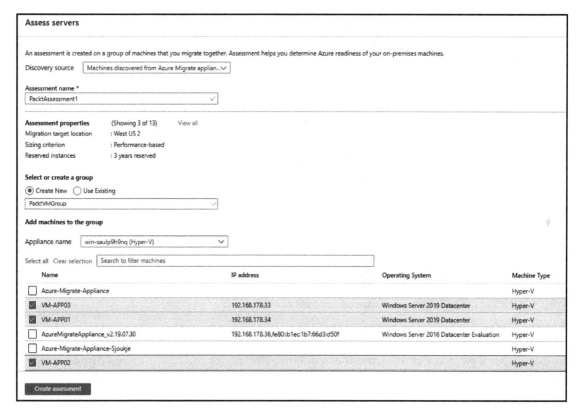

Selecting VMs

4. Click **Create assessment**.

5. It will take some time before the assessment is ready.

6. Once the assessment has been created, you can view it by going to **Servers | Azure Migrate: Server Assessment | Assessments**:

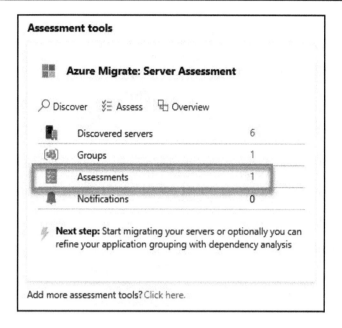

Reviewing the assessment

7. Select the assessment from the list. You will get an overview of the assessed machines, as shown in the following screenshot:

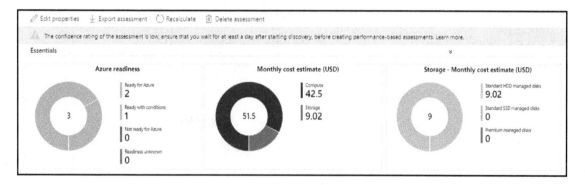

Overview of the assessment

8. Click on **Export assessment** from the top menu to download the assessment as an Excel file.

In this section, we created and viewed an assessment. In the upcoming sections, we are going to migrate the VMs to Azure. We will start by preparing the Hyper-V host server.

Prepare Hyper-V host

In this section, we are going to prepare the Hyper-V host so that it can migrate the VMs that we assessed previously to Azure. To do so, follow these steps:

1. In the Azure Migrate project overview blade in the Azure portal, under **Migration goals**, select **Servers | Azure Migration | Server Migration | Discover**:

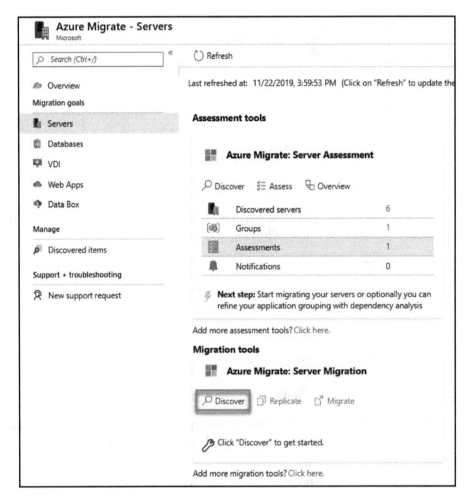

Azure Migrate: Server Migration

2. A new blade will open where you can specify what type of machines you want to migrate. Ensure that you select the following values:

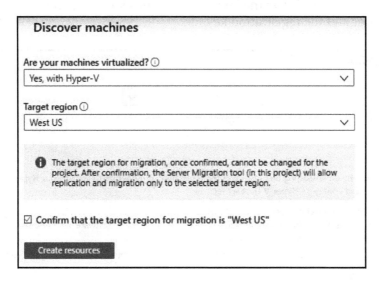

Selecting the required machine types for migration

3. Click **Create resources**. This will start the creation of a deployment template, which creates an Azure Site Recovery vault in the background.

4. Now that the deployment template has been created, we can download the Hyper-V replication provider software installer. This is used to install the replication provider on the Hyper-V servers. Download the Hyper-V Replication provider and the registration key file:

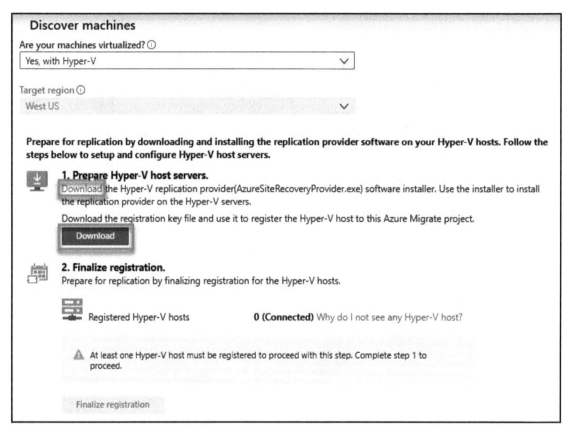

Downloading the Hyper-V replication provider software

5. The registration key is needed to register the Hyper-V host with Azure Migrate Server Migration. Note that the key is valid for 5 days after it is generated.

6. Copy the provider setup file and registration key file for each Hyper-V host (or cluster node) running the VMs you want to replicate. Now, run the AzureSiteRecoveryProvider.exe file. In the first screen of the installer, you will be asked whether you want to use Microsoft update. Click **yes**.

7. In the next screen, you have to provide an installation directory. Leave the default as it is and click **Install**.

8. After installation, you need to register the server in the Key Vault that was automatically created when we created the Azure Migrate project. Click **Register**.

9. Now, you need to specify the vault settings. First, import the key file that we downloaded in the previous step. This will automatically fill in the **Subscription**, **Vault name**, and **Hyper-V site name**:

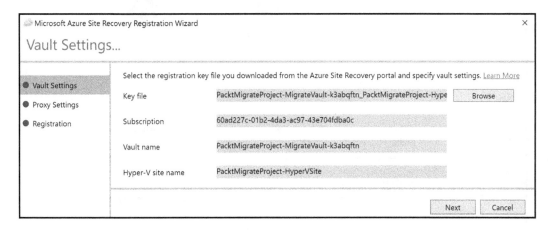

Registering the Key Vault

10. Click **Next**.

11. In the next screen, you have to specify whether you want to connect to Azure Site Recovery directly or by using a proxy. Keep the default setting as it is and click **Next**:

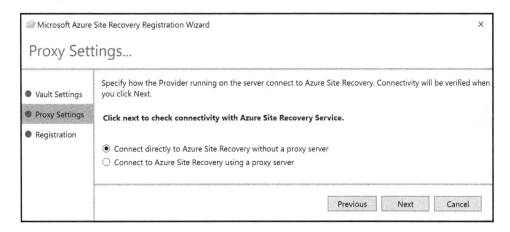

Connecting to Azure Site Recovery

12. The server will be registered and all the settings configured. You can close the installer by clicking **Finish**.

13. Now, go back into Azure portal, go to the discover machines blade, and click the **Finalize registration** button:

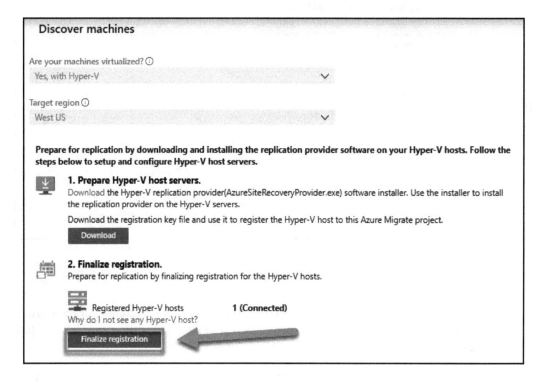

Finalize registration

14. Now, the registration has been finalized and the virtual machines have been discovered. This can take up to 15 minutes.

Now that we have prepared the Hyper-V host for migration, we are going to replicate (migrate) the servers to Azure.

Replicating the Hyper-V VMs

In this section, we are going to replicate the VMs to Azure Site Recovery. To do so, follow these steps:

 For this part of the demonstration, you should have a resource group with a storage account, VNet, and subnet created in the same region as the target region of the discovery, which we selected in the *Prepare Hyper-V host* discovery step in the previous section. In this demonstration, this is the West US region.

1. Open the Azure Migrate project from the Azure portal. Then, under **Migration goals**, click **Servers | Azure Migrate: Server Migration** and then click **Replicate**:

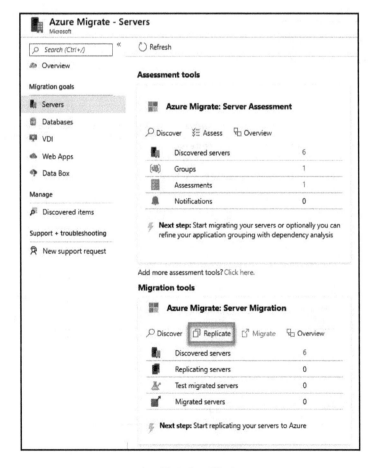

Azure Migrate: Server Migration

2. In the **Replicate** blade, add the following values:
   - **Are your machines virtualized? Yes, with Hyper-V**.

3. Then, click **Next: Virtual Machines**. Add the following values to the **Virtual machines** blade:
   - **Import migration settings from an Azure Migrate assessment?: Yes, apply migration settings from an Azure Migrate assessment**.
   - Select the group that we created earlier, as well as the assessment.
   - Select the VMs that you want to migrate:

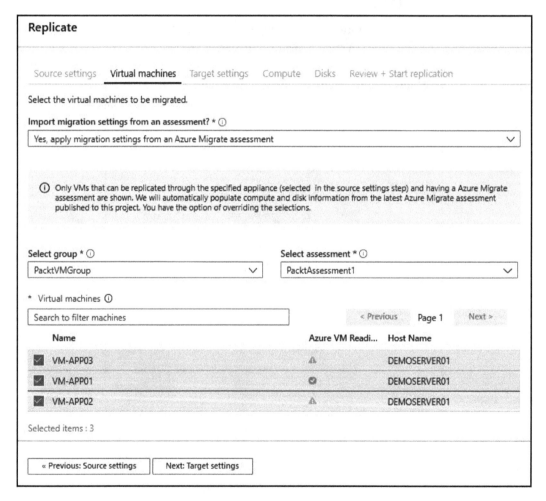

Selecting the assessment as input

4. Click **Next: target settings**.
5. In **Target settings**, the target region that you'll migrate to will be automatically selected. Select the subscription, the resource group, the storage account, and the virtual network and subnet that the Azure VMs will reside in after migration. You can also select whether you want to use the Azure hybrid benefit here:

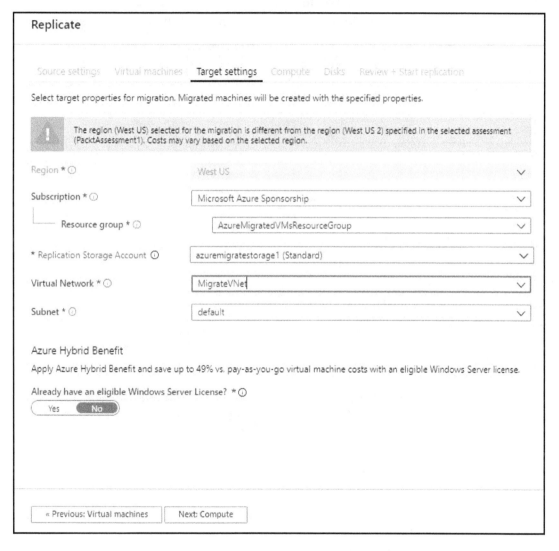

Target settings

6. Click **Next: Compute**.
7. In **Compute**, review the VM name, size, OS disk type, and availability set:
    1. **VM size**: If the assessment recommendations are used, the VM drop-down will contain the recommended size. Otherwise, Azure Migrate picks a size based on the closest match in the Azure subscription. You can also pick a size manually.
    2. **OS type**: Pick the OS type. You can choose between Windows or Linux.
    3. **OS disk**: Specify the OS (boot) disk for the VM.
    4. **Availability set:** If the VM should be in an Azure availability set after migration, specify the set. The set must be in the target resource group you specify for the migration:

Compute settings

8. Click **Next: Disks**.
9. In **Disks**, specify whether the VM disks should be replicated to Azure and select the disk type (standard SSD/HDD or premium-managed disks) in Azure:

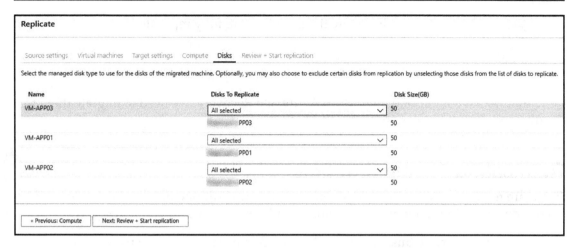

Selecting the required disks

10. Then, click **Next: Review + start replication**.
11. Click **Replicate**.
12. When the replication process has finished, you will see an overview of the replication VMs. Under **Migration goals | Servers | Azure Migrate: Server Migration | Replicating server**, you will see a list of all the replicated VMs and whether they have been replicated successfully. You can also view the health of the replication:

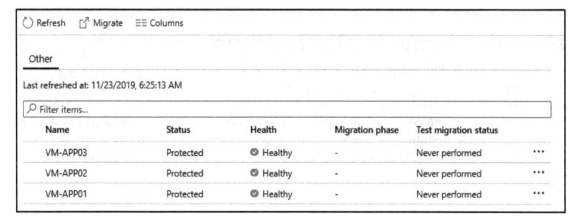

Replication overview

It can take a while before the machines are fully replicated.

Now that we have replicated the VMs to Azure Site Recovery, we need to migrate them to Azure.

Replicating for the first time

If you are replicating VMs for the first time in the Azure Migrate project, the Azure Migration Server Migration tool will automatically provide the following resources:

- **Azure Service bus**: The Azure Migrate Server Migration tool uses the Azure Service Bus to send replication orchestration messages to the appliance.
- **Gateway storage account**: Server Migration uses the gateway storage account to store state information about the VMs that are being replicated.
- **Log storage account**: The Azure Migrate appliance uploads replication logs for VMs to a log storage account. Then, the replication information will be applied to the replicated managed disks.
- **Key vault**: The Azure Migrate appliance uses the key vault to manage connection strings for the service bus, as well as the access keys for the storage accounts that are used in replication.

Migrating Hyper-V VMs to Azure

For the actual migration, there are two steps: a test migration and a migration. To make sure everything's working as expected without impacting the on-premises machines, it is recommended to do a test migration. During a test migration, the on-premises machines remain operational and can continue replicating. You can also use the replicated test Azure VM to validate the migration process, perform app testing, and address any issues before full migration. It is recommended to do this at least once for every machine before it gets migrated.

Running a test migration

To do a test migration, follow these steps:

1. In the Azure Migrate project, under **Migration goals** | **Servers** | **Azure Migrate: Server Migration**, navigate to **Overview**:

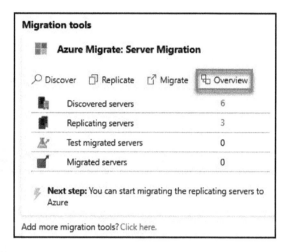

Azure Migrate: Server Migration

2. From the **Overview** blade of **Azure Migrate: Server Migration**, click the **Test migration** button:

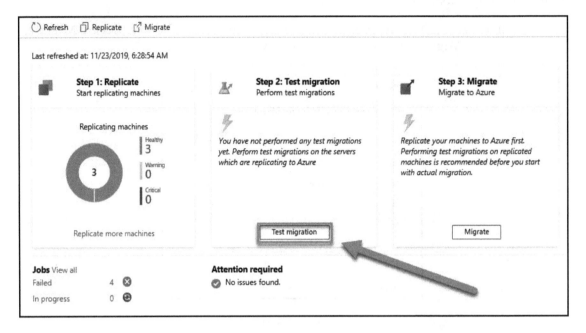

Test migration

3. Select the VM that you want to migrate. Then, from the **Overview** page, select **Test migration** from the top menu:

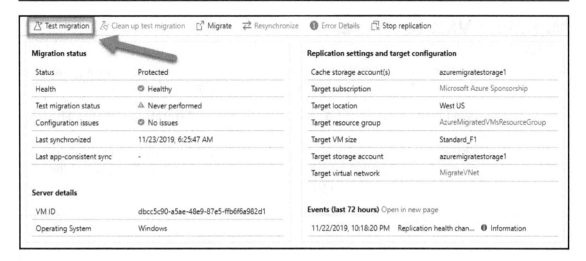

Starting test migration for the VM

4. Select the virtual network that we created before we replicated the VMs and start the test migration by clicking the **Test migration** button.

5. After the migration has finished, you can view the migrated Azure VM by going to **Virtual machines** in the Azure portal. The machine name has a suffix of - Test:

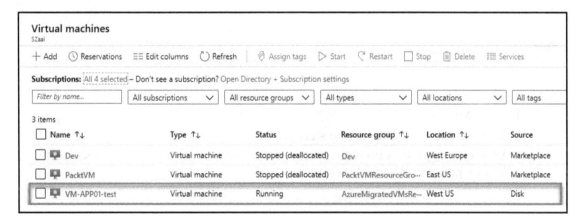

Migrated VM after test migration

6. Clean up the test migration after finishing the test migration. You can also remove the test VM.

Now that we have executed a test migration, we can migrate the VM to Azure.

Migrating VMs to Azure

In this final part of this demonstration, we are going to migrate the VM. We did a successful test migration in the previous step, which means we can start migrating the VMs properly. The migration of VMs is also done by the Azure Migrate: Server Migration tool:

1. From the **Overview** blade of **Azure Migrate: Server Migration** click the **Migrate** button.
2. In the **Migrate** blade, you need to specify whether you want to shut down the machines before migration to minimize data loss. Select **Yes**. Then, select the machines that you want to migrate:

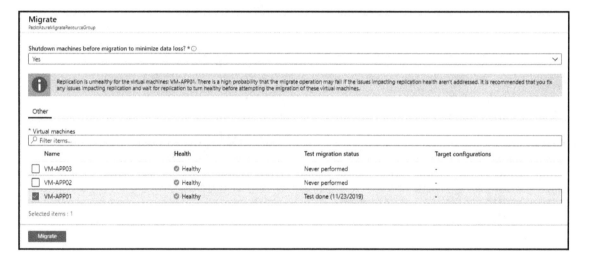

Selecting the VMs to migrate

3. Click **Migrate**.
4. The migration process will be started.
5. When the migration process has completed, you can view the migrated Azure VM by going to **Virtual Machines** in the Azure portal:

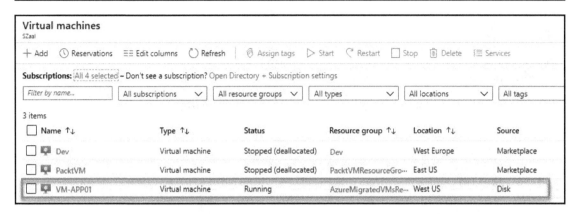

Migrated VM

 It can take a while before the VMs are fully migrated.

In this section, we migrated a VM to Azure. That concludes this chapter.

Summary

In this chapter, we covered the first part of the *Implement Workloads and Security* objective. We learned how to use Azure Migrate so that we can migrate, as well as the different features and capabilities that it has to offer. We also assessed and migrated VMs from a Hyper-V environment to Azure using Azure Migrate.

In the next chapter, we will continue with this objective by covering how to configure serverless computing.

Questions

Answer the following questions to test your knowledge of the information contained in this chapter. You can find the answers in the *Assessments* section at the end of this book:

1. Can you use Azure Migrate to migrate web applications?
    1. Yes
    2. No

2. Is Azure Migrate capable of visualizing cross-server dependencies so that groups of VMs can be migrated together?
    1. Yes
    2. No

3. Azure Migrate cannot be used to migrate physical machines.
    1. Yes
    2. No

Further reading

Check out the following links to find out more about the topics that were covered in this chapter:

- **About Azure Migrate**: https://docs.microsoft.com/en-us/azure/migrate/migrate-services-overview
- **Migrating physical or virtualized servers to Azure**: https://docs.microsoft.com/en-us/azure/migrate/tutorial-migrate-physical-virtual-machines
- **Migrating VMware VMs to Azure (agentless)**: https://docs.microsoft.com/en-us/azure/migrate/tutorial-migrate-vmware

Configuring Serverless Computing

9

In the previous chapter, we covered the first part of the *Implement Workloads and Security* objective. In this chapter, you'll learn how to migrate your environments using Azure Site Recovery. Then, you'll learn how to create and manage objects, how to manage a Logic App resource, how to manage Azure Function app settings, how to manage Event Grid, and how to manage Service Bus.

The following topics will be covered in this chapter:

- Creating and managing objects
- Managing a Logic App resource
- Understanding Azure Event Grid
- Understanding Azure Service Bus

Technical requirements

The demonstrations in this chapter use Azure PowerShell (`https://docs.microsoft.com/en-us/powershell/azure/install-az-ps?view=azps-1.8.0`) and Visual Studio Code (`https://code.visualstudio.com/download`).

The source code for our sample application can be downloaded from `https://github.com/PacktPublishing/Microsoft-Azure-Architect-Technologies-Exam-Guide-AZ-300/tree/master/Chapter09`.

Creating and managing objects

Azure offers a variety of services that we can use to build applications. One of the possibilities it offers is to create serverless applications. Serverless computing is the abstraction of servers, infrastructure, and operating systems. Serverless is consumption-based, which means that you don't need to anticipate any capacity. This is different from using PaaS services. With PaaS services, you still pay for the reserved compute.

In the upcoming sections, we are going to cover serverless services in Azure such as Azure Functions, Azure Logic Apps, Azure Event Grid, and Azure Service Bus. Then, we are going to create an Azure Function, deploy some applications with ARM templates, and learn how to manage these services from the Azure portal.

Azure Functions

Azure Functions is a serverless compute service that's used to run small pieces of code in the cloud. You can simply write the code you need in order to execute a certain task, without the need to create a whole application or manage your own infrastructure.

Azure Functions can be created from the Azure portal and from Visual Studio 2019 and can be created in a variety of programming languages. At the time of writing this book, the following languages are supported:

Language	1.x	2.x	3.x
C#	GA (.NET Framework 4.7)	GA (.NET Core 2.2)	Preview (.NET Core 3.1)
JavaScript	GA (Node 6)	GA (Node 8 and 10)	GA (Node 8 and 10)
F#	GA (.NET Framework 4.7)	GA (.NET Core 2.2)	GA (.NET Core 3.1)
Java	N/A	GA (Java 8)	GA (Java 8)
PowerShell	N/A	GA (PowerShell Core 6)	GA (PowerShell Core 6)
Python	N/A	GA (Python 3.6 and 3.7)	GA (Python 3.6 and 3.7)
TypeScript	N/A	GA (Supported through transpiling to JavaScript)	GA (Supported through transpiling to JavaScript)

Functions can be created using ARM templates as well. They can be deployed on Windows or Linux and by using continuous deployment. At the time of writing this book, Linux is still in preview.

With Azure Functions, you can build solutions that process data, integrate various systems, work with the **Internet of Things** (**IoT**), and simple APIs and microservices applications. You can create a small task, such as image or order processing, and call this task from other applications or execute it based on a certain schedule. For that, Azure Functions provides triggers such as `HTTPTrigger`, `TimerTrigger`, `CosmosDBTrigger`, `BlobTrigger`, `QueueTrigger`, `EventGridTrigger`, `EventHubTrigger`, `ServiceBusQueueTrigger`, and `ServiceBusTopicTrigger`.

Azure Functions uses an Azure storage account to store any code files and configuration bindings. It uses the standard Azure Storage, which provides blob, table, and queue storage for storing the files and triggers. However, you can use the same App Service plans for the functions that you use for web apps and APIs. Azure Functions can also be deployed in **App Service environments** (**ASEs**). When using these App Service plans or an ASE to host your functions, the function will become non-serverless. This happens due to the compute power being prelocated and therefore prepaid.

Creating an Azure Function

To create an Azure Function in the Azure portal, perform the following steps:

1. Navigate to the Azure portal by opening `https://portal.azure.com`.
2. Click on **Create a resource** and type `Function` into the search bar. Select **Function App** and click **Create** to create a new function.
3. A new blade will open, where you have to specify the properties for the function app. Add the following properties:
   - **Subscription**: Select a subscription here.
   - **Resource group**: Create a new resource group named `PacktFunctionApp`.
   - **Function App Name**: Name it `PacktFunctionApp`.
   - **Publish**: Code (you can also select a Docker Container to host your app in).
   - **Runtime Stack**: Select **.NET Core**.
   - **Location**: Select **Central US**.

4. Click **Review + Create** and then **Create** to create the function app.

5. Once the app has been created, open the resource in the Azure portal. This will navigate you to the settings of the function app. To create a new function, click **+**, which can be found next to **Functions** in the top left menu, and select **In-portal** to build your function directly into the Azure portal:

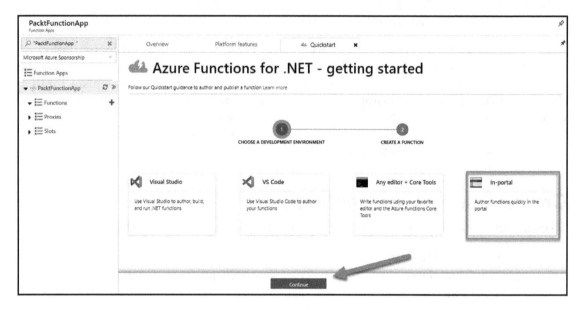

Creating a new function in the Azure portal

6. Next, we need to select a trigger template. For this demo, we're going to select the **Webhook + API** trigger template. After that, click **Create**:

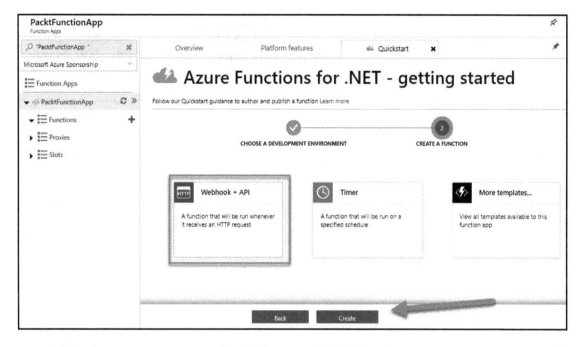

Selecting the Webhook + API trigger template

7. The sample for your Azure Function will be generated. Since the exam doesn't cover coding the Azure Function, we are going to keep the default code for this demo.

8. By using the **Webhook + API** trigger, this function can be called manually or from other applications by using the function URL. To obtain this URL, click the **Get function URL** link at the top of the screen. You can use this URL to start executing the function:

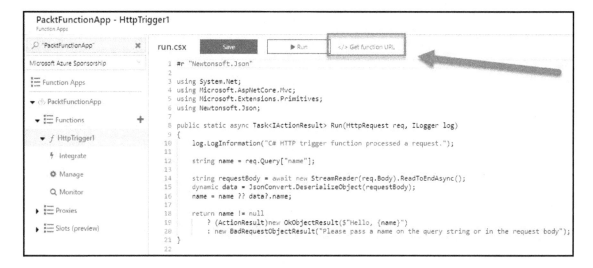

Obtaining the function URL

9. By default, the function URL consists of an application security key. You can change this authentication level in the settings if you want to:

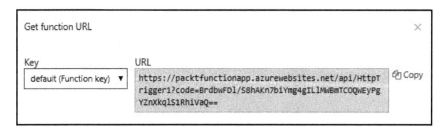

Displaying the function URL

10. You can also test the function from the Azure portal. Click **Test** from the right-hand menu. A test value will already be provided for you. After that, click on **Run** from the lower right of the screen to test the function:

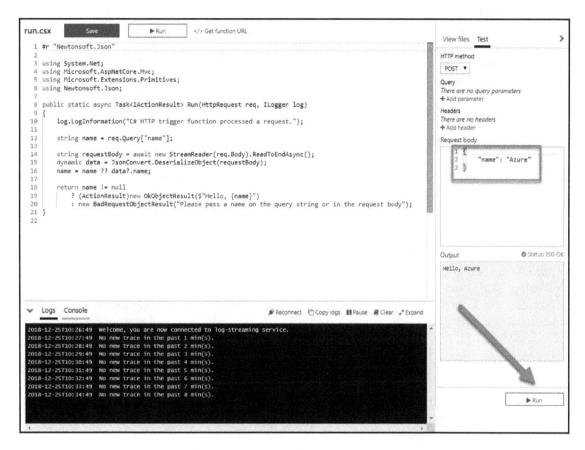

Testing the function

The function app is provided as an ARM template on GitHub. You can download it and deploy it inside your environment. It is recommended that you get familiar with the properties inside the template because there is a possibility that this will be part of the exam.

Azure Logic Apps

Logic Apps is another serverless service provided by Azure. They differ from Azure Functions because Logic Apps are used for creating workflows. They manage durable processes, while Azure Functions are usually used for a short-lived chain element in a broader chain. They are used to execute short pieces of code that handle a single function in that broader chain. Azure Functions are completely code-based, while Logic Apps can be created using a visual designer. Both Logic Apps and Azure Functions can be used to integrate services and applications.

Logic Apps can also be used to automate business processes. You can create them in the Azure portal and developers can create them from Visual Studio as well. For both, the visual designer is used to moderate the process. Logic Apps offers connectors that can integrate a number of cloud services and on-premises resources and applications. For Logic Apps, there is also a connector available to call an Azure Function from a Logic App.

These connectors can connect to different Azure services, third-party cloud services, different data stores and databases, and **line-of-business** (**LOB**) applications. Azure Logic Apps provide a number of pre-built connectors that you can leverage inside your workflow. Besides that, developers can also create their own connectors using Visual Studio. Besides using the Visual Editor, you can create and make adjustments to the Workflow Definition Language schema manually. This schema is created using JSON and can be created from scratch using Visual Studio or can be adjusted inside the Azure portal. Some capabilities can only be added to the schema directly and cannot be made from the Visual Editor. Examples of this include date and time formatting and string concatenation. Logic App definition files can be added to ARM templates and deployed using PowerShell, CLI, or REST APIs.

 You can refer to the following article for an overview of all the available connectors for Azure Logic Apps: https://docs.microsoft.com/en-us/azure/connectors/apis-list.

Deploying the Logic App ARM template

In this demo, we are going to deploy the Logic App ARM template, which can be downloaded from the GitHub repository that was provided in the *Technical requirements* section at the beginning of this chapter. The Logic App reads out RSS information on the CNN website and sends out an email from an Office 365 email account with the RSS item details. To deploy the Logic App ARM template, perform these steps:

1. Download the ARM template from the GitHub repository. If you want to look at the properties of the template, you can use Visual Studio Code or Notepad. The download link for Visual Studio Code is provided in the *Technical requirements* section as well. Create a new folder on your C drive and name it MyTemplates. Save the ARM templates in this directory.

2. We are going to deploy this template using PowerShell. Open PowerShell and add the following code (replace the subscription name):

   1. First, we need to log into the Azure account:

   ```
   Connect-AzAccount
   ```

   2. If necessary, select the right subscription:

   ```
   Select-AzSubscription -SubscriptionId "********-****-
   ****-****-***********"
   ```

   3. Create a resource group:

   ```
   New-AzResourceGroup -Name PacktLogicAppResourceGroup -
   Location EastUS
   ```

   4. Deploy the template inside your Azure subscription as follows:

   ```
   New-AzResourceGroupDeployment `
       -Name PacktDeployment `
       -ResourceGroupName PacktLogicAppResourceGroup `
       -TemplateFile c:\MyTemplates\template.json
   ```

3. After deployment, you need to go to the Logic App settings and configure an Outlook account that can be used to send out the email. By default, the account details will be empty. To configure an account, open `PacktLogicApp` in the **Logic App Designer** and open the **Connections** step. There, click **Invalid connection** and connect to an Office 365 account, as shown in the following screenshot:

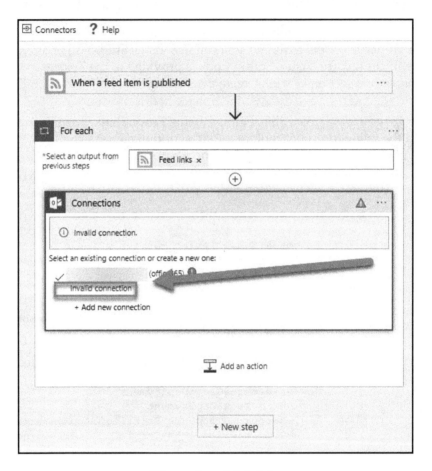

Adding an email account to the Logic App

You should get familiar with the different parts of the ARM template as they could be part of the exam questions.

Managing a Logic App resource

Now that the Logic App has been deployed and in place, we can take a look at how to manage it. You can use a variety of logging and monitoring capabilities to do so, all of which will be covered in this section.

Monitoring, logging, and alerts

After deploying and executing your Logic App, you can look at the run and trigger history, performance, and status tabs in the Azure portal. You can also set up diagnostic logging for real-time monitoring and more debugging capabilities for your Logic App. You can also enable alerts to get notifications about problems and failures.

Viewing runs and trigger history

To view the runs and trigger history for your Logic App, perform the following steps:

1. Navigate to the Azure portal by opening `https://portal.azure.com`.
2. Click on **All Resources** in the left menu and select the resource group for the Logic App.
3. A new blade will open with an overview of all of the resources that are part of the Logic App resource group.
4. Select the Logic App itself. A new blade will open with an overview page of the Logic App.
5. In the section that follows, under **Runs history**, you will see the runs of the Logic App. To get details about a certain run, select one of the runs from the list.

6. The **Logic App Designer** will open. Here, you can select each step to get more details about their input and output:

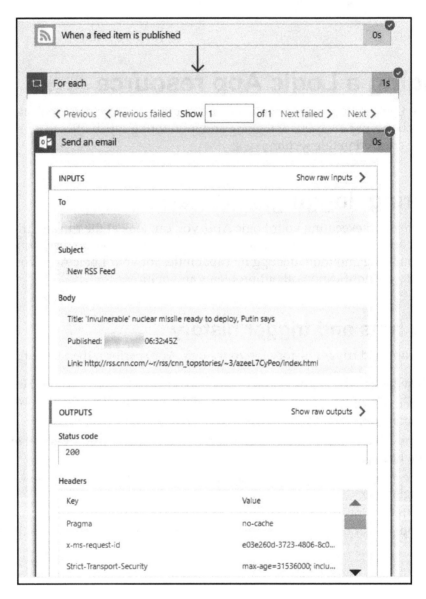

Logic App detailed monitoring

7. To get more details about the triggered event, go back to the **Overview** pane. Then, under see **Trigger History**, select the trigger event. Now, you can view various details, such as input and output information:

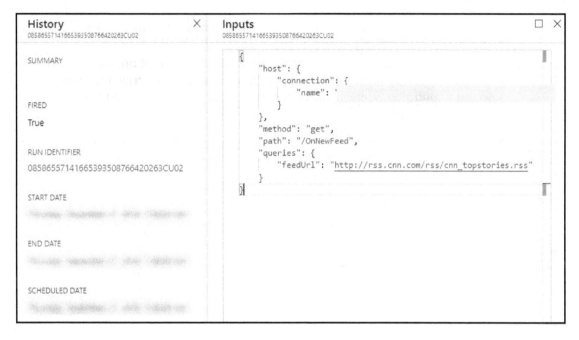

Logic App trigger history

Setting up alerts

In the case of problems and failures, you can set up alerts for Logic Apps. To set this up, perform the following steps:

1. On the Logic App overview pane in the Azure portal, from the left-hand side menu under **Monitoring**, select **Alerts**.

2. Click **New alert rule** at the top of the screen. In the pane that opens, you can add a condition. Here, you can select a signal that the alerts subscribe to. Once you've selected a condition, you can add a threshold and select the period for monitoring the metric:

Setting a condition for your alert

3. After that, you can create a new action group or select an existing one. Action groups allow you to trigger one or more actions so that you can notify others about an alert. You can select the following action types:

Setting an action group for your alert

4. Finally, you need to specify an alert title, a description, and a severity. Then, you need to enable the rule.

Accessing on-premises data

You can access on-premises data from your Logic App as well. For this, you can use the on-premises data gateway. The on-premises data gateway can connect on-premises environments to a number of Azure services, such as Azure Analysis Services, Azure Logic Apps, Microsoft Flow, Power Apps, and Power BI. For the on-premises side, there are a number of products that can be connected to the gateway, such as SQL Server, SQL Analysis Services, and SharePoint.

 For an overview of all of the on-premises data sources that are supported for the on-premises gateway, you can refer to `https://docs.microsoft.com/en-us/azure/analysis-services/analysis-services-datasource`.

To use the on-premises data gateway, a client needs to be installed on the on-premises environment. The client consists of a Windows Service that is responsible for setting up the connection with Azure. In Azure, a gateway cloud service needs to be created. The client then communicates with the gateway cloud service using the Azure Service Bus.

When a request for data is created by one of the Azure Services, the cloud gateway service creates a query and encrypts the on-premises credentials. This query and its credentials are then sent to a queue inside the gateway. Afterwards, the gateway sends the query to the Azure Service Bus.

The on-premises client polls the Azure Service Bus regularly. When a message is waiting inside the Service Bus, it decrypts the credentials from the on-premises data source. From there, it will run the query on it to retrieve the data. The following diagram illustrates this:

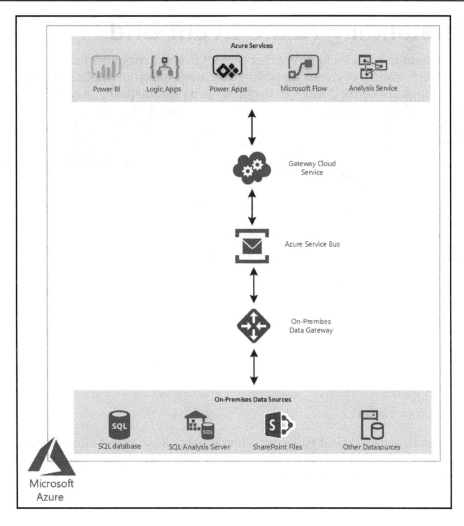

Azure on-premises data gateway

Now that we have seen how to manage a Logic App, let's look at Azure Event Grid.

Understanding Azure Event Grid

Azure Event Grid is a service in Azure that enables event management across different Azure resources. Instead of creating a polling mechanism in your application that polls for changes, the apps are notified when an event happens automatically. Azure Event Grid offers the throughput of millions of events per second and a 24-hour retrying mechanism. You can filter events based on publishing paths in order to receive only the events that are relevant to your application or resource. Events can be created without using code if you configure them in the Azure portal. You can create custom events as well, which can be created in your custom applications, PowerShell, or CLI.

Azure Event Grid offers the following built-in event sources:

- Azure Subscriptions (management operations)
- Resource Groups (management operations)
- Container Registry
- Event Hubs
- IoT Hub
- Media Services
- Storage Blob
- Azure Maps
- Service Bus
- Custom Topics

For Event Handlers, Event Grid currently offers Webhooks, Azure Automation, Azure Functions, Logic Apps, Event Hubs, Queue Storage, Microsoft Flow, Hybrid Connections, and Service Bus (Preview):

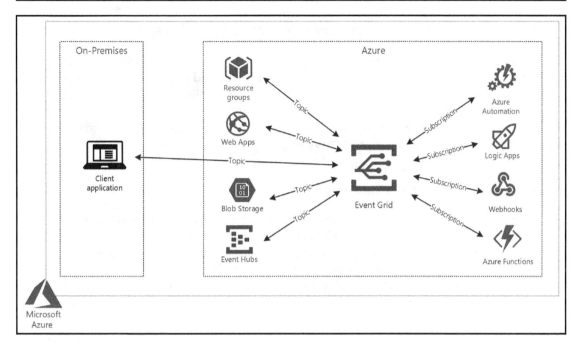

Azure Event Grid

 New publishers and event handlers are added rapidly to Azure Event Grid, so keep an eye on `https://docs.microsoft.com/en-us/azure/event-grid/overview`.

Event domains

An event domain is a management tool for a large number of Event Grid topics that are related to the same application. This allows you to publish events to thousands of topics at once. They also provide authorization and authentication control over each topic.

An event domain also handles partitioning, so, instead of needing to publish events to each topic individually, customers can publish all of their events to the domain's endpoint. The Event Grid takes care of ensuring that each event will be sent to the correct topic.

Understanding Azure Service Bus

Azure Service Bus is a fully managed enterprise integration message broker. It is mostly used for integration scenarios such as decoupling services and applications from each other. For those scenarios, it offers message queuing and publish/subscribe messaging. You can use it for IoT solutions as well, in combination with the Azure IoT Hub. It offers a reliable and secure platform for asynchronous data and state transfer, where data is transferred between applications and services using messaging. A message can be a JSON, XML, or text file.

Azure Service Bus offers the following key capabilities:

- **Queues**: With queues, you can decouple message communication between applications and services with asynchronous messaging. A queue offers first in, first out message delivery, where each message is delivered to one consumer. All of the messages are stored inside the queue, so it isn't necessary for applications to be connected to the queue at the same time. Messages can be grouped together using a session ID. This way, messages can be isolated and processed by dedicated clients.
- **Topics and subscriptions**: This offers the same functionalities as queues, except there can be multiple consumers. This uses the publish/subscribe pattern, where the message is sent to a topic. Applications don't connect to that topic directly; instead, they connect to the subscription. The subscription then connects to the topic. These subscriptions can have filters that only subscribe to a subset of messages, named filter expressions.
- **WCF relays**: WCF relays offer a gateway that you can use to connect your on-premises WCF Services to Azure, without having to open a firewall connection on your network.

Azure Service Bus geo-disaster recovery

When entire Azure regions or data centers experience downtime, it is critical for your messaging solutions to continue to operate in a different data center or region. That's why *geo-disaster recovery* and *geo-replication* are important features.

Setting up geo-disaster recovery

The disaster recovery feature uses metadata disaster recovery and relies on primary and secondary disaster recovery namespaces.

Metadata means that it replicates only the entities such as queues, topics, subscriptions, and the service properties that are part of the service bus namespace. The actual messages are not replicated. For the primary and secondary namespaces, the former is the *active* namespace and receives the messages. The latter is a *passive* namespace and doesn't receive the messages. The metadata is kept in sync between both the namespaces. Therefore, both can receive these messages. To make sure that only the active namespace received the messages, you need to configure an *alias*. This is basically a disaster recovery configuration. By configuring an alias, a **fully qualified domain name (FQDN)** connection string is provided, which can be used by applications to connect to the namespace.

To set up the initial failover, you have to perform the following steps:

1. **Set up a primary namespace**: First, you must create a primary namespace. This can be an existing namespace.
2. **Set up a secondary namespace**: Then, you need to create the secondary namespace.
3. **Create pairing**: After that, you pair the two of them. This will create an alias that you can use to connect to the Service Bus. Only new namespaces can be added to the failover pairing.
4. **Monitoring**: Finally, you have to set up some monitoring to determine whether failover is necessary. Typically, automatic failover isn't possible because the service is part of a large ecosystem. Failovers must be performed in sync with other applications or infrastructure components.

If you initiate the actual failover, follow these steps:

1. You want to perform the failover again in the case of a second outage. Therefore, it is highly recommended to set up another passive namespace and update the pairing.
2. When the former primary namespace is available again, you can pull the messages from it. Then, you can delete the old primary namespace or use it for regular messaging outside the geo-recovery setup.

For a detailed example of how to set up geo-disaster recovery for your Service Bus solutions, you can refer to the following GitHub page: `https://github.com/Azure/azure-service-bus/tree/master/samples/DotNet/Microsoft.ServiceBus.Messaging/GeoDR/SBGeoDR2/`.

Summary

In this chapter, we covered the second part of the *Implementing and Managing Application Services* objective. We covered how to create and manage different application services in Azure such as Azure Functions and Azure Logic Apps, as well as Azure Event Grid and Azure Service Bus.

In the next chapter, we will cover the third part of this exam objective by managing App Service plans.

Questions

Answer the following questions to test your knowledge of the information contained in this chapter. You can find the answers in the *Assessments* section at the end of this book:

1. You want to create a small task, such as processing an image, which can be called from other applications. Is Logic Apps the most suitable option for this?
   - Yes
   - No

2. You want to set up geo-disaster recovery for Azure Service Bus. Do you need to set up an alias manually?
   - Yes
   - No

3. With Azure Logic Apps, you can connect to Azure resources and on-premises data.
   - Yes
   - No

Further reading

Check out the following links to find out more about the topics that were covered in this chapter:

- **Azure Functions Documentation**: `https://docs.microsoft.com/en-us/azure/azure-functions/`
- **Monitoring statuses, setting up diagnostics logging, and turning on alerts for Azure Logic Apps**: `https://docs.microsoft.com/en-us/azure/logic-apps/logic-apps-monitor-your-logic-apps#find-events`
- **Azure Event Grid Documentation**: `https://docs.microsoft.com/en-us/azure/event-grid/`
- **Service Bus Documentation**: `https://docs.microsoft.com/en-us/azure/service-bus/`
- **Azure Service Bus Geo-Disaster Recovery**: `https://docs.microsoft.com/en-us/azure/service-bus-messaging/service-bus-geo-dr`

10
Implementing Application Load Balancing

In the previous chapter, we covered the second part of the *Implementing Workloads and Security* objective. We covered how to configure serverless computing by looking at how to manage Azure Logic Apps, Azure Functions, and more.

This chapter covers the third part of this objective. In this chapter, we are going to learn how to configure an application gateway and load balancing rules, how to implement frontend IP configurations, and how to manage application load balancing. We will also look at Azure Front Door.

The following topics will be covered in this chapter:

- Understanding Azure Application Gateway
- Configuring an application gateway
- Implementing frontend IP configurations
- Configuring load balancing rules
- Managing application load balancing
- Understanding Azure Front Door

Technical requirements

The example in this chapter use Azure PowerShell (`https://docs.microsoft.com/en-us/powershell/azure/install-az-ps?view=azps-1.8.0`).

The source code for our sample application can be downloaded from `https://github.com/PacktPublishing/Microsoft-Azure-Architect-Technologies-Exam-Guide-AZ-300/tree/master/Chapter10`.

Understanding Azure Application Gateway

Azure Application Gateway is a web traffic load balancer that can be used to manage traffic to web applications. This web traffic load balancer operates at the application layer (Layer 7 in the OSI network reference stack).

It offers web load balancing, which is for HTTP(S) only. Traditional load balancers operate at the transport layer (Layer 4 in the OSI network reference stack), and route traffic—based on the source IP address and a port number—to a destination IP address and a port number. With Azure Application Gateway, traffic can be routed based on the incoming URL as well. For instance, if `/pictures` is part of the incoming URL, traffic can be routed to a particular set of servers that have been specifically configured for pictures. If `/audio` is part of the incoming URL, the traffic is routed to another set of servers, configured specifically for audio files. The following diagram shows the workflow of Azure Application Gateway:

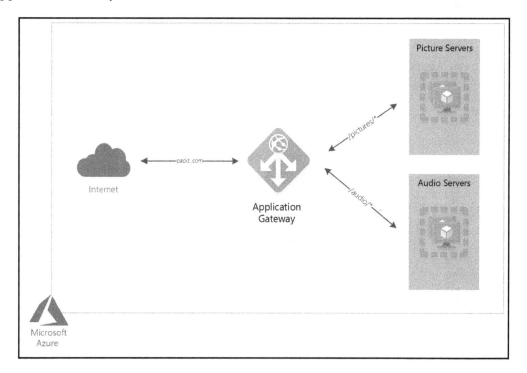

Azure Application Gateway

Azure Application Gateway offers the following features and capabilities:

- **Web application firewall**: One of the features of the Application Gateway is its **web application firewall** (**WAF**). It offers centralized protection of web apps from common vulnerabilities and exploits. It is based on rules from the **Open Web Application Security Project** (**OWASP**) 3.0 or 2.2.9. Common exploits include cross-site scripting attacks and SQL injection attacks. With **WAF**, you can centralize the prevention of such types of attacks, which makes security management a lot easier and gives a better assurance to the administrators than if this is handled in the application code. And, by patching a known vulnerability at a central location instead of in every application separately, administrators can react a lot faster to security threats.

- **URL Path-Based Routing**: This allows you to route traffic, based on URL paths, to different backend server pools.

- **Autoscaling**: Azure Application Gateway also offers a public preview of a new pricing tier, `Standard_V2`. This offers **Autoscaling**, whereby the number of application gateway or WAF deployments can scale based on incoming traffic. It also offers **Zone redundancy**, whereby the deployment can span multiple availability zones. This way, you don't have to set up multiple application gateway instances in different zones with a traffic manager. It also offers **Static VIP**, which ensures that the VIP associated with the application gateway does not change after a restart. Additionally, it offers faster deployment and update time, and five times better SSL offload performance than the other pricing tier.

- **Secure Sockets Layer (SSL) termination**: Azure Application Gateway offers SSL termination at the gateway. After the gate, the traffic will be transported unencrypted to the backend servers. This will eliminate the need for costly encryption and decryption overheads. End-to-end SSL encryption is also supported for cases that need encrypted communication, such as when an application can only accept a secure connection or for other security requirements.

- **Connection draining**: This feature will remove backend pool members during planned service updates. You can enable this setting at the backend **HTTP setting** and during rule creation. This setting can be applied to all the members of the backend pool. When this feature is enabled, Azure Application Gateway makes sure that all the deregistering instances in the pool do not receive any new requests.

- **Custom error pages**: You can create custom error pages using your customer layout and branding, instead of the default error pages that are displayed.

- **Multiple-site hosting**: With multiple-site hosting, more than one web app can be configured on the same application gateway. You can add up to 100 web apps to the application gateway, and each web app can be redirected to its own pool of backend servers.

- **Redirection**: Azure Application Gateway offers the ability to redirect traffic on the gateway itself. It offers a generic redirection mechanism that can be used for global redirection, whereby traffic is redirected from and to any port you define by using rules. An example of this could be an HTTP to HTTPS redirection. It also offers **path-based redirection**, where the HTTP to HTTPS is only redirected to a specific site area, and offers redirection to external sites.

- **Session affinity**: This feature is useful when you want to maintain a user session on the same server. By using gateway-managed cookies, the gateway can direct traffic from the same user session to the same server for processing. This is used in cases where session states are stored locally on the server for the user session.

- **WebSocket and HTTP/2 traffic**: The WebSocket and HTTP/2 protocols are natively supported by Azure Application Gateway. These protocols enable full-duplex communication between the client and the server over a long-running TCP connection, without the need for polling. These protocols can use the same TCP connection for multiple requests and responses, which results in more efficient utilization of resources. These protocols work over the traditional HTTP ports 80 and 443.

- **Rewrite HTTP headers**: Azure Application Gateway can also rewrite the HTTP headers for incoming and outgoing traffic. This way, you can add, update, and remove HTTP headers while the request/response packets are moved between the client and the backend pools.

Azure Application Gateway comes in the following tiers:

- **Standard**: By selecting this tier, you are going to use the Azure Application Gateway as a load balancer for your web apps.

- **Standard v2 (Preview)**: In addition to the previous Standard tier, this tier offers autoscaling, zone redundancy, and support for static VIPs.

- **WAF**: By selecting this tier, you are going to create a web application firewall.

- **WAF v2 (Preview)**: In addition to the previous WAF tier, this tier offers autoscaling, zone redundancy, and support for static VIPs.

Azure Application Gateway comes in three different sizes. The following table shows an average performance throughput for each application gateway:

Average backend page response size	Small	Medium	Large
6 KB	7.5 Mbps	13 Mbps	50 Mbps
100 KB	35 Mbps	100 Mbps	200 Mbps

The actual throughput depends on various environment details, such as the location of backend instances, the average page size, and the processing time to serve a page.

Configuring an application gateway

You can create an Azure application gateway using the Azure portal, PowerShell, or CLI. In this demo, we are going to create an Azure application gateway from PowerShell.

In this section, we are going to set up the required network resources, virtual machines, backend servers, frontend IP address, and the application gateway itself. It will take a while (30 minutes upwards) to run the full script.

The code for this example has been split into multiple sections. You can download the whole script from GitHub using the link provided in the *Technical requirements* section at the beginning of this chapter.

First, we need to connect to our Azure account and select the subscription. If you are using Azure Cloud Shell, you don't need to log in to your Azure account using the administrator credentials. Take the following steps:

1. First, we need to log in to the Azure account, as follows:

   ```
   Connect-AzAccount
   ```

2. If necessary, select the right subscription, as follows:

   ```
   Select-AzSubscription -SubscriptionId "********-****-****-****-
   ***********"
   ```

Creating network resources

Next, we need to create a resource group and the required network resources. We need to create two subnets – one for the application gateway and one for the backend pool – which we will create later in this demo. Take the following steps:

1. Create a resource group, as follows:

   ```
   New-AzResourceGroup -Name PacktApplicationGateway -Location
   EastUS
   ```

2. Create the network resources, as follows:

   ```
   $PacktAGSubnet = New-AzVirtualNetworkSubnetConfig `
     -Name PacktAGSubnet `
     -AddressPrefix 10.0.1.0/24
   ```

3. Create the subnets, as follows:

   ```
   $PacktBackendSubnetConfig = New-AzVirtualNetworkSubnetConfig `
     -Name PacktBackendSubnetConfig `
     -AddressPrefix 10.0.2.0/24
   ```

4. Create the VNet, as follows:

   ```
   $vnet = New-AzVirtualNetwork `
     -ResourceGroupName PacktApplicationGateway `
     -Location eastus `
     -Name PacktVNet `
     -AddressPrefix 10.0.0.0/16 `
     -Subnet $PacktAGSubnet, $PacktBackendSubnetConfig
   ```

5. Create the public IP address, as follows:

   ```
   $pip = New-AzPublicIpAddress `
     -ResourceGroupName PacktApplicationGateway `
     -Location eastus `
     -Name PacktAGPublicIPAddress `
     -AllocationMethod Dynamic
   ```

Creating the backend servers

Finally, for the backend, we are going to create two VMs that are going to be used as backend servers for the application gateway. We are also going to deploy IIS and a web page to it for testing purposes. During execution, you will be prompted to provide a username and password for the VMs. Take the following steps:

1. Set the credentials and the VM settings, as follows:

```
$vnet = Get-AzVirtualNetwork -ResourceGroupName
PacktApplicationGateway -Name PacktVNet
$cred = Get-Credential
for ($i=1; $i -le 2; $i++)
{
# Create a virtual machine
 $nic = New-AzNetworkInterface `
 -Name PacktNic$i `
 -ResourceGroupName PacktApplicationGateway ` -Location eastus
`
 -SubnetId $vnet.Subnets[1].Id
 $vm = New-AzVMConfig `
 -VMName PacktVM$i `
 -VMSize Standard_D2
 $vm = Set-AzVMOperatingSystem `
 -VM $vm `
 -Windows `
 -ComputerName PAcktVM$i `
 -Credential $cred `
 -ProvisionVMAgent
 $vm = Set-AzVMSourceImage `
 -VM $vm `
 -PublisherName MicrosoftWindowsServer `
 -Offer WindowsServer `
 -Skus 2016-Datacenter `
 -Version latest
 $vm = Add-AzVMNetworkInterface `
 -VM $vm `
 -Id $nic.Id
 $vm = Set-AzVMBootDiagnostic `
 -VM $vm `
 -Disable
```

2. Create the VMs and install IIS on the VMs, as follows:

```
New-AzVM -ResourceGroupName PacktApplicationGateway -Location
eastus -VM $vm
Set-AzVMExtension `
```

```
-ResourceGroupName PacktApplicationGateway `
-ExtensionName IIS `
-VMName PacktVM$i `
-Publisher Microsoft.Compute `
-ExtensionType CustomScriptExtension `
-TypeHandlerVersion 1.4 `
-SettingString '{"commandToExecute":"powershell Add-
WindowsFeature Web-Server; powershell Add-Content -Path
\"C:\\inetpub\\wwwroot\\Default.htm\" -Value
$($env:computername)"}' `
-Location EastUS
}
```

In the next section, we will look at IP configurations.

Implementing frontend IP configurations

Now, we need to create the IP configurations and the frontend port. The IP configurations consist of associating the subnet that was created previously with the application gateway and assigning the public IP address to the gateway as well. We are also going to assign port 80, which can be used to access the application gateway. Take the following steps:

1. Create the IP configurations and the frontend port, as follows:

```
$vnet = Get-AzVirtualNetwork `
 -ResourceGroupName PacktApplicationGateway `
 -Name PacktVNet
$subnet=$vnet.Subnets[0]
$gipconfig = New-AzApplicationGatewayIPConfiguration `
 -Name PacktAGIPConfig `
 -Subnet $subnet
$fipconfig = New-AzApplicationGatewayFrontendIPConfig `
 -Name PacktAGFrontendIPConfig `
 -PublicIPAddress $pip
$frontendport = New-AzApplicationGatewayFrontendPort `
 -Name PacktFrontendPort `
 -Port 80
```

Creating the backend pool

Now, we have to create the backend pool for the application gateway and assign port 80 to it, so that it can be accessed by the application gateway. Take the following steps:

1. Create the backend pool and settings, as follows:

```
$address1 = Get-AzNetworkInterface -ResourceGroupName
PacktApplicationGateway -Name PacktNic1
$address2 = Get-AzNetworkInterface -ResourceGroupName
PacktApplicationGateway -Name PacktNic2

$backendPool = New-AzApplicationGatewayBackendAddressPool `
  -Name PacktGBackendPool `
  -BackendIPAddresses
$address1.ipconfigurations[0].privateipaddress,
$address2.ipconfigurations[0].privateipaddress

$poolSettings = New-AzApplicationGatewayBackendHttpSettings `
  -Name PacktPoolSettings `
  -Port 80 `
  -Protocol Http `
  -CookieBasedAffinity Enabled `
  -RequestTimeout 120
```

2. Next, we need to create the listener and add a rule. A listener is required to allow the application gateway to route the traffic appropriately to the backend pool. First we need to create a new listener and assign the frontend configuration and frontend port that we created previously to it. Then, we need to create a rule, which is required for the listener to know which backend pool is used for the incoming traffic. Create the listener and add the rule, as follows:

```
$defaultlistener = New-AzApplicationGatewayHttpListener `
  -Name PacktAGListener `
  -Protocol Http `
  -FrontendIPConfiguration $fipconfig `
  -FrontendPort $frontendport
$frontendRule = New-AzApplicationGatewayRequestRoutingRule `
  -Name rule1 `
  -RuleType Basic `
  -HttpListener $defaultlistener `
  -BackendAddressPool $backendPool `
  -BackendHttpSettings $poolSettings
```

Creating the application gateway

Lastly, we will create the application gateway itself. Proceed as follows:

1. Create the application gateway, as follows:

```
$sku = New-AzApplicationGatewaySku -Name Standard_Medium -Tier
Standard -Capacity 2

New-AzApplicationGateway `
  -Name PacktAppGateway `
  -ResourceGroupName PacktApplicationGateway `
  -Location eastus `
  -BackendAddressPools $backendPool `
  -BackendHttpSettingsCollection $poolSettings `
  -FrontendIpConfigurations $fipconfig `
  -GatewayIpConfigurations $gipconfig `
  -FrontendPorts $frontendport `
  -HttpListeners $defaultlistener `
  -RequestRoutingRules $frontendRule `
  -Sku $sku
```

 It will take approximately 30 minutes before the whole script is executed.

Testing the application gateway

You can test the application gateway by requesting the public IP address of the gateway and pasting it into a browser window. Take the following steps:

1. To get the public IP address, add the following line of code to PowerShell:

```
Get-AzPublicIPAddress -ResourceGroupName
PacktApplicationGateway -Name PacktAGPublicIPAddress
```

2. Paste this IP address into a browser window to test the application gateway. If you open an in-private browser and call the same URL, you will see that the request is routed to the second VM, as shown in the following screenshot:

Testing the application gateway

In the next section, we will learn how to configure the load balancing rules.

Configuring load balancing rules

You can also configure load balancing rules from the Azure portal. In the following demo, we are going to create a new routing rule that routes all the traffic that is coming in on port 81 to `PacktVM2`. First, we need to create a new backend pool; then, we can add a listener that picks up the traffic and calls the rule to route the traffic to the right backend server. To configure this, take the following steps:

1. Navigate to the Azure portal by opening `https://portal.azure.com/`.
2. Open the application gateway resource that we created in the previous section.
3. First, we need to create a backend pool. This will be associated with the new rule in the upcoming steps.
4. Under **Settings**, select **Backend pools** and click **Add** in the top menu, as shown in the following screenshot:

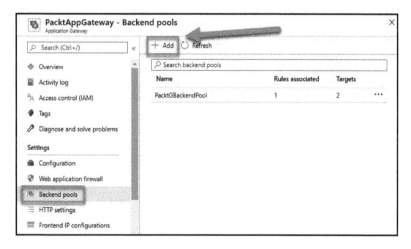

Creating a backend pool

5. Add the following values, as shown in the following screenshot:
    - **Name:** `Packt2BackendPool`
    - **Add backend pool without targets:** No
    - **Target type:** Select **Virtual machine**; **Target:** `PacktNic2`
6. Click **Add**:

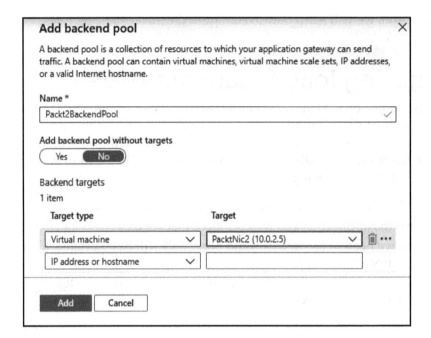

Backend pool settings

7. Next, create the listener. Under **Settings**, select **Listeners** and click **Basic** in the top menu, as shown in the following screenshot:

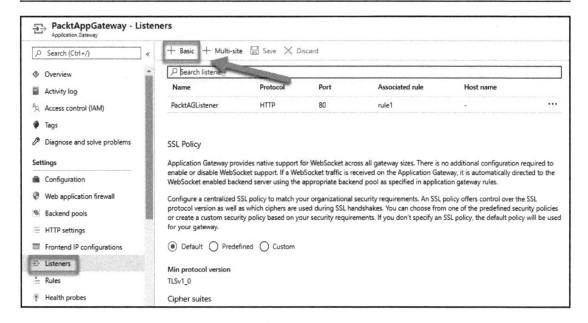

Creating a listener

8. Fill in the following values, as shown in the following screenshot:

- **Listener name:** `Packt2AGListener`
- **Frontend IP: Public**
- **Port**: `81`
- **Protocol: HTTP**

9. Click **OK**:

Listener settings

10. Now, under **Settings**, select **Rules** and, in the top menu, select **Basic** to create a new rule, as shown in the following screenshot:

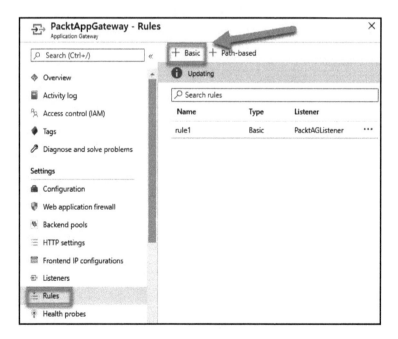

Creating a new rule

11. Add the following settings:
    - **Name:** `Rule2`
    - **Listener:** `Packt2AGListener`
    - **Backend pool:** `Packt2BackendPool`
    - **HTTP settings:** `PacktPoolSettings`

12. Click **OK**:

Rule settings

13. You can test the rule by navigating to the following URL in the browser: `http://<public-ip-address>:81`. You will be redirected to `PacktVM2`.

Next, we will look at how to manage application load balancing.

Managing application load balancing

In the previous sections, we covered how to create and manage frontend IP configurations, listeners, and rules. There are a couple of additional features that can be managed for the application gateway from the Azure portal, PowerShell, and CLI, such as monitoring, WAF, and health probes.

Health probes

By default, the health of all the resources in the backend pool of Azure Application Gateway are monitored. When resources are considered unhealthy, they are automatically removed from the pool. They are monitored continuously and added back to the backend pool when they become available and respond to health probes again.

Azure Application Gateway offers default health probes and custom health probes. When a custom health probe is not created, Azure Application Gateway automatically configures a default health probe. The default health probe will monitor the resources in the backend pool by making an HTTP request to the IP addresses that have been configured for the backend pool. When HTTPS is configured, the probe will make an HTTPS request to test the health of the backend. The default health probe will test the resources in the backend pool every 30 seconds. A healthy response will have a status code between 200 and 399.

Custom health probes allow you to have more granular control over health monitoring. When using custom probes, you can configure the probe interval, the URL and path to test, and how many failed responses to accept, before marking the backend pool instance as unhealthy.

Monitoring

By using Azure Application Gateway, you can monitor resources, as follows:

- **Backend health**: The health of the individual servers in the backend pools can be monitored using the Azure portal, PowerShell, and CLI. An aggregated health summary can be found in the performance diagnostic logs as well. The backend health report shows the output of the application gateway health probe to the backend instances. When probing is not successful and the backend cannot receive traffic, it's considered unhealthy.
- **Metrics**: Metrics is a feature for certain Azure resources, whereby you can view performance counters in the portal. Azure Application Gateway provides seven metrics so that we can view performance counters: Current connections, Healthy host count, Unhealthy host count, Response Status, Total Requests, Failed Requests, and Throughput.

- **Logs**: Azure provides different kinds of logs so that we can manage and troubleshoot application gateways. All the logs can be extracted from Azure Blob Storage and viewed in different tools, such as Azure Monitor Logs, Excel, and Power BI. The following types of logs are supported:
  - **Activity log**: All operations that are submitted to your Azure subscription are displayed in the Azure activity logs (formerly known as operational logs and audit logs). These logs can be viewed from the Azure portal, and they are collected by default.
  - **Performance log**: This log reflects how the application gateway is performing. It is collected every 60 seconds, and it captures the performance information for each instance, including throughput in bytes, failed request count, total requests served, total requests served, and healthy and unhealthy backend instance count.
  - **Firewall log**: In cases where the application gateway is configured with the web application firewall, this log can be viewed to display the requests that are logged through either Detection or Prevention mode.
  - **Access log**: You can use this log to view application gateway access patterns and analyze important information. It is collected every 300 seconds. This information includes the caller's IP, response latency, requested URL, return code, and bytes in and out. This log contains one record per instance of the application gateway.

Logs can be stored using one of the following three options:

- **Storage account**: When logs need to be stored for a longer duration, storage accounts are the best solution. When they are stored in a storage account, they can be reviewed when needed.
- **Event Hubs**: Using Event Hubs, you can integrate the logs with other **security information and event management** (**SIEM**) tools to get alerts about your resources.
- **Azure Monitor Logs**: Azure Monitor Logs is the best solution for real-time monitoring of your application or for looking at trends.

Some basic monitoring can also be done from the overview blade of the application gateway. There, you can find the sum total requests, sum failed requests, sum throughput, and more.

Turning on the web application firewall

You can turn on the web application firewall after provisioning the application gateway. WAF can be configured in the following modes:

- **Detection mode**: The application gateway WAF will monitor and log all threat alerts to a log file. You need to make sure that the WAF log is selected and turned on. The WAF will not block the incoming requests when WAF is configured in Detection mode.
- **Prevention mode**: In this mode, intrusions and attacks that have been detected by rules are actively blocked by the application gateway. The connection is terminated and the attacker will receive a *403 unauthorized access* exception. Prevention mode continues to log such attacks in the WAF logs.

To enable WAF, take the following steps:

1. Open the Application Gateway resource again.
2. Under **Settings**, select **Web application firewall**. In the WAF blade, you have to switch the tier from **Standard** to **WAF**. We created an application gateway using the Standard tier in our PowerShell script. Then, you can select **Detection** or **Prevention** regarding the **Firewall mode**, and configure the required settings, as follows:

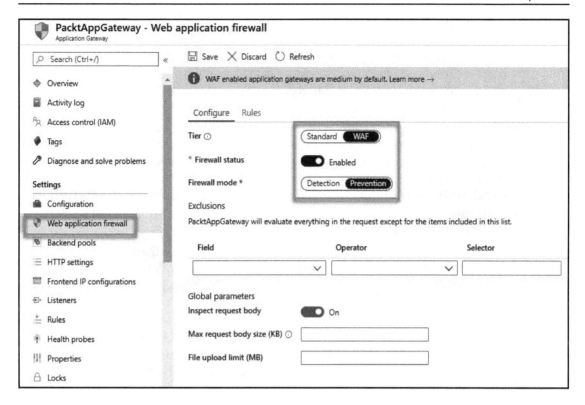

WAF

In this section, we covered three different ways of managing the Azure application load balancer. In the next section, we are going to cover Azure Front Door.

Understanding Azure Front Door

Azure Front Door offers a service that also works at the application layer (Layer 7). It is an **Application Delivery Network** (**ADN**) as a service, and it offers various load balancing capabilities for your applications.

Both Azure Front Door and Azure Application Gateway are Layer 7 (HTTPS/HTTPS) load balancers. The difference between the two is that Front Door is a global service, whereas Application Gateway is a regional service. This means that Front Door can load balance between different scale units across multiple regions. Application Gateway is designed to load balance between different VMs/containers that are located inside the same scale unit.

Azure Front Door offers the following features and capabilities:

- **Accelerate application performance**: End users can quickly connect to the nearest Front Door **Point of Presence (POP)** using the split TCP-based anycast protocol. It then uses Microsoft's global network to connect the application to the backend.

- **Smart health probes**: Front Door increases application availability with smart health probes. These probes will monitor the backends for both availability and latency, and provide instant automatic failover when a backend goes down. This way, you can run planned maintenance operations on your applications without any downtime. Traffic is redirected to alternative backends during maintenance.

- **URL Path-Based Routing**: This allows you to route traffic to backend pools based on the URL paths of the request.

- **Multiple-site hosting**: This allows you to configure more than one web application on the same Front Door configuration. This allows a more efficient topology for deployments. Azure Front Door can be configured to route a single web application to its own backend pool or to route multiple web applications to the same backend pool.

- **Session affinity**: Azure Front Door offers managed cookies, which can be used to keep a user session on the same application backend. This feature is suitable in scenarios where the session state is saved locally on the backend for a user session.

- **Custom domains and certificate management**: If you want your own domain name to be visible in the Front Door URL, a custom domain is necessary. This can be useful for branding purposes. Also, HTTPS for custom domain names is supported and can be done by uploading your own SSL certificate or by implementing Front Door-managed certificates.

- **Secure Sockets Layer (SSL) termination**: Front Door offers SSL termination, which speeds up the decryption process and reduces the processing burden on backend servers. Front Door supports both HTTP and HTTPS connectivity between Front Door environments and your backends. Thus, you can also set up end-to-end SSL encryption, if this is required.

- **URL redirection**: To ensure that all the communication between the users and the application occurs over an encrypted path, web applications are expected to automatically redirect any HTTP traffic to HTTPS. Azure Front Door offers the functionality to redirect HTTP traffic to HTTPS. It also allows you to redirect traffic to a different hostname, redirect traffic to a different path, or redirect traffic to a new query string in the URL.

- **Application layer security**: The Front Door platform is protected by Azure DDoS Protection Basic. It also allows you to create rate-limiting rules to battle malicious bot traffic and configure custom web application firewall rules for access control. This can protect your HTTP/HTTPS workload from exploitation based on client IP addresses, HTTP parameters, and country code.

- **URL rewrite**: You can configure an optional custom forwarding path to support URL rewrite in Front Door. This path can be used when the request is made from the frontend to the backend. You can configure host headers when forwarding this request.

- **Protocol support—IPv6 and HTTP/2 traffic**: Front Door natively offers end-to-end IPv6 connectivity and the HTTP/2 protocol. The HTTP/2 protocol enables full-duplex communication between application backends and a client over a long-running TCP connection.

In this section, we covered Azure Front Door. This concludes this chapter.

Summary

In this chapter, we covered the third part of the *Implementing workloads and security* objective by learning how to configure an application gateway and load balancing rules, how to implement frontend IP configurations, and how to manage application load balancing. We also covered Azure Front Door.

In the next chapter, we will continue with this objective by learning how to integrate our on-premises network with an Azure virtual network.

Questions

Answer the following questions to test your knowledge of the information contained in this chapter. You can find the answers in the *Assessments* section at the end of this book:

1. Azure Application Gateway can be used as a load balancer and a web application firewall.
    1. Yes
    2. No

2. You can use Azure Application Gateway to route traffic based on specific URLs.
    1. Yes
    2. No

3. You don't need frontend IP configurations for Azure Application Gateway to function properly.
    1. Yes
    2. No

Further reading

Check out the following links to find out more about the topics that were covered in this chapter:

- **Azure Application Gateway documentation**: `https://docs.microsoft.com/en-us/azure/application-gateway/`
- **Quickstart: Direct web traffic with Azure Application Gateway—Azure portal**: `https://docs.microsoft.com/en-us/azure/application-gateway/quick-create-portal`
- **Web application firewall (WAF)**: `https://docs.microsoft.com/en-gb/azure/application-gateway/waf-overview`
- **Backend health, diagnostic logs, and metrics for Application Gateway**: `https://docs.microsoft.com/en-us/azure/application-gateway/application-gateway-diagnostics`
- **Application Gateway health monitoring overview**: `https://docs.microsoft.com/en-us/azure/application-gateway/application-gateway-probe-overview`

11
Integrating On-Premises Networks with Azure Virtual Network

In the previous chapter, we covered the third part of the *Implementing Workloads and Security* objective. We covered how to implement application load balancing by learning how to configure an application gateway, load balancing rules, and more.

This chapter continues with this objective by covering how to integrate your on-premises network with an Azure Virtual Network. In this chapter, we are going to focus on VPN connections from your on-premises environment to Azure and from Azure to Azure as well. You will learn how to create an Azure VPN gateway, as well as how to configure a **Site-to-Site** (**S2S**) VPN using an on-premises server and the Azure VPN gateway. At the end of this chapter, we are going to look at how to manage on-premises connectivity with Azure.

The following topics will be covered in this chapter:

- Understanding Azure VPN gateway
- Creating and configuring an Azure VPN gateway
- Creating and configuring the S2S VPN
- Verifying on-premises connectivity

Technical requirements

The examples in this chapter use Azure PowerShell (https://docs.microsoft.com/en-us/powershell/azure/install-az-ps?view=azps-1.8.0).

The source code for our sample application can be downloaded from `https://github.com/PacktPublishing/Microsoft-Azure-Architect-Technologies-Exam-Guide-AZ-300/tree/master/Chapter11`.

Understanding Azure VPN gateway

Azure VPN provides a secure gateway that can be used for sending encrypted traffic over the internet and between an Azure Virtual Network and an on-premises location. This gateway can be used to send encrypted traffic between different Azure Virtual Networks and Microsoft networks.

For each virtual network, you can only have one VPN gateway. You can, however, create multiple connections to the same VPN gateway. When creating multiple connections, all of the VPN tunnels will share the available gateway bandwidth.

A **virtual network gateway** is created with two or more virtual machines that are deployed in a **gateway subnet**. This is a specific subnet that is created for the VPN connection. The VMs that are deployed in the gateway subnet are created at the same time the virtual network gateway is created. The VMs are then configured to contain specific gateway services and routing tables that connect to the gateway in Azure. It isn't possible to configure the gateway services and routing tables manually.

Azure VPN gateway offers the following pricing tiers:

- **Basic**: This tier provides a maximum of 10 S2S/VNet-to-VNet tunnels and a maximum of 128 **Point-to-Site** (**P2S**) connections. The average bandwidth is 100 Mbps.
- **VpnGw1**: This tier provides a maximum of 30 S2S/VNet-to-VNet tunnels and a maximum of 128 P2S connections. The average bandwidth is 650 Mbps.
- **VpnGw2**: This tier provides a maximum of 30 S2S/VNet-to-VNet tunnels and a maximum of 128 P2S connections. The average bandwidth is 1 Gbps.
- **VpnGw3**: This tier provides a maximum of 30 S2S/VNet-to-VNet tunnels and a maximum of 128 P2S connections. The average bandwidth is 1.25 Gbps.

S2S VPNs

A S2S VPN gateway connection is a connection over an IPsec/IKE (IKEv1 or IKEv2) VPN tunnel. These connections can be used for hybrid configurations and cross-premises configurations. They were designed to create a secure connection between a location and your virtual network over the internet. This location can be something such as an office. Once the S2S VPN connection has been configured, you can connect every device from that location to Azure using the same VPN location.

A S2S connection requires a compatible VPN device located on-premises that has a public IP address assigned to it. It should not be located behind a NAT.

 For more information about the various compatible VPN devices, you can refer to the following documentation: https://docs.microsoft.com/en-us/azure/vpn-gateway/vpn-gateway-vpn-faq#s2s.

The following diagram shows a S2S VPN connection from an on-premises environment to Azure:

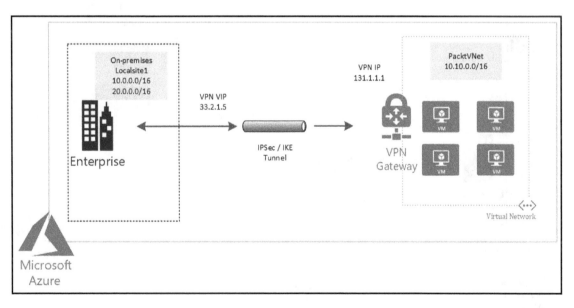

S2S VPN

In the next section, we are going to look at **multi-site VPNs**.

Multi-site VPNs

A multi-site VPN is a variation of the S2S connection. You use this type of connection for connecting to multiple on-premises sites from your virtual network gateway. It is required that multi-site connections use a route-based VPN type gateway. All connections through the gateway will share the available bandwidth. This is because each virtual network can only have one VPN gateway.

The following diagram shows a multi-site VPN connection from an on-premises environment to Azure:

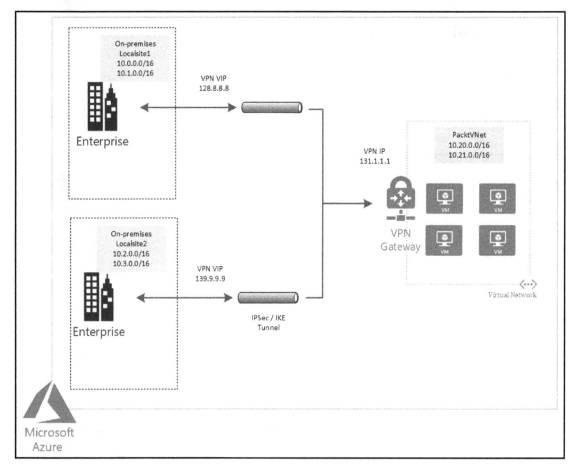

Multi-site VPN

In the next section, we are going to look at **Point-to-Site** (**P2S**) VPNs.

P2S VPNs

A P2S VPN gateway connection is designed to create a secure connection between an individual client and your virtual network over the internet. It is established from the client computer and is useful for people who are working from different locations, such as from their home or from a hotel. PS2 VPN is also the best solution if you only have a few clients to connect to a virtual network.

A P2S connection does not require an on-premises, public-facing IP address like S2S VPN connections do. You can use P2S connections together with S2S connections over the same VPN gateway. You need to make sure that the configuration requirements for both connections are compatible so that you can use both connection types over the same gateway.

The following diagram shows a P2S VPN connection from an on-premises environment to Azure:

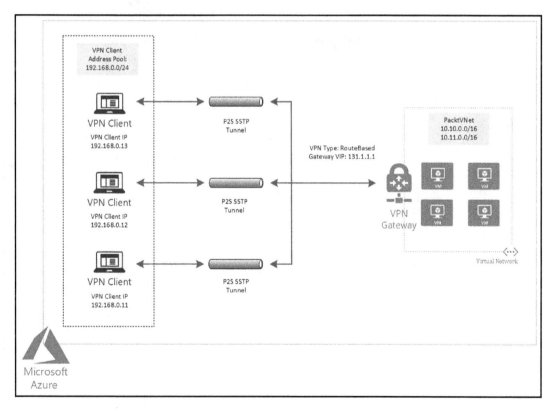

P2S VPN

In the next section, we are going to look at **ExpressRoute**.

ExpressRoute

ExpressRoute offers a private connection that is facilitated by a connectivity provider. ExpressRoute connections don't go over the public internet; instead, they use a more reliable connection. These types of connections offer lower latencies, higher security, and faster speeds than connections that go over the internet. Also, Microsoft provides stronger SLAs for the ExpressRoute connection. You can use these to extend your on-premises networks to Azure and Office 365. Connections can be made from an any-to-any (IP VPN) network, a virtual cross-connection at a colocation facility, and a point-to-point Ethernet network connection.

ExpressRoute uses a virtual network gateway, which is configured with a gateway type of ExpressRoute instead of VPN. By default, the traffic is not encrypted, but you can create a solution that encrypts the traffic that goes over the ExpressRoute circuit.

The following diagram shows an ExpressRoute connection from an on-premises environment to Azure:

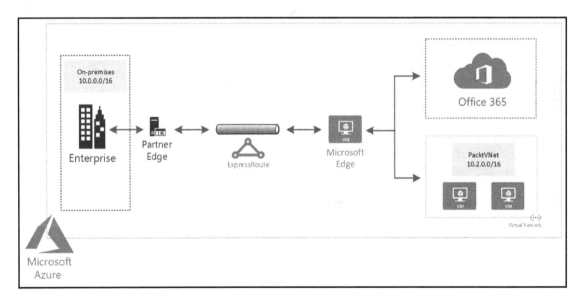

ExpressRoute

Now that we have looked at the different types of VPN connections you can configure, we are going to create and configure an Azure VPN gateway.

Creating and configuring an Azure VPN gateway

In the upcoming sections, we are going to configure an Azure VPN gateway, configure a S2S VPN, and verify the connectivity between Azure and the on-premises environment.

We are going to use Windows Server 2012 with **Routing and Remote Access Service** (**RRAS**) enabled on it to serve as the compatible VPN device that is installed on the on-premises environment.

Creating and configuring the on-premises VPN device

First, we are going to set up Windows Server 2012 and activate RRAS on it to set up the VPN. For this demonstration, I've created a virtual machine on my laptop with Windows Server 2012 R2 installed on it. To enable RRAS, perform the following steps:

Make sure that the network adapter is set to bridged mode. The VPN gateway in Azure can't connect to a VPN that is behind a NAT.

1. Go to **Server Manager** | **Manage** | **Add Roles and Features** to enable RRAS:

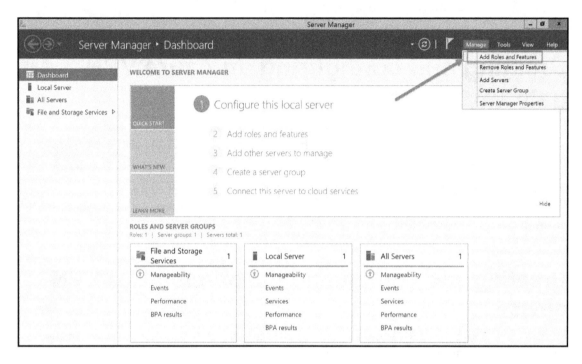

Enabling RRAS on Windows Server 2012

2. Click **Next** on the first screen of the **Add Roles and Features Wizard**. On the next screen, select **Role-based or feature-based installation** and click **Next**. Select the server and click **Next**. On the **Server Roles** screen, select **Remote Access** and click **Next**:

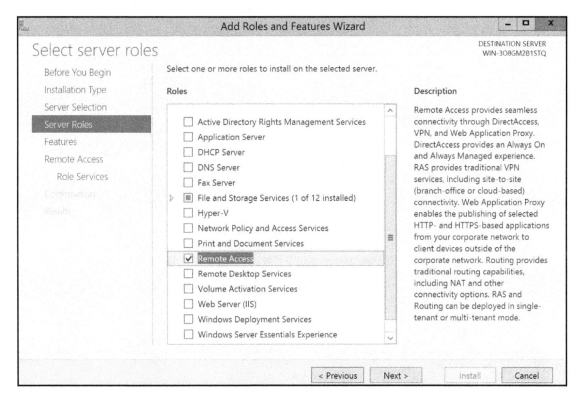

Enabling Remote Access

3. On the **Features** screen, we can click **Next** immediately. On the **Remote Access** screen, click **Next**:

Remote Access

4. On the **Role Services** screen, select **DirectAccess and VPN (RAS)**.
   A window will pop up, asking you to add the required features. Click **Add features** and then click **Next**:

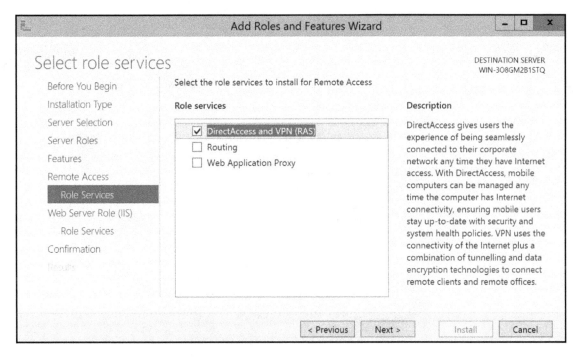

Role Services

5. On the **Web Server Role (IIS)** screen, click **Next**. On the IIS role services screen, keep all of the default settings as they are and click **Next** again. On the last screen, verify the settings and click the **Install** button:

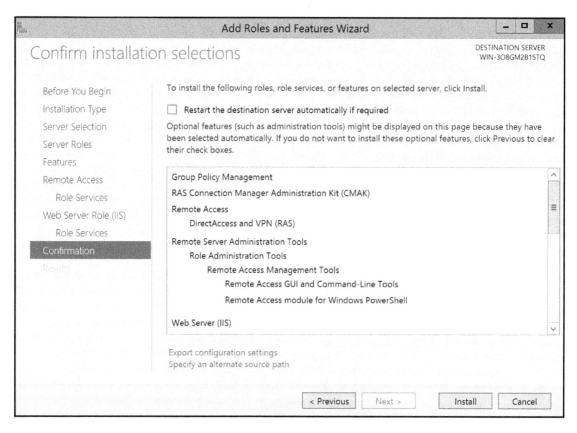

Confirmation

The next step is to configure a VNet.

Creating a virtual network

Now that we've gone through the configuration process for the on-premises VPN device, we are going to create a VNet. To do so, perform the following steps:

1. Navigate to Azure portal by opening `https://portal.azure.com/`.
2. Select **Create a resource** | **Networking** | **Virtual network**.
3. In the **Create virtual network** blade, add the following values:
   - **Name**: PacktVPNVNet.
   - **Address space**: `172.17.0.0/16`.
   - **Subscription**: Pick a subscription.
   - **Resource group**: Create a new resource group and name it `PacktVPNResourceGroup`.
   - **Location**: **East US**.
   - **Subnet name**: Frontend.
   - **Address range**: `172.17.0.0/24`.
4. Click **Create** to create the VNet.
5. Now, we need to create a **Gateway subnet** that contains the reserved IP addresses that will be used by the virtual network gateway services. Open the VNet resource and, under **Settings**, click **Subnets** and then click **+ Gateway subnet**, which can be found in the top menu.
6. In the **Add subnet** blade, adjust the address range to `172.17.255.0/27`.
7. Click **OK**.

Creating an Azure VPN gateway

Now, we are going to configure the Azure VPN gateway. Perform the following steps:

1. Navigate to Azure portal by opening `https://portal.azure.com/`.
2. Select **Create a resource** and type `Virtual network gateway` into the search box.
3. In the **Create virtual network gateway**, add the following values:
   - **Subscription**: Pick a subscription.
   - **Name**: `PacktVnetGateway`.
   - **Region**: **East US**.
   - **Gateway type**: **VPN**.
   - **VPN type**: **Route-based**.
   - **SKU**: `VpnGw1`.
   - **Generation**: Generation 1.
   - **Virtual network**: Click **Virtual network/Choose a virtual network**. Select `PacktVPNVNet`.
   - **Public IP address**: Here, you need to set the public IP address that is associated with the VPN gateway. The Azure VPN gateway only supports dynamically assigned IP addresses. However, once the IP address is associated with the VPN gateway, it will not change. The IP address will only change when the VPN gateway is recreated or deleted. Leave **Create new** selected.
   - **Public IP address name**: `PacktVNetGWIP`.
   - **Enable active-active mode**: Disabled
   - **Configure BGP ASN**: Disabled:

Create virtual network gateway

Basics   Tags   Review + create

Azure has provided a planning and design guide to help you configure the various VPN gateway options. Learn more.

Project details

Select the subscription to manage deployed resources and costs. Use resource groups like folders to organize and manage all your resources.

Subscription * | Microsoft Azure Sponsorship   ∨ |

Resource group ⓘ   PacktVPNResourceGroup (derived from virtual network's resource group)

Instance details

Name * | PacktVnetGateway   ✓ |

Region * | (US) East US   ∨ |

Gateway type * ⓘ   ◉ VPN   ◯ ExpressRoute

VPN type * ⓘ   ◉ Route-based   ◯ Policy-based

SKU * ⓘ | VpnGw1   ∨ |

Generation ⓘ | Generation1   ∨ |

VIRTUAL NETWORK

Virtual network * ⓘ | PacktVPNVNet   ∨ |

                           ❶ Only virtual networks in the currently selected subscription and region are listed.

Gateway subnet address range   172.17.255.0/27

Public IP address

Public IP address * ⓘ   ◉ Create new   ◯ Use existing

Public IP address name * | PacktVNetGWIP   ✓ |

Public IP address SKU   Basic

Assignment   ◉ Dynamic   ◯ Static

Enable active-active mode * ⓘ   ◯ Enabled   ◉ Disabled

Configure BGP ASN * ⓘ   ◯ Enabled   ◉ Disabled

Azure recommends using a validated VPN device with your virtual network gateway. To view a list of validated devices and

---

Review + create   < Previous   Next : Tags >   Download a template for automation

Gateway settings

4. Click **Review + create** and then **Create** to create the Azure VPN gateway.
5. We need the public IP address for the VPN gateway later in this demonstration, so go to the overview of the Azure VPN gateway when it has been created. In there, copy the public IP address to Notepad:

Obtaining the public IP address

6. Once you've created the gateway, open the **Overview** page of the VNet resource that we created earlier. The VPN gateway will be displayed on the **Overview** page:

VPN gateway in VNet

The Azure VPN gateway has been created, which means we can now set up the S2S VPN connection with the on-premises environment.

Creating and configuring the S2S VPN

To create the S2S VPN, we are going to connect the VPN gateway with the on-premises environment we created earlier with RRAS enabled on it. This will serve as a compatible VPN device.

To be able to complete this step, we need the public IP address of the on-premises environment. I used VMware for this demonstration and set it up in bridged mode. This way, the public IP address of your provider is used. You can check the public IP address using multiple tools, such as `https://www.whatsmyip.org/`.

Creating the local network gateway

First, we need to create a local network gateway. This refers to the on-premises location where we have Windows Server 2012 R2 installed with RRAS enabled.

To create the local network gateway, perform the following steps:

1. Navigate to Azure portal by opening `https://portal.azure.com/`.
2. Select **Create a resource** and type `Local network gateway` into the search box. Select **Local network gateway** from the list and create a new one.
3. On the **Create local network gateway** screen, add the following values:
    - **Name**: `PacktOnPremisesGateway`.
    - **IP address**: Here, you need to fill in the public IP address from the on-premises VPN device where Azure needs to connect to.
    - **Address space**: `82.173.0.0/16`. This represents the address ranges for the on-premises network. You can add multiple address ranges.
    - **Configure BGP settings**: Don't select this.
    - **Subscription**: Select the same subscription that we used for the previous examples.

- **Resource group**: Select the resource group that we already created, that is, `PacktVPNResourceGroup`.
- **Location:** Select the same location where the VNet resides, that is, **East US**:

Local network gateway settings

4. Click **Create**.

Configuring the on-premises VPN device

As we described in the previous section, S2S connections require a compatible VPN device. We already configured this in the first step. Now, we need to configure this to connect to the Azure VPN gateway.

To configure RRAS so that it can connect to Azure, we need the following artifacts:

- **Shared key**: We are going to create a shared key that is used for connecting to the on-premises device.
- **The public IP address of the Azure VPN gateway**: This is the public IP address that we copied to Notepad.

To create a new connection, perform the following steps:

1. Open the local gateway that we created previously. Then, under **Settings**, select **Connections**. Click the **Add** button at the top of the screen.
2. In the **Add connection** blade, add the following values:
   - **Name**: `PacktVNetToSite`.
   - **Virtual network gateway**: Click **Choose a local network gateway** and select `PacktVNetGateway`.
   - **Local network gateway**: This is a fixed value.
   - **Shared Key**: This value must be the same as the one for your local on-premises device. Fill this in with `Packt123`.
   - **Protocol**: Leave the default as it is, that is, IKEv2:

Add connection

3. Click **OK** to create the connection.

4. Now, you can select the connection from the **Connections** page. From there, you can download the configuration package that will be used to configure the on-premises VPN device. Click **Download configuration** from the top menu:

Downloading the configuration package

5. Since we are using RRAS, which is part of Windows Server, we need to select the following values:
   - **Device vendor**: **Generic Samples**
   - **Device family**: **Device Parameters**
   - **Firmware version**: **1.0**

6. Click **Download configuration**.

7. The configuration package consists of a text file with all the necessary configuration values in it.

Switch over to the on-premises VM with Windows Server 2012 R2 on it and RRAS enabled. Perform the following steps on the VPN device with the Azure VPN gateway:

1. Download the script from GitHub. This link is provided in the *Technical requirements* section, which can be found at the beginning of this chapter. We are going to use this script to configure RRAS. We need to make some adjustments to the script so that we can add the Azure VPN gateway and local network addresses. You can use the IP address and the subnet address from the downloaded configuration file as input.

2. The first part of the script gives us some additional information about the script and creates the `Invoke-WindowsApi` function:

```
# Windows Azure Virtual Network

# This configuration template applies to Microsoft RRAS running
on Windows Server 2012 R2.
# It configures an IPSec VPN tunnel connecting your on-premise
VPN device with the Azure gateway.

# !!! Please notice that we have the following restrictions in
our support for RRAS:
# !!! 1. Only IKEv2 is currently supported
# !!! 2. Only route-based VPN configuration is supported.
# !!! 3. Admin privileges are required in order to run this
script

Function Invoke-WindowsApi(
    [string] $dllName,
    [Type] $returnType,
    [string] $methodName,
    [Type[]] $parameterTypes,
    [Object[]] $parameters
    )
```

3. Now, we are going to build the dynamic assembly and define the method:

```
{
  ## Begin to build the dynamic assembly
  $domain = [AppDomain]::CurrentDomain
  $name = New-Object Reflection.AssemblyName 'PInvokeAssembly'
  $assembly = $domain.DefineDynamicAssembly($name, 'Run')
  $module = $assembly.DefineDynamicModule('PInvokeModule')
  $type = $module.DefineType('PInvokeType',
"Public,BeforeFieldInit")

  $inputParameters = @()

  for($counter = 1; $counter -le $parameterTypes.Length;
$counter++)
  {
      $inputParameters += $parameters[$counter - 1]
  }

  $method = $type.DefineMethod($methodName,
'Public,HideBySig,Static,PinvokeImpl',$returnType,
$parameterTypes)
```

4. Next, we need to apply the `P/Invoke` constructor, thereby creating the temporary type and invoking the method:

```
## Apply the P/Invoke constructor
$ctor =
[Runtime.InteropServices.DllImportAttribute].GetConstructor([st
ring])
$attr = New-Object Reflection.Emit.CustomAttributeBuilder
$ctor, $dllName
$method.SetCustomAttribute($attr)

## Create the temporary type, and invoke the method.
$realType = $type.CreateType()

$ret = $realType.InvokeMember($methodName,
'Public,Static,InvokeMethod', $null, $null, $inputParameters)

return $ret
}
```

5. Then, we are going to prepare the parameter values and invoke the API:

```
Function Set-PrivateProfileString(
    $file,
    $category,
    $key,
    $value)
{
    ## Prepare the parameter types and parameter values for the
Invoke-WindowsApi script
    $parameterTypes = [string], [string], [string], [string]
    $parameters = [string] $category, [string] $key, [string]
$value, [string] $file

    ## Invoke the API
    [void] (Invoke-WindowsApi "kernel32.dll" ([UInt32])
"WritePrivateProfileString" $parameterTypes $parameters)
}
```

6. Now, we are going to install the RRAS role on the server:

```
# Install RRAS role
Import-Module ServerManager
Install-WindowsFeature RemoteAccess -IncludeManagementTools
Add-WindowsFeature -name Routing -IncludeManagementTools

# !!! NOTE: A reboot of the machine might be required here
after which the script can be executed again.
```

7. As we can see, the S2S VPN is installed from here:

```
# Install S2S VPN
Import-Module RemoteAccess
if ((Get-RemoteAccess).VpnS2SStatus -ne "Installed")
{
   Install-RemoteAccess -VpnType VpnS2S
}
```

8. Next, we need to add and configure it:

```
# Add and configure S2S VPN interface

Add-VpnS2SInterface `
 -Protocol IKEv2 `
 -AuthenticationMethod PSKOnly `
 -NumberOfTries 3 `
 -ResponderAuthenticationMethod PSKOnly `
 -Name <IP address of your Azure gateway> `
 -Destination <IP address of your Azure gateway> `
 -IPv4Subnet @("<IP range of your subnet in Azure>:100") `
 -SharedSecret <shared key>

Set-VpnServerIPsecConfiguration `
 -EncryptionType MaximumEncryption

Set-VpnS2Sinterface `
 -Name <IP address of your Azure gateway> `
 -InitiateConfigPayload $false `
 -Force
```

9. In the last part of the script, we are going to set the connection to be persistent, restart the RRAS server, and dial-in to the Azure gateway:

```
# Set S2S VPN connection to be persistent by editing the
router.pbk file (required admin privileges)
Set-PrivateProfileString $env:windir\System32\RRAS\router.pbk
"<IP address of your Azure gateway>" "IdleDisconnectSeconds"
"0"
Set-PrivateProfileString $env:windir\System32\RRAS\router.pbk
"<IP address of your Azure gateway>" "RedialOnLinkFailure" "1"

# Restart the RRAS service
Restart-Service RemoteAccess

# Dial-in to Azure gateway
Connect-VpnS2SInterface `
 -Name <IP address of your Azure gateway>
```

This script will also enable RRAS on your server. We did this manually in one of the first sections, so we have skipped this part.

Now, we have finished configuring the on-premises VPN device. In the next section, we are going to verify on-premises connectivity.

Verifying on-premises connectivity

There are two different ways to verify on-premises connectivity: using the RRAS console on-premises or in the Azure portal.

To verify the connection using the RRAS console, open Windows search and type in `Remote Access Management`. Then, open the node that's displayed in the following screenshot. As you can see, RRAS is connected to the Azure VPN gateway:

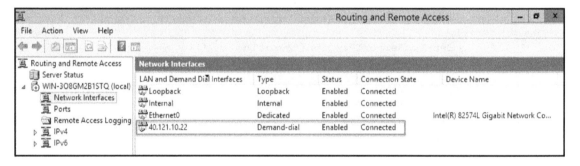

Verifying the connection in the RRAS console

To verify the connection from Azure portal, perform the following steps:

1. Navigate to Azure portal by opening `https://portal.azure.com/`.
2. Open the `PAcktVnetGateway` resource. Then, under **Settings**, select **Connections**. Now, you will be able to see that the `PacktVNetToSite` connection is connected, as shown in the following screenshot:

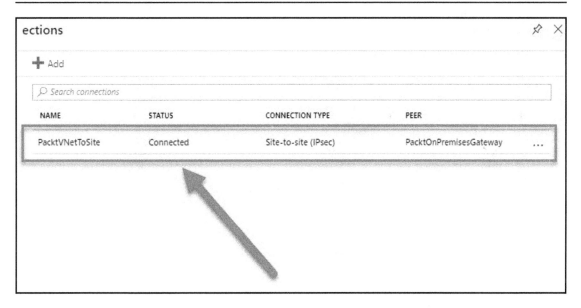

Verifying the connection in Azure portal

In this demonstration, we configured an Azure VPN gateway, configured a S2S VPN, and verified the connectivity between Azure and the on-premises environment.

Summary

In this chapter, we covered the fourth part of the *Implement Workloads and Security* objective by covering how to create and configure an Azure VPN gateway, how to create and configure S2S VPNs, and how to verify on-premises connectivity with Azure.

In the next chapter, we will continue with the fifth part of this objective by covering how to manage **role-based access control** (**RBAC**).

Questions

Answer the following questions to test your knowledge of the information contained in this chapter. You can find the answers in the *Assessments* section at the end of this book:

1. ExpressRoute traffic is encrypted by default.
   - Yes
   - No

2. Your organization has a requirement for employees to connect from locations other than the office. Do you need to set up a P2S VPN connection for this?
   - Yes
   - No

3. When you set up the on-premises VPN device for a S2S connection, your server isn't allowed to be behind a NAT.
   - Yes
   - No

Further reading

Check out the following links to find out more about the topics that were covered in this chapter:

- **Azure VPN Gateway Documentation**: https://docs.microsoft.com/en-us/azure/vpn-gateway/
- **Creating a VNet with a Site-to-Site VPN Connection Using PowerShell**: https://docs.microsoft.com/en-us/azure/vpn-gateway/vpn-gateway-create-S2S-rm-powershell
- **Creating a Virtual Network with a Site-to-Site VPN Connection Using CLI**: https://docs.microsoft.com/en-us/azure/vpn-gateway/vpn-gateway-howto-S2S-resource-manager-cli
- **ExpressRoute Overview**: https://docs.microsoft.com/en-us/azure/expressroute/expressroute-introduction
- **Creating and modifying an ExpressRoute Circuit**: https://docs.microsoft.com/en-us/azure/expressroute/expressroute-howto-circuit-portal-resource-manager

12
Managing Role-Based Access Control (RBAC)

In the previous chapter, we covered the fourth part of the *Implement Workloads and Security* objective by learning how to integrate our on-premises network with an Azure virtual network by configuring an Azure VPN Gateway, setting up a site-to-site VPN, and more.

This chapter will cover the fifth part of the *Implement Workloads and Security* objective by covering **role-based access control (RBAC)**. You'll learn how to configure access to Azure resources by assigning RBAC roles from the Azure portal. You'll also learn how to configure management access by assigning global administrators to your Azure subscription and other resources. Then, you'll learn how to create custom roles that you can apply when custom permissions are needed by your users. Finally, you will learn about Azure policies and how you can apply them to your Azure resources.

The following topics will be covered in this chapter:

- Understanding RBAC
- Configuring access to Azure resources by assigning roles
- Configuring management access to Azure
- Creating a custom role
- Azure Policy
- Implementing and assigning Azure policies

Technical requirements

The examples in this chapter use Azure PowerShell (https://docs.microsoft.com/en-us/powershell/azure/install-az-ps?view=azps-1.8.0).

The source code for the sample application can be downloaded from `https://github.com/ PacktPublishing/Microsoft-Azure-Architect-Technologies-Exam-Guide-AZ-300/tree/ master/Chapter12`.

Understanding RBAC

With RBAC, you can manage who has access to the different Azure resources inside of your tenant. You can also set what the users can do with different Azure resources.

It's good practice to assign permissions using the principle of least permissions; this involves giving users the exact permissions they need to do their jobs properly. Users, groups, and applications are added to roles in Azure, and those roles have certain permissions. You can use the built-in roles that Azure offers, or you can create custom roles in RBAC.

The roles in Azure can be added to a certain scope. This scope can be an Azure subscription, an Azure resource group, or a web application. Azure then uses access inheritance; that is, roles that are added to a parent resource give access to child resources automatically. For instance, a group that is added to an Azure subscription gets access to all the resource groups and underlying resources that are in that subscription as well. A user that is added to a **virtual machine** (**VM**) only gets access to that particular VM.

Let's start by looking at built-in roles.

Built-in roles

Azure offers various built-in roles that you can use to assign permissions to users, groups, and applications. RBAC offers the following three standard roles that you can assign to each Azure resource:

- **Owner**: Users in this role can manage everything and create new resources.
- **Contributor**: Users in this role can manage everything, just like users in the owner role, but they can't assign access to others.
- **Reader**: Users in this role can read everything, but they are not allowed to make any changes.

Aside from the standard roles, each Azure resource also has roles that are scoped to particular resources. For instance, you can assign users, groups, or applications to the SQL security manager so that they can manage all the security-related policies of the Azure SQL Server. Alternatively, you can assign them to the VM contributor role, where they can manage the VMs, but not the VNet or storage accounts that are connected to a VM.

 For an overview of all the built-in roles that Azure offers, refer to `https:/ /docs.microsoft.com/en-us/azure/role-based-access-control/built- in-roles`.

While these built-in roles usually cover all possible use cases, they can never account for every requirement in an organization. To allow for flexibility in role assignment, RBAC lets you make custom roles. We'll look at this feature in more detail in the next section.

Custom roles

You can also create custom roles in RBAC when none of the built-in roles suit your needs. Custom roles can be assigned to the exact same resources as built-in roles and can only be created using PowerShell, the CLI, and the REST API. You can't create them in the Azure portal. In each Azure tenant, you can create up to 2,000 roles.

Custom roles are defined in JSON and, after deployment, they are stored inside the Azure AD tenant. By storing them inside the Azure AD tenant, they can be used in all the different Azure subscriptions that are connected to the Azure AD tenant.

Configuring access to Azure resources by assigning roles

If a user in your organization needs permissions to access Azure resources, you need to assign the user to the appropriate role in Azure. In this section, we are going to assign administrator access to a user for a VM. First, we need to run a script in Azure Cloud Shell to create the VM. Let's get started:

1. Navigate to the Azure portal by opening `https://portal.azure.com/`.
2. Open Azure Cloud Shell.

3. First, we need to create a new resource group:

```
az group create --location eastus --name PacktVMResourceGroup
```

4. Then, we need to create the VM:

```
az vm create \
    --resource-group PacktVMResourceGroup \
    --name VM1 \
    --image win2016datacenter \
    --admin-username packtuser \
    --admin-password PacktPassword123
```

5. Now that we have the VM in place, we can configure access to the VM for the user. Open the `PacktVMResourceGroup` resource group and select **VM1** from the list.

6. You will be redirected to the VM settings blade.

7. In the settings blade, select **Access control (IAM)** from the left menu and click on **Add** | **Add a role assignment**, which can be found in the top menu:

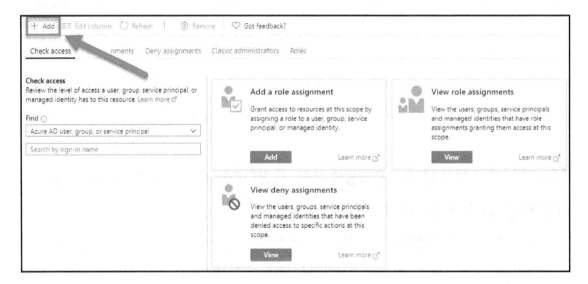

Access control settings

8. In the **Add role assignment** blade, specify the following values:

The Add role assignment blade

9. Click on **Save**.
10. The user now has administrator permissions on the VM.

In this section, we assigned administrator access to a user for a VM. Now, we're going to learn how to configure management access to Azure.

Configuring management access to Azure

Management access to Azure can be configured at the subscription level. To do this, perform the following steps:

1. Navigate to the Azure portal by opening `https://portal.azure.com`.
2. Select **All services** from the left menu and type `subscriptions` into the search box. Then, select **Subscriptions**.

3. Select the subscription that you want to grant management access to from the list.
4. In the subscription settings blade, select **Access control (IAM)** and click on **Add** | **Add co-administrator**, which can be found in the top menu:

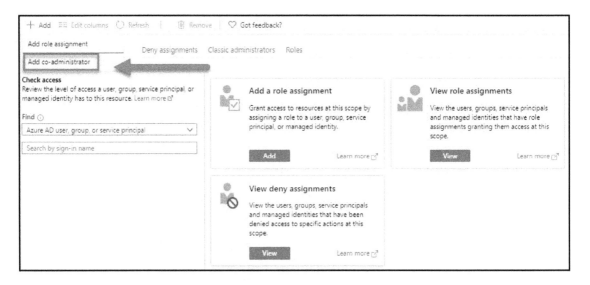

The access control settings

5. In the **Add co-administrator** blade, specify the following values:

Adding a co-administrator

6. Click on **Add**.

Now that we have configured management access to Azure, we are going to look at how to create a custom role for our users.

Creating a custom role

In the following example, we will create a custom role that can only restart VMs in Azure. For this, you need to create a JSON file that will be deployed using PowerShell. We are going to be assigning that role to a user account inside the JSON file. Let's get started:

1. You can define the custom role by using the following JSON code. You should set the Id to null since the custom role gets an ID assigned to it when it's created. We will add the custom role to two Azure subscriptions, as follows (replace the subscriptions in the AssignableScopes part with your subscription IDs):

```
{
"Name": "Packt Custom Role",
 "Id": null,
 "IsCustom": true,
 "Description": "Allows for read access to Azure Storage, Network
and Compute resources and access to support",
     "Actions": [
          "Microsoft.Compute/*/read",
          "Microsoft.Storage/*/read",
          "Microsoft.Network/*/read",
          "Microsoft.Resources/subscriptions/resourceGroups/read",
          "Microsoft.Support/*"
     ],
     "NotActions": [
     ],
     "AssignableScopes": [
     "/subscriptions/********-****-****-****-**********",
     "/subscriptions/********-****-****-****-**********"
     ]
}
```

2. Save the JSON file in a folder named CustomRoles on the C: drive of your computer. Then, run the following PowerShell script to create the role. First, log into your Azure account, as follows:

```
Connect-AzAccount
```

3. If necessary, select the right subscription:

```
Select-AzSubscription -SubscriptionId "********-****-****-****-
************"
```

4. Then, create the custom role in Azure by importing the JSON file into PowerShell:

```
New-AzRoleDefinition -InputFile
"C:\CustomRoles\PacktCustomRole.json"
```

In this section, we created a custom role that can only restart VMs in Azure. Now, we're going to take a look at how we can create policies using Azure Policy.

Azure Policy

With Azure Policy, you can create policies that enforce rules over your Azure resources. This way, resources stay compliant with service-level agreements and corporate standards. With Azure Policy, you can evaluate all the different Azure resources for non-compliance. For example, you can create a policy to allow only a certain size of VM in your Azure environment. When the policy is created, Azure will check all the new and existing VMs to see whether they apply to this policy.

Azure Policy differs from RBAC because Azure Policy focuses on resource properties for existing resources and during deployment, while RBAC focuses on user actions at different scopes. For example, a user can be added to the owner role in a resource group, which will give the user full rights to that resource group.

Azure offers built-in policies and custom policies. Some examples of these built-in policies are as follows:

- **Allowed VM SKUs**: This policy specifies a set of VM sizes and types that can be deployed in Azure.
- **Allowed locations**: This policy restricts the available locations where resources can be deployed.

- **Not allowed resource types**: This policy prevents certain resource types from being deployed.
- **Allowed resource types**: This policy defines a list of resource types that you can deploy. Resource types that are not on the list can't be deployed inside the Azure environment.
- **Allowed storage account SKUs**: This policy specifies a set of storage account SKUs that can be deployed.

If the built-in policies don't match with your requirements, you can create a custom policy instead. Custom policies are created in JSON and look similar to the following example. The first part of the code sets the different properties:

```json
{
    "properties": {
        "displayName": "Deny storage accounts not using only HTTPS",
        "description": "Deny storage accounts not using only HTTPS. Checks
the supportsHttpsTrafficOnly property on StorageAccounts.",
        "mode": "all",
        "parameters": {
            "effectType": {
                "type": "string",
                "defaultValue": "Deny",
                "allowedValues": [
                    "Deny",
                    "Disabled"
                ],
                "metadata": {
                    "displayName": "Effect",
                    "description": "Enable or disable the execution of the
policy"
                }
            }
        }
    },
```

In the following part of the code, we are looking at the policy rule:

```json
        "policyRule": {
            "if": {
                "allOf": [
                    {
                        "field": "type",
                        "equals": "Microsoft.Storage/storageAccounts"
                    },
                    {
                        "field":
"Microsoft.Storage/storageAccounts/supportsHttpsTrafficOnly",
```

```
                      "notEquals": "true"
                  }
              ]
          },
          "then": {
              "effect": "[parameters('effectType')]"
          }
      }
    }
}
```

Policies are assigned at the management group level, the subscription level, or the resource group level.

Implementing and assigning Azure policies

To implement Azure policies, you have to assign them. In this section, we are going to assign an **Allowed location** policy to an Azure resource group. To do so, follow these steps:

1. Navigate to the Azure portal by opening `https://portal.azure.com`.
2. Open the `PacktVMResourceGroup` resource group.
3. Then, under **Settings**, select **Policies.**
4. Click on the **Getting started** menu item. You will see a page that looks similar to the following:

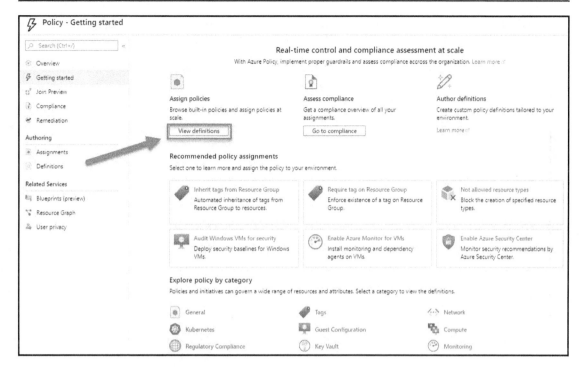

Getting started with Azure policies

5. The first step is to view and select the policy definition. To do so, select the **View definitions** button, as shown in the preceding screenshot.

6. You will be taken to the available built-in and custom policies inside your subscription. On the right-hand side, type `Locations` into the search bar:

Searching for a locations policy

7. Then, select the **Allowed locations** policy; you will be redirected to a blade where you can view the policy definition in JSON and assign the policy:

```
Allowed locations
Policy definition

⟶ Assign    ✏ Edit definition    ⧉ Duplicate definition    🗑 Delete definition

Name            : Allowed locations
Description     : This policy enables you to restrict the locations your organization can specify when deploying resources. Use to enforce your geo-com
Available Effects : Deny
Category        : General

Definition    Assignments (0)    Parameters

 9        },
10        "parameters": {
11          "listOfAllowedLocations": {
12            "type": "Array",
13            "metadata": {
14              "description": "The list of locations that can be specified when deploying resources.",
15              "strongType": "location",
16              "displayName": "Allowed locations"
17            }
18          }
19        },
20        "policyRule": {
21          "if": {
22            "allOf": [
23              {
24                "field": "location",
25                "notIn": "[parameters('listOfAllowedLocations')]"
26              },
27              {
28                "field": "location",
29                "notEquals": "global"
30              },
31              {
32                "field": "type",
33                "notEquals": "Microsoft.AzureActiveDirectory/b2cDirectories"
34              }
35            ]
36          },
37          "then": {
38            "effect": "deny"
39          }
40        }
41      },
42      "id": "/providers/Microsoft.Authorization/policyDefinitions/e56962a6-4747-49cd-b67b-bf8b01975c4c",
43      "type": "Microsoft.Authorization/policyDefinitions",
44      "name": "e56962a6-4747-49cd-b67b-bf8b01975c4c"
45    }
```

Policy definition

8. Click on **Assign** in the top menu.

9. To assign the policy, you have to fill in the following values:
    1. In the **Basics** tab, apply the following values:
        1. **Scope**: Select a subscription and, optionally, a resource group. I've selected the `PacktVMResourceGroup` resource group for this demonstration:

Add the resource group

2. In the **Parameters** tab, apply the following values:

   1. **Allowed locations**: Only select **East US**, as shown in the following screenshot:

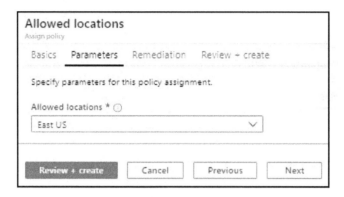

Setting the allowed locations

3. Click **Review + create** and then **Create**.

10. Now, when we add a new resource to the resource group (such as a new VM) and set the location to West Europe, we will notice a validation error on the top-left of the screen. When you click on it, you will see the following details on the right-hand side of the screen:

Validation error

In this section, we learned how to assign a policy in Azure. This concludes this chapter.

Summary

In this chapter, we covered the fifth part of the *Managing Azure Subscriptions and Resources* objective by learning how to configure access to Azure resources by assigning roles, how to configure management access, how to create a custom role, how to assign RBAC roles, and how to implement and assign Azure policies.

In the next chapter, we will cover the last part of this objective by learning how to implement **Multi-Factor Authentication** (**MFA**).

Questions

Answer the following questions to test your knowledge of the information contained in this chapter. You can find the answers in the *Assessments* section at the end of this book:

1. With Azure Policy, can you assign permissions to users, giving them access to your Azure resources?
    - Yes
    - No

2. Suppose that you want to check whether all the VMs inside your Azure subscription use managed disks. Can you use Azure Policy for this?
    - Yes
    - No

3. Are custom policies created in XML?
    - Yes
    - No

Further reading

Check out the following links to find out more about the topics that were covered in this chapter:

- **What is Role-Based Access Control (RBAC) for Azure Resources?**: https://docs.microsoft.com/en-us/azure/role-based-access-control/overview
- **Troubleshooting RBAC for Azure Resources**: https://docs.microsoft.com/en-us/azure/role-based-access-control/troubleshooting
- **Overview of the Azure Policy Service**: https://docs.microsoft.com/en-us/azure/governance/policy/overview
- **Creating a Custom Policy Definition**: https://docs.microsoft.com/en-us/azure/governance/policy/tutorials/create-custom-policy-definition

13
Implementing Multi-Factor Authentication (MFA)

In the previous chapter, we covered the fifth part of the *Implementing Workloads and Security* objective. We've covered how to manage **role-based access control** (**RBAC**), how to configure access to Azure resources by assigning RBAC roles from the Azure portal, and more.

This chapter covers the last part of this objective, by covering how to configure user accounts for **multi-factor authentication** (**MFA**), how to configure fraud alerts, how to configure bypass options, how to configure trusted IPs, and how to configure verification methods.

The following topics will be covered in this chapter:

- Understanding Azure MFA
- Configuring user accounts for MFA
- Configuring verification methods
- Configuring fraud alerts
- Configuring bypass options
- Configuring trusted IPs

Understanding Azure MFA

MFA is a security feature that requires more than one method of authentication. You can use it to add an additional layer of security to the signing in of users. It enables two-step verification, where the user first signs in using something they know (such as a password), and then signs in with something they have (such as a smartphone), or some human characteristic (such as biometrics).

Azure MFA maintains simplicity for users, but also helps to keep data and applications safe by providing additional security and requiring a second form of authentication. It offers a variety of configuration methods set by an administrator that determines whether users are challenged for MFA or not.

Azure MFA is part of the following offerings:

- **Azure Active Directory (AD) Premium license**: With this license, you can use Azure MFA Service (cloud) and Azure MFA Server (on-premises). The latter is most suitable in scenarios where an organization has ADFS installed and needs to manage infrastructure components.
- **Azure AD Global Administrators**: A subset of the MFA features is available for administrator accounts in Azure.
- **MFA for Office 365**: A subset of the MFA features is available for Office 365 users.

With Azure MFA, you can use the following verification methods:

Verification method	Description
Voice call	A call is made to the registered phone of the user. The user needs to enter a PIN for verification.
Text message	A text message is sent to the user's mobile phone containing a six-digit code. The user needs to fill in this code on the login page.
Mobile app notification	A request for verification is sent to the user's smartphone. When necessary, the user will enter a PIN and then select **Verify**.
Mobile app verification code	The mobile app on the user's smartphone will display a verification code, which will refresh every 30 seconds. The user will select the most recent code and will enter it on the login page.
Third-party tokens	Azure MFA Server can be configured to accept third-party security tokens.
App passwords	Only in certain cases. Certain non-browser apps do not support MFA; if a user has been enabled for MFA and attempts to use non-browser apps, they are unable to authenticate. An app password allows users to continue to authenticate. If MFA is enforced through Conditional Access policies and not through per-user MFA, you cannot create app passwords. Applications that use Conditional Access policies to control access do not need app passwords.

In the upcoming sections, we will enable MFA for the Azure AD tenant, configure user accounts, configure fraud alerts, and configure bypass options.

 For the demos in this chapter, I will use an Azure Active Directory Premium P2 license.

Enabling MFA for an Azure AD tenant

The following are the three different options for enabling MFA for your users, data, and applications:

- **Using a Conditional Access policy**: You can use Conditional Access policies to enable MFA. This can be enabled at the user or application level. You can also enable MFA for security groups or for all external users using a Conditional Access policy. This is available for premium Azure AD licenses.
- **At the user level**: This option is covered in more detail in the next section of this chapter. This is the traditional method for enabling MFA. With this method, the user needs to perform MFA every time they sign in. It will override Conditional Access policies when these are set.
- **Using Azure AD Identity Protection**: With this option, you will create an Azure AD Identity Protection risk policy based on the sign-in risk for all of your cloud applications. This will also override Conditional Access policies, if they've been created. This option requires an Azure AD P2 license.

Configuring user accounts for MFA

Azure MFA is enabled in Azure AD at the user level. To enable MFA for a user account in Azure AD, take the following steps:

1. Navigate to the Azure portal by opening `https://portal.azure.com/`.
2. Go to **All services** in the left menu, then type `Azure Active Directory`, and open the Azure AD resource.
3. In the Azure AD blade, under **Manage**, select **Users**.
4. In the **All users** blade, select **Multi-Factor Authentication** in the top menu.

5. You then will be redirected to the **multi-factor authentication** portal. In there, select a user and click **Enable** at the right side of the screen:

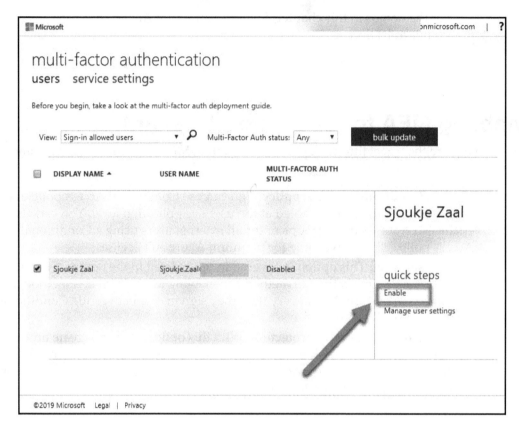

Enable MFA for a user

6. After clicking the link, you will receive the following warning:

Warning

7. Click **enable multi-factor auth** to activate MFA for this user.

Now that we have enabled MFA for the user, we can look at how to configure the verification methods.

Configuring verification methods

Verification methods are also configured in the Azure MFA portal, just as you enabled MFA for the user account in the previous step:

1. With the MFA portal still open, select **service settings** in the top menu:

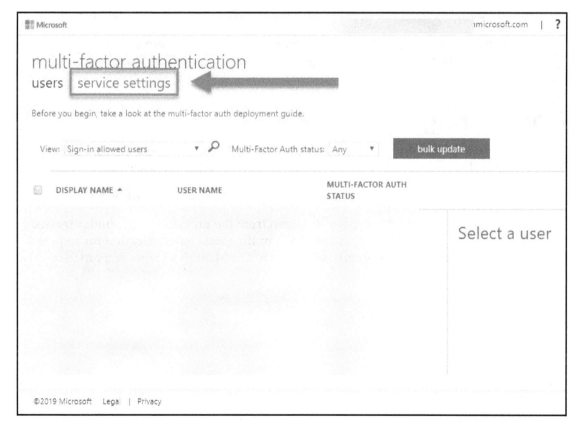

MFA portal service settings

2. Under **verification options**, you can select the methods that you want to enable for your users. By default, all verification options are enabled:

verification options (learn more)

Methods available to users:
- ☑ Call to phone
- ☑ Text message to phone
- ☑ Notification through mobile app
- ☑ Verification code from mobile app or hardware token

MFA verification options

3. If you want to disable options, uncheck the checkbox and click the **Save** button.

We have seen how to configure the verification methods that users are allowed to use with MFA in Azure. In the next section, we are going to look at how to configure trusted IPs.

Configuring trusted IPs

Trusted IPs are used by administrators of an Azure AD tenant. This option will bypass the MFA for users that sign in from a trusted IP, such as the company intranet.

Trusted IPs can be configured from the **service settings** page from the MFA portal:

1. With the **server settings** page still open from the previous demo, under **trusted ips**, check the checkbox that says **Skip multi-factor authentication for requests from federated users on my intranet**. Then, add an IP address or a range of IP addresses to the list:

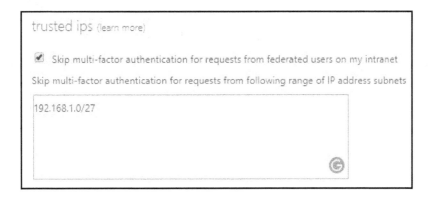

Trusted IP settings

2. Click the **Save** button to save your settings.

In the next section, we are going to cover how to configure fraud alerts in the Azure portal.

Configuring fraud alerts

With the fraud alert feature, users can report fraudulent attempts to access their resources using their phone or the mobile app. This is an MFA Server (on-premises) feature.

Fraud alerts are configured from the Azure portal, in the Azure Active Directory settings:

1. Navigate to the Azure portal by opening `https://portal.azure.com`.
2. Select **All services** in the left menu, then type `Azure Active Directory` in the search bar, and open the settings:
   - Under **Manage**, select **Security**.
   - Then in the **Security** blade, select **MFA**.
3. The **Getting started** blade is automatically opened. Under **Settings**, select the **Fraud alert**.

4. The **Fraud alert** settings page is opened. In here, you can enable users to submit fraud alerts:

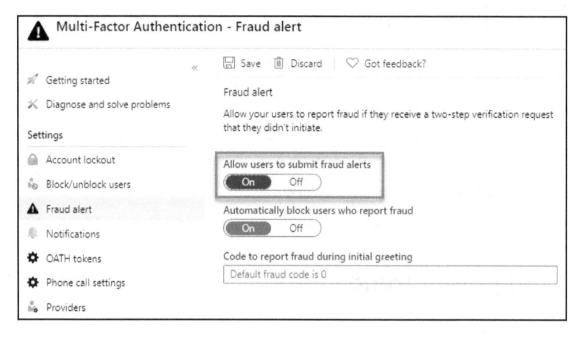

Enable submitting fraud alerts

5. Click the **Save** button to save the settings.

We've now seen how we can allow users to submit fraud alerts. In the next section, we will cover how to configure bypass options.

Configuring bypass options

With the one-time bypass feature, users can authenticate one time and bypass the MFA. This setting is temporary, and after a specified number of seconds, it will expire automatically. This can be a solution in cases when a phone or mobile app doesn't receive a phone call or notification.

This setting is also configured from the Azure Active Directory settings in the Azure portal as follows:

1. Navigate to the Azure portal by opening `https://portal.azure.com`.
2. Select **All services** in the left menu, then type `Azure Active Directory` in the search bar, and open the settings.
3. Under **Manage**, select **Security.**
4. Then in the **Security** blade, select **One-time bypass.** Click the **Add** button in the top menu:

One-time bypass

5. On the settings page, enter the username, including the full domain name, such as `username@domain.com`. Specify the number of seconds that the bypass should last and the reason for the bypass.
6. Click the **Add** button. The time limit will go into effect immediately.

We've now covered how to authenticate one time and bypass the MFA using the one-time bypass feature.

Summary

In this chapter, we covered the last part of the *Implement Workloads and Security* objective by how to configure user accounts for MFA, how to configure fraud alerts, how to configure bypass options, how to configure trusted IPs, and how to configure verification methods.

In the next chapter, we will start with a new objective, *Creating and Deploying Apps*, and in the first chapter of this objective, we are going to cover how to create web apps by using PaaS.

Questions

Answer the following questions to test your knowledge of the information in this chapter. You can find the answers in the *Assessments* section at the end of this book:

1. Can you allow trusted IP addresses to bypass MFA?
   1. Yes
   2. No

2. MFA cannot be enabled using Conditional Access policies:
   1. Yes
   2. No

3. Are fraud alerts part of the MFA Server (on-premises) offering?
   1. Yes
   2. No

Further reading

You can check the following links for more information about the topics that are covered in this chapter:

- **How it works: Azure Multi-Factor Authentication**: `https://docs.microsoft.com/en-us/azure/active-directory/authentication/concept-mfa-howitworks`
- **Deploy cloud-based Azure Multi-Factor Authentication**: `https://docs.microsoft.com/en-us/azure/active-directory/authentication/howto-mfa-getstarted`
- **Configure Azure Multi-Factor Authentication settings**: `https://docs.microsoft.com/en-us/azure/active-directory/authentication/howto-mfa-mfasettings`

Section 3: Creating and Deploying Apps

3

As this section's objective, you will learn how to create web apps using PaaS and how to design and develop apps that run in containers.

This section contains the following chapters:

14
Creating Web Apps by Using PaaS

In the previous chapter, we covered the last part of the *Implementing Workloads and Security* objective by learning how to configure user accounts for **multi-factor authentication (MFA)**, how to configure fraud alerts, bypass options, trusted IPs, and verification methods.

This chapter introduces the *Create and Deploy Apps* objective. In this chapter, we are going to learn how to create web apps using PaaS. We are going to cover App Services and App Service plans. We are also going to create an Azure App Service web app and learn about web apps for containers. Next, we are going to create an App Service background task using WebJobs. Finally, we are going to enable diagnostics logging.

The following topics will be covered in this chapter:

- Understanding App Services
- Understanding App Service plans
- Understanding Web Apps for Containers
- Understanding WebJobs
- Understanding diagnostics logging

Technical requirements

The examples in this chapter use Azure PowerShell (https://docs.microsoft.com/en-us/powershell/azure/install-az-ps?view=azps-1.8.0) and Visual Studio 2019 (https://visualstudio.microsoft.com/vs/).

The source code for our sample application can be downloaded from `https://github.com/PacktPublishing/Microsoft-Azure-Architect-Technologies-Exam-Guide-AZ-300/tree/master/Chapter14`.

Understanding App Services

App Services in Azure is part of Azure's PaaS and serverless solution, and you can use these services to host web apps, API apps, mobile apps, and logic apps. You can also host them inside App Service plans. Basically, this means that your apps are running on virtual machines that are hosted and maintained by Azure.

Azure App Services offer the following capabilities:

- **Multiple languages and frameworks**: Azure App Services supports ASP.NET, ASP.NET Core, Java, Ruby, Node.js, PHP, and Python. You can also run PowerShell and other scripts, which can be executed in App Services as background services.
- **DevOps optimization**: You can set up **continuous integration and continuous deployment** (**CI/CD**) with Azure DevOps, GitHub, BitBucket, Docker Hub, and Azure Container Registry. You can use the test and staging environments to deploy your apps, and you can manage these apps using PowerShell or the CLI.
- **Global scale with high availability**: You can scale up or out manually or automatically. This will be covered in the *Scaling out* and *Scaling up* sections later in this chapter.
- **Security and compliance**: App Services is ISO, SOC, and PCI compliant. You can authenticate users using Azure Active Directory or with social media logins, such as Google, Facebook, Twitter, and Microsoft accounts. You can also create IP address restrictions.
- **Visual Studio integration**: Visual Studio provides tools that can be used to create, deploy, and debug apps in App Services easily.
- **API and mobile features**: For RESTful API scenarios, Azure App Services provides turnkey **cross-origin resource sharing** (**CORS**) support. It also simplifies mobile app scenarios by enabling push notifications, offline data synchronization, authentication, and more.
- **Serverless code**: You can run scripts and code snippets on-demand without the need to provision or manage an infrastructure, and you only have to pay for the resources that you are using (see `Chapter 9`, *Configuring Serverless Computing*, for more information).

Understanding App Service plans

App Services are hosted in App Service plans. You can configure all of the required settings, such as the compute resources, which region you want to deploy your apps to, and the costs inside an App Service plan. You can choose between free plans—the one that's the most suitable for development applications where you share all of the resources with other customers—to paid plans—where you can set the available CPU, whether to host your apps on Linux or Windows VMs, and more.

Azure offers the following service plan options:

- **Dev/Test**: Free and shared are both part of this service plan option. Your app runs in a shared environment on the same VM as other apps. This environment can also include apps from other Azure customers and users. Each app has a CPU quota and there is no ability to scale up or out. The free App Service plan can host up to 10 apps, and the shared plan can host up to 100 apps. These App Service plans are most suited for development and test apps or apps with less traffic. There is no SLA support for these two plans. The shared service plan offers the ability to add custom domains. The service plan is shown here:

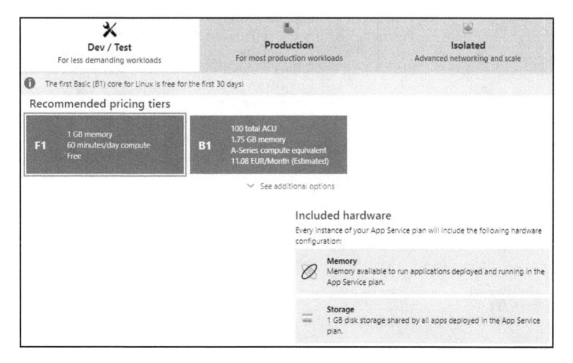

Dev/Test App Service plans

- **Production**:
    - **Basic**: The basic tier is the first tier, and is where you can choose between different pricing ranges. It offers three tiers, and the available cores and RAM doubles for every tier. Apps run on dedicated Linux or Windows VMs and the compute resources are only shared between apps that are deployed inside the same App Service plan. All the apps inside the same App Service plan reside in an isolated environment that supports SSL and custom domains. The Basic tier can host an unlimited amount of apps with a maximum of three instances, and offers scaling to three instances, but you need to do this manually. This tier is most suitable for development and test environments and applications with less traffic.
    - **Standard**: The Standard tier also has three tiers to choose from. It offers custom domains and SSL support, can also host an unlimited amount of apps, offers autoscaling for up to 10 instances, and offers five deployment slots, which can be used for testing, staging, and production apps. It also provides daily backups and Azure Traffic Manager.
    - **Premium**: Premium offers two types of tiers: Premium and Premium V2. They both offer all of the features of the Standard tier, but the Premium tier offers extra scaling instances and deployment slots. The Premium V2 tier runs on Dv2-series VMs, which have faster processors and SSD drives.
    This drastically increases the performance of your application. This tier can host an unlimited amount of apps and offers autoscaling for up to 20 instances. The dedicated compute plans in the Azure portal are shown here:

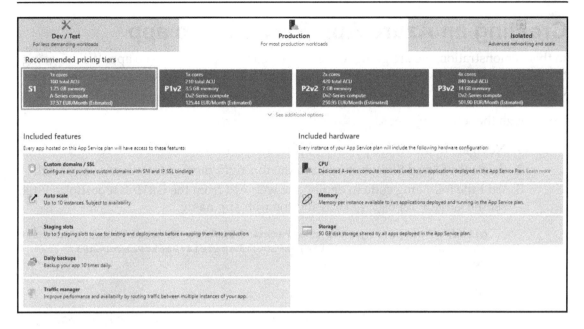

Production App Service plans

- **Isolated**: The isolated tier offers full isolation for your applications by providing a private environment with dedicated VMs and virtual networks. This tier can host an unlimited amount of apps, and you can scale up to 100 instances. These can be 100 instances in one App Service plan, or 100 different App Service plans. To create a private environment, App Services uses an **App Service environment** (**ASE**). All the apps run on Dv2-series virtual machines, so this tier offers high-performance capabilities. The isolated App Service plan is most suitable for apps that need complete isolation because of high-security demands, for instance, but want to use all of the capabilities that Azure Web Apps offers, such as autoscaling and deployment slots. Inline creation of App Service environments is not allowed for App Service creation, so you have to create an ASE separately.

Now that we have some basic information about App Services and the different App Service plans that Azure has to offer, we are going to create an Azure App Service web app.

Creating an Azure App Service web app

In this demonstration, we are going to create an Azure App Service web app. We are going to deploy a web API from GitHub to Azure using the CLI. Then, we are going to use Azure Cloud Shell for deployment.

Go through the following steps:

1. Navigate to the Azure portal by opening `https://portal.azure.com/`.
2. Select the **Cloud Shell** button from the top-right menu bar in the Azure portal.
3. Add the following code to deploy the web API from the GitHub repository. First, set the GitHub repository URL and the web app name:

   ```
   gitrepo="https://github.com/PacktPublishing/Microsoft-Azure-Archite
   ct-Technologies-Exam-Guide-AZ-300/Chapter14/PacktPubToDoAPI"
   webappname="PacktPubToDoAPI"
   ```

4. Create a resource group:

   ```
   az group create --location eastus --name PacktWebAppResourceGroup
   ```

5. Create an App Service plan in the free tier:

   ```
   az appservice plan create --name $webappname --resource-group
   PacktWebAppResourceGroup --sku FREE
   ```

6. Create a web app:

   ```
   az webapp create --name $webappname --resource-group
   PacktWebAppResourceGroup --plan $webappname
   ```

7. Deploy the code from the GitHub repository:

   ```
   az webapp deployment source config --name $webappname --resource-
   group PacktWebAppResourceGroup \
   --repo-url $gitrepo --branch master --manual-integration
   ```

8. Open a browser and add the following URL:

   ```
   https://packtpubtodoapi.azurewebsites.net/api/ToDo
   ```

You will see the following output in the browser:

Now, we have deployed the web API inside an Azure Web App. In the next section, we are going to create documentation for the API.

Creating documentation for the API

It can be challenging for developers to understand the different methods of a web API when it is consumed. This problem can be solved by using Swagger, which is an open source software framework tool that offers developers support for automated documentation, code generation, and test-case generation. This tool generates useful documentation and help pages for web APIs. It also provides benefits such as client SDK generation, API discoverability, and interactive documentation.

Swagger is a language-agnostic specification for describing REST APIs. It offers the ability for both users and computers to understand the capabilities of a service without any direct access to the implementation (source code, network access, documentation, and so on). This reduces the amount of time that's needed to accurately document service, and it minimizes the amount of work that is needed to connect disassociated services to it.

Swagger uses a core specification document, which is called `swagger.json`. It is generated by the Swagger toolchain (or third-party implementations of it) based on the service at hand. It describes how to access the API with HTTP(s) and what its capabilities are.

In this demonstration, we are going to create documentation for the API using Swagger. This can be created directly in Visual Studio using a NuGet package. Go through the following steps:

1. Clone or download the API sample application from the GitHub page that was referenced at the beginning of this chapter in the *Technical requirements* section.
2. Open the solution in Visual Studio.
3. In Visual Studio, in the top menu, go to **Tools** | **NuGet Package Manager**.

4. Open the **Browse** tab and search for `Swashbuckle.AspNetCore`. Select the package and install it for your application.

5. Wait for the package to be installed. Then, open `Startup.cs` and import the following namespace:

```
using Microsoft.OpenApi.Models;
```

I needed to install version 5.0 (prerelease) of the `Swashbuckle.AspNetCore` NuGet package before I was able to import the namespace. By selecting **Include prerelease**, this version will be displayed in the list.

6. Add the following line of code to the `ConfigureServices` method in `Startup.cs`:

```
services.AddSwaggerGen(c =>
{
    c.SwaggerDoc("v1", new OpenApiInfo { Title = "To Do API",
Version = "v1" });
});
```

7. Add the following lines of code to the `configure` method in `Startup.cs`:

```
// Enable middleware to serve generated Swagger as a JSON
endpoint.
app.UseSwagger();

// Enable middleware to serve swagger-ui (HTML, JS, CSS, etc.),
// specifying the Swagger JSON endpoint.
app.UseSwaggerUI(c =>
{
    c.SwaggerEndpoint("/swagger/v1/swagger.json", "My To Do API
v1");
});
```

8. Now, run your application. When the API is displayed in the browser, replace the URL with the following:

```
https://localhost:44377/swagger/index.html
```

9. The Swagger page will be displayed. This will look as follows:

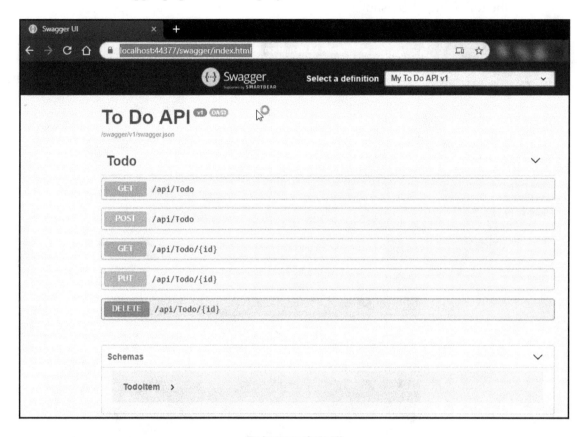

The Swagger page for the API

10. You can drill down into the different methods by clicking on them, as shown in the following screenshot:

Different API methods

11. Now, you can publish this API directly from Visual Studio to the Web App that we created in the previous demonstration. Therefore, in the **Solution Explorer** of Visual Studio, right-click on the project name and select **Publish...**:

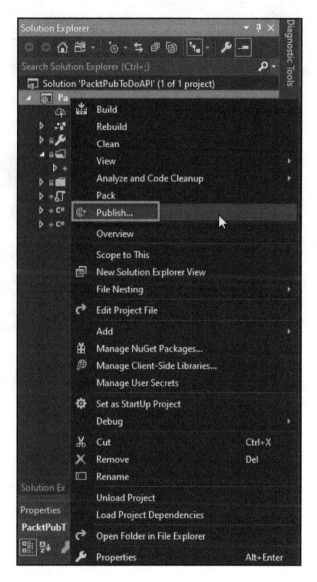

Publishing the API

12. On the first screen of the wizard, select **App Service,** then **Select Existing,** and click **Publish**:

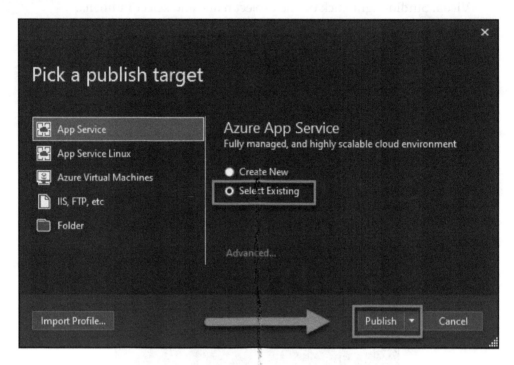

Publishing to an existing App Service

13. On the next screen, select the subscription where the API will be deployed, select **PAcktPubToDoAPI**, and click **OK**:

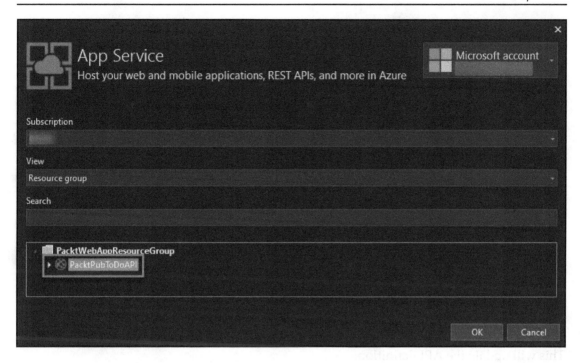

Selecting the subscription and API

The API will be published and the browser opened to display the root URL of the Web App.

14. To display the API, append the following to the URL:

    ```
    https://<our-azure-webapp-url/api/ToDo
    ```

15. To display the Swagger page, append the following to the root URL of the web API:

    ```
    https://<your-azure-webapp-url/swagger/index.html
    ```

Now, we can navigate to the Azure portal by opening `https://portal.azure.com/`.

Go to the **App Service** overview page. Then, under API, select **API definition**. Here, we can add the definition to the App Service. Add the Swagger URL to the textbox and click **Save**:

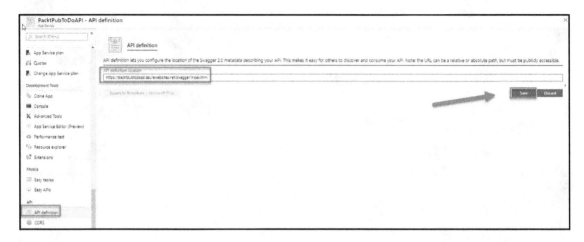

Adding the definition to the App Service

This will update the API definition.

This concludes this demonstration. In the next section, we are going to cover Web Apps for containers.

Understanding Web App for Containers

Web Apps for containers is part of the Azure App Service on Linux offering. You can pull web app container images from Docker Hub or a private Azure Container Registry, and Web App for Containers will deploy the containerized app with all the dependencies to Azure. The platform automatically takes care of OS patching, capacity provisioning, and load balancing. Container image deployments can be automated and simplified using **continuous integration/continuous deployment** (**CI/CD**) capabilities with Docker Hub, Azure Container Registry, and Visual Studio Team Services.

Docker is based on open standards, which means it can run on all major Linux distributions (and Windows Server 2016). Docker containers are lightweight sandboxes on top of your OS. When your application is deployed inside a Docker container, the app cannot see or access all the other applications or processes that are running on the same OS. You can compare this to creating different VMs to host different types of workloads or applications, but without the overhead of the virtualization itself. Docker containers also share the same OS and infrastructure, whereas VMs need to have their own OS installed inside their own infrastructure.

With containers, you share the underlying resources of the Docker host and you build a Docker image that includes everything you need to run the application. You can start with a basic image and then add everything you need. Docker containers are also extremely portable. You can deploy a Docker container, including all its settings, such as configuration settings, a specific runtime, framework, and tooling on a VM with Docker installed. Then, you can easily move that same container to the Azure App Service on Linux, and the application will still run as expected. This solves the it-works-on-*my*-machine problem that (mostly) all developers face. This makes Docker not a virtualization technology, but an application-delivery technology.

Docker containers are very suitable for building applications using the microservices architecture, where parts of an application are loosely coupled and divided into separate services that all collaborate with each other. Each service can then be deployed into a separate container and written in their own programming language using their own configuration settings. A service can consist of a Web App, a web API, or a mobile backend. You can easily deploy multiple copies of a single application. The only thing to be aware of is that they all share the same OS. If your application needs to run on a different OS, you still have to use a VM.

In the next demo, we are going to create an App Service Web App for Containers.

Creating an App Service Web App for Containers

In this demonstration, we are going to create a Web App for Containers. This can be created from the Azure portal. Let's go through the following steps:

1. Navigate to the Azure portal by opening `https://portal.azure.com/`.
2. Click **Create a resource**, type `Web App for Containers` into the search bar, and create a new one.

3. Add the following values, as shown in the following screenshot:
   - Subscription: Select a subscription.
   - Resource Group: PacktContainerResourceGroup.
   - Name: PacktContainerApp.
   - Publish: Docker Container.
   - Operating system: Linux.
   - Region: East US.
   - App Service Plan/Location: A new App Service plan will automatically be created. If you want to pick an existing one or change the default settings, you can click on it and change the settings:

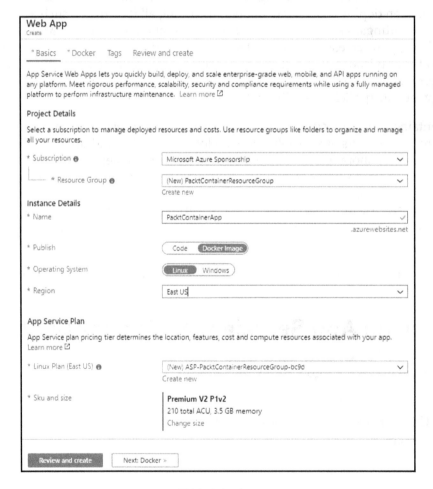

Web App basic settings

4. Next, click the **Docker** tab and select the following:

- **Options**: **Single Container** (you can select **Docker Compose (preview)** here as well). You can define and run multi Docker containers using **Docker Compose**. It uses a YAML file to configure the application's services.
- **Image Source**: **Quickstart**. Here, you can select **Quickstart**, **Azure Container Registry**, **Docker Hub**, or **Private Registry**.
- **Sample**: **Static site**:

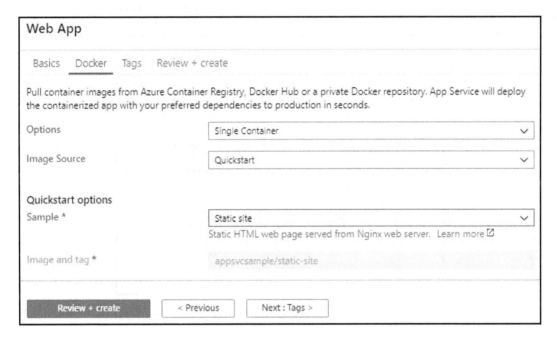

Docker settings

5. Click **Review and create** and then **Create**.

6. After it has been created, go to the overview page of **PacktContainerApp**. In the top menu, on the right-hand side, copy the URL:

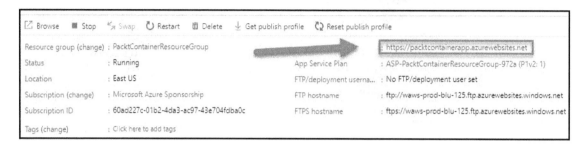

PacktContainerApp

7. Open a browser and navigate to the URL. You will see a static page similar to the one shown in the following screenshot:

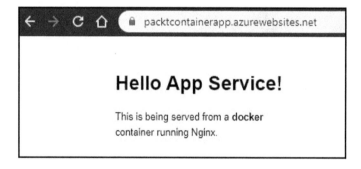

Sample app

In this demonstration, we deployed a container app. In the next section, we are going to create an App Service background task using WebJobs.

Understanding WebJobs

Another feature of Azure App Services is WebJobs. With WebJobs, you can run scripts or programs as background processes on Azure App Service web apps, APIs, and mobile apps, without any additional costs. Some scenarios that would be suitable for WebJobs are long-running tasks, such as for sending emails and file maintenance, such as aggregating or cleaning up log files, queue processing, RSS aggregation and image processing, and other CPU-intensive work. You can upload and run executable files such as the following:

- `.ps1` (using PowerShell)
- `.cmd`, `.bat`, and `.exe` (using Windows CMD)
- `.sh` (using Bash)
- `.py` (using Python)
- `.php` (using PHP)
- `.js` (using Node.js)
- `.jar` (using Java)

There are two different types of WebJobs:

- **Continuous**: This starts immediately after creating the WebJob. The work inside the WebJob is run inside an endless loop to keep the job from ending. By default, continuous WebJobs run on all the instances that the web app runs; however, you can configure the WebJob so that it runs on a single instance as well. Continuous WebJobs support remote debugging.
- **Triggered**: This starts on a schedule, but when triggered manually, it runs on a single instance that is selected by Azure for load balancing. A triggered WebJob doesn't support remote debugging.

 At the time of writing, WebJobs aren't yet supported for App Service on Linux.

Web Apps can time out after 20 minutes of inactivity. The timer can only be reset when a request is made to the Web App. The Web App's configuration can be viewed by making requests to the advanced tools site or in the Azure portal. If your app runs continuous or scheduled (timer triggered) WebJobs, enable **Always On** to ensure that the WebJobs run reliably. The **Always On** feature is only available in the Basic, Standard, and Premium plans.

In the next demonstration, we are going to create a background task using WebJobs.

Creating an App Service background task using WebJobs

In this demonstration, we are going to create a continuous WebJob that executes a console application. This application will listen for queue messages when it starts up. To create the storage account and the queue, you can run the `CreateStorageAccountQueue` PowerShell script that's been added to the GitHub repository of this book. To find out where to download the script, take a look at the *Technical requirements* section at the beginning of this chapter.

Once you have created the storage account, open Visual Studio 2019 and go through the following steps:

1. Create a new console application (.NET Core) project and name it `HelloWorldWebJob`.

2. First, we need to add two NuGet packages. Open the **NuGet Package Manager** and install the following packages:

    ```
    Microsoft.Azure.WebJobs
    Microsoft.Azure.WebJobs.Extensions
    ```

3. In `Program.cs`, add the following `using` statement:

    ```
    using Microsoft.Extensions.Hosting;
    ```

4. Open `Program.cs` and replace the `Main` method with the following code:

    ```
    static void Main(string[] args)
    {
        var builder = new HostBuilder();
        builder.ConfigureWebJobs(b =>
            {
                b.AddAzureStorageCoreServices();
    ```

```
        });
    var host = builder.Build();
    using (host)
    {
        host.Run();
    }
}
```

5. The next step is to set up console logging, which uses the ASP.NET Core logging framework. Therefore, we need to install the following NuGet packages:

```
Microsoft.Extensions.Logging
Microsoft.Extensions.Logging.Console
```

6. In `Program.cs`, add the following `using` statement:

```
using Microsoft.Extensions.Logging;
```

7. Call the `ConfigureLogging` method on `HostBuilder`. The `AddConsole` method adds console logging to the configuration:

```
builder.ConfigureLogging((context, b) =>
{
    b.AddConsole();
});
```

8. In version 3.x, the `Storage` binding extension needs to be installed explicitly. Import the following NuGet package:

```
Microsoft.Azure.WebJobs.Extensions.Storage
```

9. Update the `ConfigureWebJobs` extension method so that it looks like the following:

```
builder.ConfigureWebJobs(b =>
{
    b.AddAzureStorageCoreServices();
    b.AddAzureStorage();
});
```

10. Add a new class to the project and name it `Functions.cs`. Replace the code with the following:

```
using Microsoft.Azure.WebJobs;
using Microsoft.Extensions.Logging;

namespace HelloWorldWebJob
{
```

```
public class Functions
{
    public static void
ProcessQueueMessage([QueueTrigger("webjob")] string message,
ILogger logger)
    {
        logger.LogInformation(message);
    }
}
}
```

11. Next, add a JavaScript JSON configuration file to the project and name it `appsettings.json`. Select the `appsettings.json` file in **Solution Explorer** and in the **Properties** window, set **Copy to Output Directory** to **Copy if newer**.

12. Switch to the Azure portal and go to the overview page of the storage account that we created in PowerShell. In the left navigation, under **Settings**, select **Access keys**. In there, copy the first connection string:

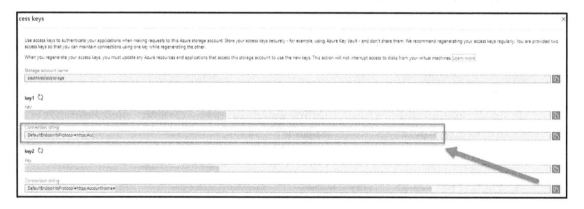

Copying access key

13. Add the following code to the `appsettings.json` file. Replace the value with the storage account **Connection string**:

```
{
    "AzureWebJobsStorage": "{storage connection string}"
}
```

14. Switch back to the Azure portal and open the overview page of the storage account. Select **Storage Explorer** in the left menu and go to **Queues** | **webjob**. In the top menu, select **+ Add Message**:

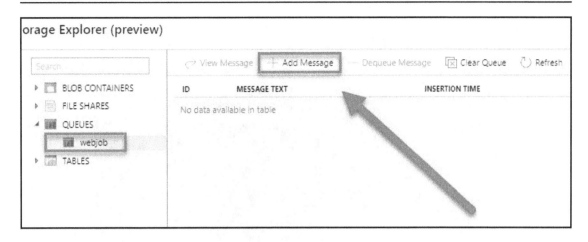

Storage Explorer

15. In the dialog, enter `Hello World` and then select **OK**. Now, run the project in Visual Studio and wait until the message is found. This can take up to two minutes because of the queue polling exponential backoff in the WebJobs SDK. The output in the console application will look as follows:

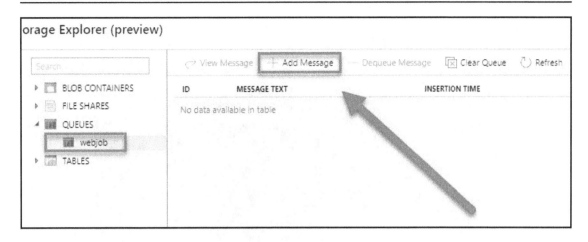

Output in the console application

16. To create an executable for the project, we need to publish it. Right-click on the project name in the **Solution Explorer** and select **Publish**. In the wizard, select **Folder**, click the arrow next to **Publish**, and select **Create profile**:

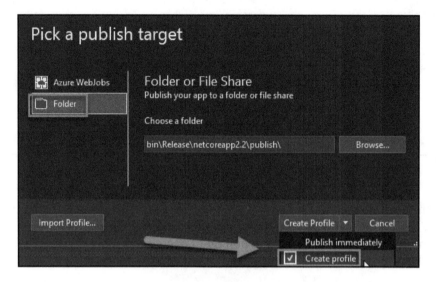

Publishing the WebJob

17. On the next screen of the wizard, select the **Edit** button:

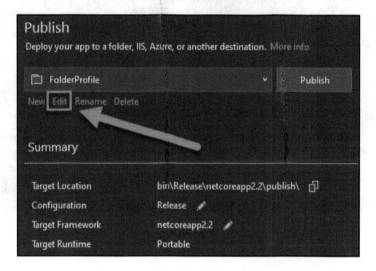

Editing the profile

18. On the next screen, set the **Target Runtime** to **win-x64** and click **Save**:

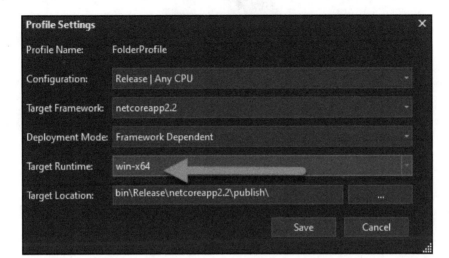

Profile Settings ✕

Profile Name: FolderProfile

Configuration: Release | Any CPU

Target Framework: netcoreapp2.2

Deployment Mode: Framework Dependent

Target Runtime: win-x64

Target Location: bin\Release\netcoreapp2.2\publish\   ...

Save   Cancel

Changing the target runtime

19. Click **Publish**.
20. The WebJob executable will now be published in the target location folder.

Now that we have created a console application that listens to the queue trigger, we can upload the executable to Azure App Services and create a new WebJob.

Deploying the WebJob to Azure App Services

Now that we have created the WebJob, we can deploy to Azure App Services. Go through the following steps:

1. Navigate to the Azure portal by opening `https://portal.azure.com/`.
2. Navigate to the overview page of the `PacktPubToDoAPI` Web App that we created in the previous demo.
3. Under **Settings**, select **WebJobs**. Then, in the top menu, click **+ Add**.
4. On the next screen, add the following values:
   - **Name:** `HelloWorldWebJob`.
   - **File Upload:** Select the `HellWorldWebJob` executable; you can find it in the `bin` folder of the Visual Studio solution.
   - **Type: Triggered**.

- **Triggers**: Manual:

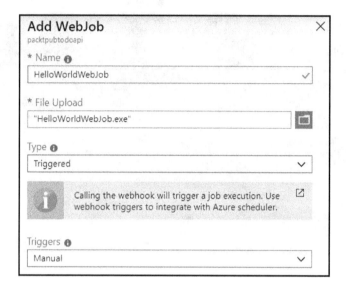

WebJob settings

5. Then, click **OK**. The WebJob will be created.

That concludes this demo. In the next and last section of this chapter, we are going to enable diagnostic logs for the `PacktPubToDoAPI` Web App.

Understanding diagnostic logging

Azure provides built-in diagnostics to assist with debugging an App Service app. App Service offers diagnostic logging for both the web server and the web application. These logs are separated into **web server diagnostics** and **application diagnostics**.

Web server diagnostics

Web server diagnostics offers the following types of logs that can be enabled and disabled:

- **Web server logging**: This type of log provides information using the W3C extended log file format to log information about HTTP transactions. This is useful for determining the overall site metrics, such as how many requests are coming from a specific IP address and the number of requests that are handled.

- **Detailed error logging**: This type of log provides detailed information for any request that results in an HTTP status code of 400 or greater. This log contains information that can help you investigate why the server returned the error code. For each error in the app's filesystem, one HTML file is generated.
- **Failed request tracing**: This provides detailed information on failed requests. This includes the IIS components that were used to process the request and the time each component took. This is useful for improving the site's performance and isolating a specific HTTP error. One folder is generated for each error in the app's filesystem.

For web server logging, you need to select a storage account or filesystem. When selecting a storage account, you need to have a storage account in place with a blob container. You can also create a new one. If you store the logs on a filesystem, they can be downloaded as a ZIP file or accessed by FTP.

Application diagnostics

With application diagnostics, you can capture information that is produced by the app itself. To capture this information, the developer uses the `System.Diagnostics.Trace` class in the application code to log the information to the application diagnostics log. You can retrieve these logs at runtime for troubleshooting.

When you publish the application to App Service, deployment information is automatically logged with diagnostic logging without needing to be configured. This can give you information about why a deployment failed.

In the next section, we are going to enable diagnostic logging in the Azure portal.

Enabling diagnostic logging

In this section, we are going to enable diagnostic logging for the `PacktPubToDoAPI` Web App. Let's go through the following steps:

1. Navigate to the Azure portal by opening `https://portal.azure.com/`.
2. Go to the overview page of the `PacktPubToDoAPI` Web App.

3. In the left menu, under **Monitoring**, select **App Service logs**. Here, you can enable the different types of logs:

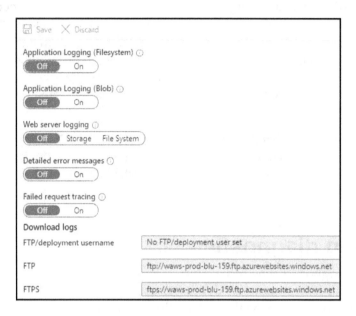

Enabling diagnostic logging

4. Enable diagnostic logging and click **Save** in the top menu.

This concludes this demo and this chapter.

Summary

In this chapter, we covered the first part of the *Implementing Workloads and Security* objective. We covered App Services and App Service plans, created an Azure App Service Web App, and looked at Web Apps for Containers. We also created an App Service background task using WebJobs and enabled diagnostic logging for the Web App.

In the next chapter, we will continue with this objective by learning how to design and develop apps that run in containers.

Questions

Answer the following questions to test your knowledge of the information contained in this chapter. You can find the answers in the *Assessments* section at the end of this book:

1. For logging information using web server logs, developers need to add additional code to their web applications.
   - Yes
   - No

2. WebJobs are also supported on Linux.
   - Yes
   - No

3. With Web App for Containers, you can only pull containers from Docker.
   - Yes
   - No

Further reading

Checkout the following links to find out more about the topics that were covered in this chapter:

- **App Service on Linux documentation**: https://docs.microsoft.com/en-us/azure/app-service/containers/
- **ASP.NET Core web API help pages with Swagger/OpenAPI**: https://docs.microsoft.com/en-us/aspnet/core/tutorials/web-api-help-pages-using-swagger?view=aspnetcore-2.2
- **Running background tasks with WebJobs in Azure App Service**: https://docs.microsoft.com/en-us/azure/app-service/webjobs-create
- **Enabling diagnostic logging for apps in Azure App Service**: https://docs.microsoft.com/en-us/azure/app-service/troubleshoot-diagnostic-logs

15
Designing and Developing Apps That Run in Containers

In the previous chapter, we covered the first part of the *Create and Deploy Apps* objective by learning how to create web apps using PaaS. Here, we covered the Azure App Services and App Service plans. We also created a web app and looked at Web Apps for Containers.

In this chapter, we are going to learn how to design and develop apps that run in containers by implementing an application that runs on an Azure Container Instance, creating a container image using a Dockerfile, and publishing it to Azure Container Registry. Then, we are going to manage the container settings from code and configure diagnostic settings for the resources. Finally, we are going to create an Azure Kubernetes Service.

The following topics will be covered in this chapter:

- Understanding Azure Container Instances
- Implementing an application that runs on an Azure Container Instance
- Creating a container image by using a Dockerfile
- Publishing an image to the Azure Container Registry
- Understanding Azure Kubernetes Service
- Creating an Azure Kubernetes Service

Technical requirements

The examples in this chapter use Azure PowerShell (`https://docs.microsoft.com/en-us/ powershell/azure/install-az-ps?view=azps-1.8.0`), Visual Studio 2019 (`https:// visualstudio.microsoft.com/vs/`), and Docker Desktop for Windows (`https://hub. docker.com/editions/community/docker-ce-desktop-windows`).

The source code for our sample application can be downloaded from `https://github.com/ PacktPublishing/Microsoft-Azure-Architect-Technologies-Exam-Guide-AZ-300/tree/ master/Chapter15`.

Understanding Azure Container Instances

In the previous chapter, we looked at Azure Web Apps for Containers, which is part of the App Service on Linux offering that makes it easy to run containerized web apps, APIs, and mobile apps inside an App Service plan.

With **Azure Containers Instances** (**ACI**), you can also run your workloads in containers. It allows you to run both Linux and Windows containers. You can deploy containers that consist of applications, databases, caches, queues, and more. Everything that runs on a VM can also run inside ACI, without the need for us to manage the infrastructure. This is all handled for you so that developers can focus on designing and building their applications. Just like Web Apps for Containers, ACI also uses Docker images to deploy the container images.

ACI is a suitable solution for any scenario that can run in isolated containers, including simple applications, build jobs, and task automation. For scenarios where you need full container orchestration, including automatic scaling, service discovery across multiple containers, and coordinated application upgrades, **Azure Kubernetes Services** (**AKS**) is recommended.

 We will cover AKS in more depth later in this chapter.

In the next section, we are going to implement an application that runs on an ACI. Then, we will create a container image using a Dockerfile and publish the image to the Azure Container Registry.

Implementing an application that runs on an ACI

In this first part of this demonstration, we are going to create a simple application that can be packaged inside a Docker container. To create a Dockerfile for this application, you need to install Docker Desktop. For the installation URL, refer to the *Technical requirements* section, which can be found at the beginning of this chapter. To create the app, follow these steps:

1. Open Visual Studio and add a new project.
2. In the new project wizard, select the **.NET Core Console App** and click **Next**.
3. Add the following values and create a new project:
      1. **Project name:** `PacktACIApp`
      2. **Location:** Pick a location
      3. **Solution name:** `PacktACIApp`
4. Click **Next**.
5. On the next screen, select **Web Application** and click **Create**.
6. We are going to use the default web application, so no code changes are required.
7. Press *F5* to run the application. The output will look as follows:

Web app output

In this section, we created an application that can be packaged inside a Docker container. We will continue with this in the next section.

Creating a container image using a Dockerfile

Now that we have our web API in place, we can create our Docker container image. We can generate this from Visual Studio directly. To do so, follow these steps:

1. Right-click the project file in the Visual Studio Solution Explorer.
2. Then, select **Add** | **Docker Support**:

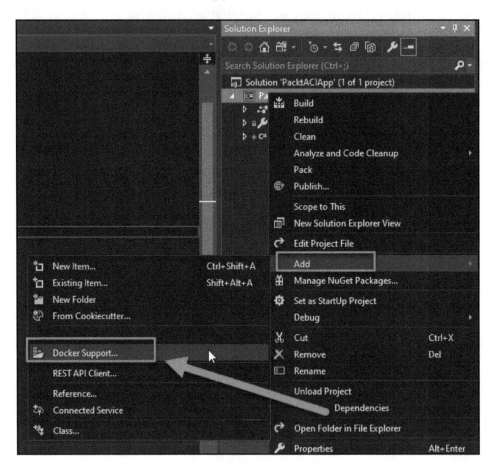

Creating a Dockerfile

3. A wizard will open where you can generate a Dockerfile. Here, select **Linux**.
4. Visual Studio creates a **Dockerfile** for you. This defines how to create the container image for your Web API project.

5. Your Dockerfile will now look as follows:

```
FROM mcr.microsoft.com/dotnet/core/aspnet:2.2-stretch-slim AS
base
WORKDIR /app
EXPOSE 80
EXPOSE 443

FROM mcr.microsoft.com/dotnet/core/sdk:2.2-stretch AS build
WORKDIR /src
COPY ["PacktACIApp/PacktACIApp.csproj", "PacktACIApp/"]
RUN dotnet restore "PacktACIApp/PacktACIApp.csproj"
COPY . .
WORKDIR "/src/PacktACIApp"
RUN dotnet build "PacktACIApp.csproj" -c Release -o /app

FROM build AS publish
RUN dotnet publish "PacktACIApp.csproj" -c Release -o /app

FROM base AS final
WORKDIR /app
COPY --from=publish /app .
ENTRYPOINT ["dotnet", "PacktACIApp.dll"]
```

6. Now, when you run your project from Visual Studio, it will run inside a Docker container. Make sure that Docker is running and click the **Docker** button on the toolbar:

Running the Dockerfile from Visual Studio

7. The browser will open once more, just like in the previous step, except now, your app will run in a container.

If you get a **Docker Volume sharing is not enabled** error when you first run your project, then open PowerShell as an administrator and run the following line of code: `docker run --rm -v c:/Users:/data alpine ls /data`. Restart Visual Studio and run the project again.

Now that we have created our Dockerfile, the next step is to deploy the image to the Azure Container Registry.

Publishing an image to the Azure Container Registry

In this section, we are going to publish the Docker image to **Azure Container Registry** (**ACR**). We can do this directly from Visual Studio as well. Let's get started:

1. Right-click the project file in the Visual Studio Solution Explorer.
2. Click **Publish**.
3. In the wizard that opens, select **Container Registry**, then **Create New Azure Container Registry**, and select **Publish immediately**:

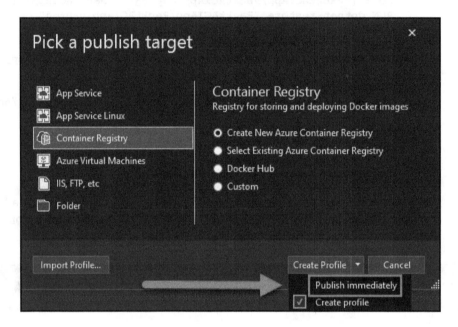

Publishing wizard

4. On the next screen, add the following settings and click **Create**:

Creating a new Container Registry

5. The Container Registry will be created, and the image will be pushed to the registry.

6. Now, navigate to the deployed ACR in the Azure portal. Under **Services**, click **Repositories**. You will see that the `packtaciapp` repository has been published. When you click on it, you will see the tag as well:

Repository with an image tag

7. Under **Settings**, click **Access Keys**. Here, copy the username and the password:

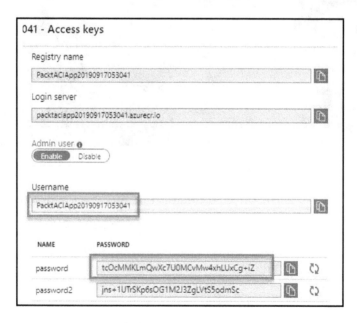

Copying the username and password

8. We will need this password in the next step of the demonstration.

In the next section, we are going to create an ACI and push the new Docker image from ACR to ACI.

Pushing the Docker image from ACR to ACI

In this part of the demonstration, we are going to use the Azure CLI to deploy and push the Docker image from the ACR to an Azure Container image. To do so, follow these steps:

1. Navigate to the Azure portal by opening `https://portal.azure.com/`.
2. Open **Azure Cloud Shell**.
3. First, we need to create a new resource group:

   ```
   az group create \
      --name PacktACIResourceGroup \
      --location eastus
   ```

4. Run the following command to create a Windows ACI and push the Docker image from ACR. The `--image` method should look similar to `{your acr name}.azurecr.io/packtaciapp:{Image Tag}` (this method is case sensitive. This will result in the following code:

   ```
   az container create \
     --name packtaciapp \
     --resource-group PacktACIResourceGroup \
     --os-type linux \
     --image packtaciapp20190917053041.azurecr.io/packtaciapp:latest \
     --ip-address public
   ```

5. When executing the preceding code, you will be prompted to provide a username and password. Here, paste in the username and password that you copied from the Container Registry settings in the previous section.
6. To display the status of the container, add the following line of code:

   ```
   az container show \
     --resource-group PacktACIResourceGroup \
     --name packtaciapp \
     --query
   "{FQDN:ipAddress.fqdn,ProvisioningState:provisioningState}" \
     --out table
   ```

7. Once the ACI has been deployed, navigate to it in the Azure portal. From the overview blade, copy the IP address:

Deployed ACI

8. Paste the IP address into a browser. The application will be displayed:

An app running in ACI

In this section, we pushed the Docker image from the ACR to an Azure container image. This concludes this demo. In the next section, we are going to look at AKS.

Understanding AKS

AKS can be used to deploy, scale, and manage Docker containers and container-based applications across a cluster of container hosts. It is based on Kubernetes (K8s), which is an open source system that's used for automating the deployment, management, and scaling of Linux-based containerized applications. Kubernetes was originally developed by Google and eliminates many of the manual processes involved in deploying and scaling containerized applications. Groups of hosts that run Linux containers can be clustered together, and Kubernetes helps you easily and efficiently manage those clusters.

Apart from this, AKS provides huge benefits. For one, it offers automation, flexibility, and reduced management overhead for administrators and developers and automatically configures all Kubernetes masters and nodes during the development process. It also configures Azure Active Directory integration (it supports Kubernetes **role-based access control (RBAC)**), configures advanced networking features such as HTTP application routing, and handles the connections to the monitoring services. Microsoft also handles all the Kubernetes upgrades when new versions become available. However, users can decide when to upgrade to the new versions of Kubernetes in their own AKS cluster to reduce the possibility of accidental workload disruption.

AKS nodes can scale up or down when needed. For additional processing power, AKS also supports node pools with **Graphics Processing Unit (GPU)**. This can be vital for compute-intensive workloads.

AKS can be accessed using the AKS management portal, the CLI, or ARM templates. It also integrates with **Azure Container Registry (ACR)** for Docker image storage and supports the use of persistent data with Azure disks.

In the next section, we are going to deploy an AKS cluster in the Azure portal.

Creating an AKS

In this section, we are going to create an AKS from the Azure portal. We will also deploy a multi-container application that includes a web frontend and a Redis instance in the cluster. To do so, follow these steps:

1. Navigate to the Azure portal by opening `https://portal.azure.com`.
2. Select **Create a resource** | **Containers** | **Kubernetes Service**.
3. On the **Basics** page, add the following values:
   - **Subscription**: Select a subscription.
   - **Resource group**: Create a new one and call it `PacktAKSResourceGroup`.
   - **Kubernetes cluster name**: `PacktAKSCluster`.
   - **Region: (US) East US**.
   - **Kubernetes version**: Leave it as the default.
   - **DNS prefix name**: `PacktAKSCluster-dns`.

- **Node size**: Leave it as the default:

Create Kubernetes cluster

Basics   Scale   Authentication   Networking   Monitoring   Tags   Review + create

Azure Kubernetes Service (AKS) manages your hosted Kubernetes environment, making it quick and easy to deploy and manage containerized applications without container orchestration expertise. It also eliminates the burden of ongoing operations and maintenance by provisioning, upgrading, and scaling resources on demand, without taking your applications offline.   Learn more about Azure Kubernetes Service

Project details

Select a subscription to manage deployed resources and costs. Use resource groups like folders to organize and manage all your resources.

* Subscription 🛈	Microsoft Azure Sponsorship	⌄
* Resource group 🛈	(New) PacktAKSResourceGroup	⌄
	Create new	

Cluster details

* Kubernetes cluster name 🛈	PacktAKSCluster	✓
* Region 🛈	(US) East US	⌄
* Kubernetes version 🛈	1.13.10 (default)	⌄
* DNS name prefix 🛈	PacktAKSCluster-dns	✓

Primary node pool

The number and size of nodes in the primary node pool in your cluster. For production workloads, at least 3 nodes are recommended for resiliency. For development or test workloads, only one node is required. You will not be able to change the node size after cluster creation, but you will be able to change the number of nodes in your cluster after creation. If you would like additional node pools, you will need to enable the "X" feature on the "Scale" tab which will allow you to add more node pools after creating the cluster.   Learn more about node pools in Azure Kubernetes Service

* Node size 🛈	**Standard DS2 v2** 2 vcpus, 7 GiB memory Change size
* Node count 🛈	◯〡〡〡〡〡〡〡〡〡〡〡〡〡〡〡〡〡〡〡〡〡〡〡〡〡〡〡〡〡〡〡〡〡〡〡〡〡〡〡 3

Review + create	< Previous	Next : Scale >

Basic settings

4. Then, select **Authentication** from the top menu. Here, we need to create a new service principal. Create a new one by leaving the default settings as they are, that is, the ones for **(new) default service principal**. You can also choose **Configure service principal** to use an existing one. If you use an existing one, you will need to provide the SPN client ID and secret.

5. Leave **Enable RBAC** under **Kubernetes authentication and authorization** enabled. This will provide you with more fine-grained control of the Kubernetes resources that are deployed in your AKS cluster:

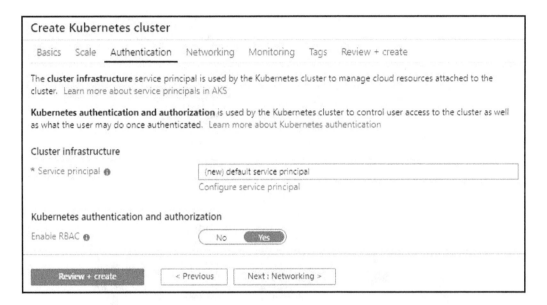

Authentication settings

6. By default, **Basic** networking is used and **Azure Monitor for containers** is enabled. Click **Review + create** and then **Create**.

7. The AKS cluster will now be created. It will take some time before the creation process finishes.

> Creating new AAD service principals may take a few minutes. When you receive an error regarding the creation of the service principal during deployment, this means the service principal hasn't been fully propagated yet. For more information, refer to the following website: `https://docs.microsoft.com/en-us/azure/aks/troubleshooting#im-receiving-errors-that-my-service-principal-was-not-found-when-i-try-to-create-a-new-cluster-without-passing-in-an-existing-one`.

Now that we have created the AKS cluster, we are going to connect to the cluster using `kubectl`.

Connecting to the cluster

In this section, we are going to connect to the cluster using `kubectl` from Azure Cloud Shell. The `kubectl` client is preinstalled in Azure Cloud Shell. Let's get started:

1. Navigate to the Azure portal by opening `https://portal.azure.com`.
2. In the top-right menu of the Azure portal, select **Azure Cloud Shell**.
3. First, we need to connect to our Kubernetes cluster. To do so, add the following line of code (the subscription method is optional):

```
az aks get-credentials \
  --resource-group PacktAKSResourceGroup \
  --name PacktAKSCluster \
  --subscription "<your-subscription-id>"
```

4. To verify the connection to your cluster, return a list of the cluster nodes:

```
kubectl get nodes
```

5. The following output displays the cluster of nodes:

```
sjoukje@Azure:~$ kubectl get nodes
NAME                        STATUS   ROLES   AGE    VERSION
aks-agentpool-18232472-0    Ready    agent   48m    v1.13.10
aks-agentpool-18232472-1    Ready    agent   48m    v1.13.10
aks-agentpool-18232472-2    Ready    agent   48m    v1.13.10
sjoukje@Azure:~$
```

Cluster of nodes

In this section, we connected to the AKS cluster using the CLI. In the next section, we are going to deploy the application.

Deploying the application

In this section, we are going to deploy the application to the cluster. For this, we need to define a Kubernetes manifest file. This defines the desired state for the cluster, such as what container images to run. We are going to use a manifest to create all the objects that are needed to deploy our sample application. This sample application is the Azure vote application and consists of a Python application and a Redis instance. The manifest will include two Kubernetes deployments: one for the frontend Python application and one for the backend Redis Cache. Two Kubernetes services will be created as well; that is, an internal service for the Redis instance and an external service so that we can access the vote application from the internet.

 In this demonstration, we are going to create the manifest file manually and deploy it manually to the cluster. However, in more real-world scenarios, you can use Azure Dev Spaces (https://docs. microsoft.com/en-us/azure/dev-spaces/) to debug your code directly in the AKS cluster. You can use Dev Spaces to work together with others on your team and across OS platforms and development environments.

1. In the Cloud Shell, use nano or vi to create a file named azure-vote.yaml.

2. Copy in the following YAML definition. Here, we have the backend application, beginning with the deployment:

```
apiVersion: apps/v1
kind: Deployment
metadata:
  name: azure-vote-back
spec:
  replicas: 1
  selector:
    matchLabels:
      app: azure-vote-back
  template:
    metadata:
      labels:
        app: azure-vote-back
    spec:
      nodeSelector:
        "beta.kubernetes.io/os": linux
      containers:
      - name: azure-vote-back
        image: redis
        resources:
          requests:
            cpu: 100m
```

```
            memory: 128Mi
        limits:
            cpu: 250m
            memory: 256Mi
    ports:
    - containerPort: 6379
      name: redis
---
```

3. Then, we have the service for the backend application:

```
apiVersion: v1
kind: Service
metadata:
  name: azure-vote-back
spec:
  ports:
  - port: 6379
  selector:
      app: azure-vote-back
---
```

Next, we have the deployment for the frontend application:

```
apiVersion: apps/v1
kind: Deployment
metadata:
  name: azure-vote-front
spec:
  replicas: 1
  selector:
    matchLabels:
        app: azure-vote-front
  template:
    metadata:
      labels:
          app: azure-vote-front
    spec:
      nodeSelector:
        "beta.kubernetes.io/os": linux
      containers:
      - name: azure-vote-front
        image: microsoft/azure-vote-front:v1
        resources:
          requests:
            cpu: 100m
            memory: 128Mi
          limits:
```

```
            cpu: 250m
            memory: 256Mi
        ports:
        - containerPort: 80
        env:
        - name: REDIS
            value: "azure-vote-back"

---
```

After this, we have the service:

```
apiVersion: v1
kind: Service
metadata:
  name: azure-vote-front
spec:
  type: LoadBalancer
  ports:
  - port: 80
  selector:
    app: azure-vote-front
```

Now, deploy the application using the `azure-vote` manifest file:

```
kubectl apply -f azure-vote.yaml
```

The application will be deployed. This will result in the following output:

The output of deploying the application

Now that we've deployed the application, we will test it.

Testing the application

When the application runs, the application frontend is exposed to the internet by a Kubernetes service. This process can take a few minutes to complete.

We can monitor its progress by using the following command in the CLI:

```
kubectl get service azure-vote-front --watch
```

When the frontend is exposed to the internet, the following output will be displayed:

Exposed service

Now, you can copy the external IP address and paste it into a browser. This will result in the following output:

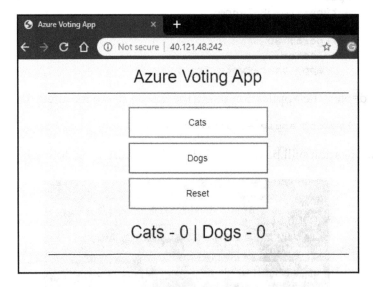

The app running in AKS

Now that we have a working app in AKS, we are going to monitor the health and logs of this application in AKS.

Monitoring the health and logs of the application

When we created the cluster, Azure Monitor for containers was enabled. This monitoring feature provides health metrics for both the AKS cluster and the pods running on the cluster. This is displayed in the Azure portal and consists of information regarding the uptime, current status, and resource usage for the Azure vote pods. Let's take a look:

1. Navigate to the Azure portal by opening `https://portal.azure.com`.
2. Go to the overview page of `PacktAKSCluster`.
3. Under **Monitoring**, select **Insights**. Then, in the top menu, choose **+ Add Filter**:

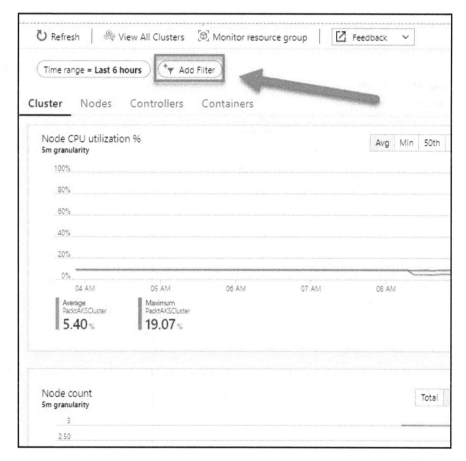

Add a new filter

4. Select **Namespace** as the property. Then, choose **<All but kube-system>**.

5. Then, from the top menu (under the filters), select **Containers**:

Containers view

6. To see the logs for the `azure-vote-front` pod, select **View container logs** from the drop-down of the containers list. These logs include the `stdout` and `stderr` streams from the container:

Opening the container logs

7. This will result in the following output:

Container logs

This concludes this section and this chapter.

Summary

In this chapter, we learned how to implement an application that runs on an ACI. We created a container image using a Dockerfile and published it to ACR. Then, we created an AKS and deployed an application to the cluster. Finally, we looked at the monitoring capabilities of AKS.

In the next chapter, we will start the *Implementing Authentication and Secure Data* objective by learning how to implement authentication.

Questions

Answer the following questions to test your knowledge of the information contained in this chapter. You can find the answers in the *Assessments* section at the end of this book:

1. You are planning to deploy an application to a container solution in Azure. You want full control over how to manage the containers. Is Azure Container Instances the right solution for this?
    1. Yes
    2. No

2. Logs in Azure Kubernetes Service can only be viewed from the CLI.
    1. Yes
    2. No

3. Can you create a Dockerfile using Visual Studio?
    1. Yes
    2. No

Further reading

Check out the following links to find out more about the topics that were covered in this chapter:

- **Azure Container Registry Documentation**: `https://docs.microsoft.com/en-us/azure/container-registry/`
- **Azure Container Instances Documentation**: `https://docs.microsoft.com/en-us/azure/container-instances/`
- **Azure Kubernetes Service (AKS)**: `https://docs.microsoft.com/en-us/azure/aks/`

4
Section 4: Implementing Authentication and Secure Data

As this section's objective, you will learn how to implement authentication and secure your data in Azure.

This section contains the following chapters:

- Chapter 16, *Implementing Authentication*
- Chapter 17, *Implementing Secure Data Solutions*

16
Implementing Authentication

In the previous chapter, we covered the last part of the *Create and Deploy Apps* objective by covering how to design and develop apps that run in containers. We've covered how to implement an application that runs on Azure Container Instances and we created an Azure Kubernetes Service and deployed an application to the cluster.

In this chapter, we are going to start with the *Implement Authentication and Secure Data* objective. We are going to cover how to implement authentication for your web apps, APIs, functions, and logic apps, using certificates, forms-based authentication, and more. We are going to implement managed identities for Azure resources service principal authentication and implement multi-factor authentication and OAuth2 authentication.

The following topics will be covered in this chapter:

- Understanding Azure App Service authentication
- Implementing Windows-integrated authentication
- Implementing authentication by using certificates
- Understanding and implementing OAuth2 authentication in Azure AD
- Implementing tokens
- Understanding managed identities
- Implementing managed identities for Azure resources service principal authentication

Technical requirements

This chapter will use Azure PowerShell (`https://docs.microsoft.com/en-us/powershell/azure/install-az-ps?view=azps-1.8.0`), Visual Studio 2019 (`https://visualstudio.microsoft.com/vs/`), and Postman (`https://www.getpostman.com/`) for examples.

The source code for our sample application can be downloaded from `https://github.com/PacktPublishing/Microsoft-Azure-Architect-Technologies-Exam-Guide-AZ-300/tree/master/Chapter16`.

Understanding Azure App Service authentication

Azure App Service provides built-in authentication and authorization support. This makes it easy to sign in users and access data, with minimal or no code changes in your web apps, APIs, Azure Functions, and mobile backends. It also extracts the need to have deeper knowledge about security, including encryption, JSON web tokens, federation, and more. This is all handled for you by Azure. However, you are not required to use App Service for authentication and authorization. You can also use security features that come with other web frameworks or write your own utilities.

The App Service authentication and authorization module runs in the same sandbox as your application code. When it is enabled, it will handle all incoming HTTP requests before they are handled by the application code.

This module handles the following things for your app:

- Authenticates users with the specified provider
- Validates, stores, and refreshes tokens
- Manages the authenticated session
- Injects identity information into request headers

This module is configured using app settings and runs completely separately for the application code. No changes to the application code, SDKs, or specific languages are required.

App Service authentication and authorization use the following security features:

- **User claims**: App Service makes the user claims available for all language frameworks. The claims are injected into the request headers. ASP.NET 4.6 apps use the `ClaimsPrincipal.Current` for this. For Azure Functions, the claims are also injected in the headers.

- **Token Store**: App Service provides a built-in token store, where tokens are stored for the users of the different apps. When you enable authentication with any provider, this token store is immediately available to your app. In most cases, you must write code to store, collect, and refresh tokens in the application. With the token store, you can just retrieve them when you need them. When they become invalid, you can tell App Service to refresh them.

- **Identity providers**: App Service can also use **federated identity**. A third-party identity provider will then manage the user identities and authentication flow for you. Five identity providers are available by default: Azure Active Directory, Microsoft Accounts, Facebook, Google, and Twitter. Besides these built-in identity providers, you can also integrate another identity provider or your own custom identity solution.

- **Logging and tracing**: When application logging is enabled, the authentication and authorization traces will be directly displayed in the log files. When an unexpected authentication error occurs, all of the details of this error can be found in the existing application logs. When failed request tracing is enabled, you can see exactly what role the authentication and authorization module may have played in a failed request.

In the upcoming section, we are going to enable this feature in the Azure portal.

Implementing Windows-integrated authentication

By configuring the authentication and authorization feature of the web app, Windows-integrated authentication is enabled. In this demonstration, we are going to enable this for a web app. First, we will deploy a web app to an Azure App Service.

Deploying the web app

In this first part of the demonstration, we are going to deploy a sample web app. We are using a sample application and will deploy this in Azure using a PowerShell script. Therefore, we have to perform the following steps:

1. First, we need to log in to the Azure account, as follows:

   ```
   Connect-AzAccount
   ```

2. If necessary, select the right subscription, as follows:

   ```
   Select-AzSubscription -SubscriptionId "********-****-****-****-***********"
   ```

3. Specify the URL for the GitHub sample application and specify the web app name:

   ```
   $gitrepo="https://github.com/Azure-Samples/app-service-web-dotnet-get-started.git"
   $webappname="PacktWebApp"
   ```

4. Create a web app:

   ```
   New-AzWebApp `
       -Name $webappname `
       -Location "East US" `
       -AppServicePlan PacktAppServicePlan `
       -ResourceGroupName PacktAppServicePlan
   ```

5. Then, configure the GitHub deployment from the GitHub repository:

   ```
   $PropertiesObject = @{
       repoUrl = "$gitrepo";
       branch = "master";
       isManualIntegration = "true";
   }
   ```

6. Deploy the GitHub web app over the newly created web app:

   ```
   Set-AzResource `
       -PropertyObject $PropertiesObject `
       -ResourceGroupName PacktAppServicePlan `
       -ResourceType Microsoft.Web/sites/sourcecontrols `
       -ResourceName $webappname/web `
       -ApiVersion 2015-08-01 `
       -Force
   ```

7. After deployment, you can obtain the web app URL from the overview blade in the Azure portal, and paste it into the browser. The output will look like the following screenshot:

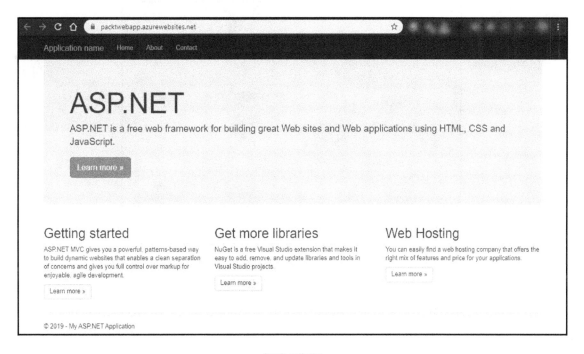

Sample application

Now that we've deployed the web app, we can enable authentication and authorization for it.

Enabling authentication and authorization

To enable authentication and authorization for your apps, perform the following steps:

1. Navigate to the Azure portal by opening `https://portal.azure.com`.
2. Go to the `PacktWebApp` that we created in the previous section.

3. In the left menu, under **Settings**, select **Authentication / Authorization**, and then turn it on, as follows:

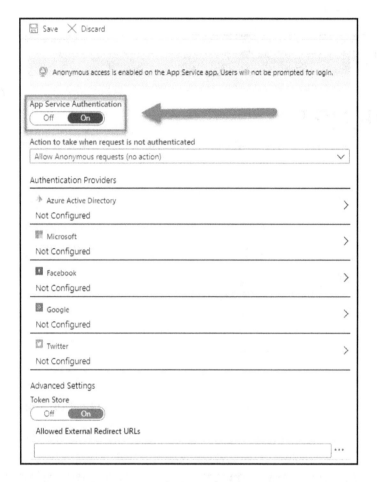

Enabling authentication/authorization

4. Under **Action to take when request is not authenticated**, you can select the following options (you can add multiple identity providers to your app; however you need to do some coding inside your app to make these multiple providers available):

- **Allow anonymous requests (no action).**
- **Log in with Azure Active Directory.**
- **Log in with Facebook.**
- **Log in with Google.**

- **Log in with a Microsoft account**.
- **Log in with Twitter**.

5. In this demo, we are going to use **Log in with Azure Active Directory**, so select this one and click the **Save** button on the top menu. Our environment is now enabled to log in to our app using Microsoft credentials.

6. We now need to configure the app to let users log in using their Azure AD credentials. Under **Authentication Providers**, select **Azure Active Directory**:

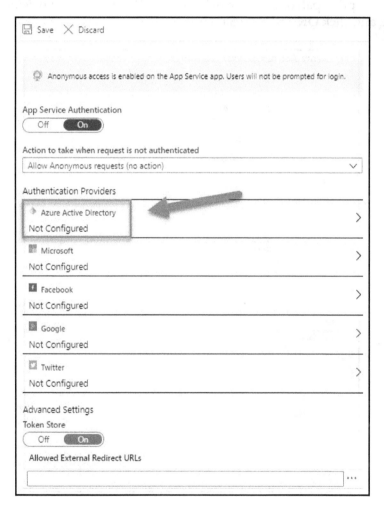

Azure AD configuration button

7. In the next blade, you can select a couple of management mode settings:
    - **Off**: There will be no Azure AD application registered for you.
    - **Express**: An Azure AD application is registered for you automatically using the express settings.
    - **Custom**: You can register an Azure AD application using custom settings that you will provide manually.

8. For this demo, select **Express**. Next, you can create a new Azure AD registration (service principal) or select an existing one. We will leave the default settings here and click **OK** and then **Save**:

Azure AD configuration settings

9. We are now ready to use Azure AD authentication in `PacktWebApp`.

10. For this demo, I've updated the original `PacktWebApp` and added the required code to be able to log in to the app using an authentication provider. This code file is added to the GitHub repository of this book. You can find the URL under the *Technical requirements* section at the beginning of this chapter.

11. To deploy the updated web app, go back to the web app overview page and under **Deployment**, select **Deployment Center**. In there, click the disconnect button in the top menu to disconnect from the current GitHub repository. When you are disconnected, select the **GitHub** tile and after that, click the **Authorize** button, as follows:

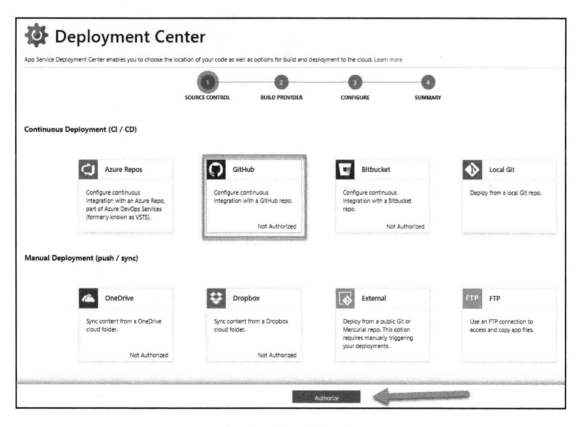

Connecting to a different GitHub repository

12. A new browser window is opened where you have to specify your GitHub credentials. Specify them, log in, and then click **Continue**.

13. For this demo, we are going to do a basic deployment, so in the next blade, select Kudu and click **Continue**:

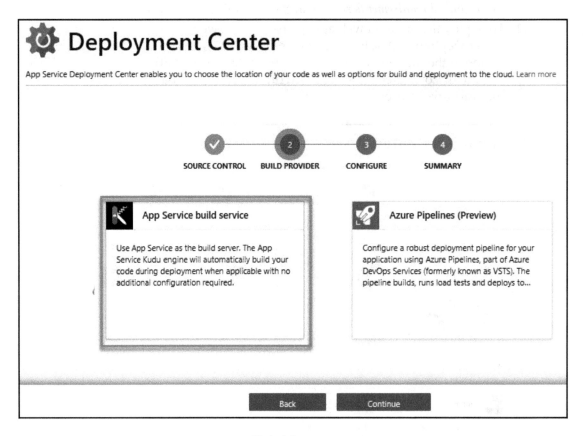

Selecting deployment type

14. In the next blade, select the **Organization**, **Repository**, and **Branch** and click **Continue** and then **Finish**:

Selecting the right repository

15. The app will be deployed inside the App Service plan now.

16. Navigate to the **Overview** blade and click the link of the URL. The website will be opened and you will have to specify a Microsoft account to log in. After you've successfully authenticated, the website will display your **Principal Name** and other information, such as claims, as shown in the following screenshot:

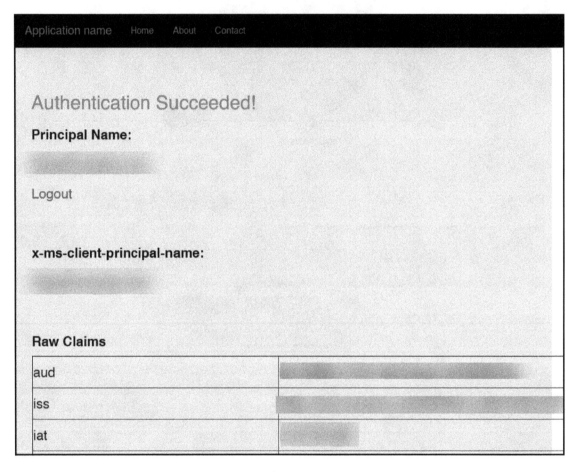

Successfully authenticated

We now have enabled authentication and authorization. In the next section, we are going to implement authentication by using certificates.

Implementing authentication by using certificates

By default, Azure secures the `*.azurewebsites.net` wildcard domain with a single SSL certificate. So, when you use the default domain that is generated for your app when you deploy it to Azure App Service, your users will access the app over a secure connection. When you use a custom domain for your app, for instance, `az-300.com`, you should assign an SSL certificate to it yourself.

You can assign SSL certificates to your app from the Azure portal. To assign a certificate, your app must run in the **Standard**, **Premium**, or **Isolated** App Service plan tiers.

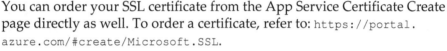

You can order your SSL certificate from the App Service Certificate Create page directly as well. To order a certificate, refer to: `https://portal.azure.com/#create/Microsoft.SSL`.

You can also create a free certificate and use this from the website at: `https://www.sslforfree.com` and convert the certificate into an SSL certificate using the website at: `https://decoder.link/converter`.

For this demo, I've added a custom domain to my web app and obtained a free certificate and converted it into an SSL certificate using the preceding websites.

To bind an SSL certificate to `PacktWebApp`, perform the following steps:

1. Navigate to the Azure portal by opening `https://portal.azure.com`.
2. Again, go to the `PacktWebApp` that we've created in the previous section.
3. In the left menu, under **Settings**, select **TLS/SSL Settings**.

4. In the TLS/SSL settings blade, click on **Private Key Certificates (.pfx)**, as follows:

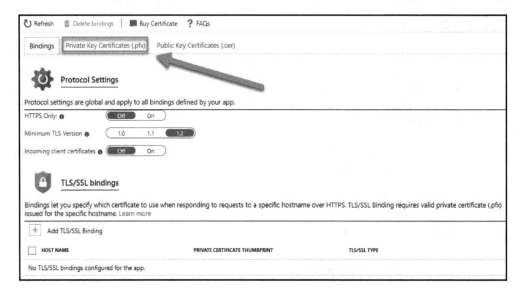

SSL settings

5. Next, click the **Upload Certificate** button, as follows:

Private certificates

6. Upload the `.pfx` file from your computer, provide the password, and click **Upload**, as follows:

Upload the .pfx file

7. The certificate is uploaded to Azure and now we have to set the SSL binding to bind it to the domain. Click **Bindings** in the top menu and then click **Add TLS/SSL Binding**, as follows:

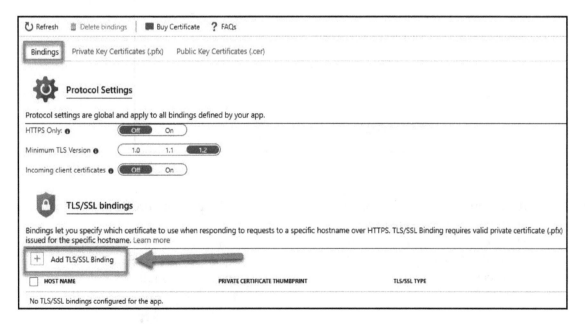

Add SSL binding

8. To bind the certificate to the domain, you need to specify the following two values:
    - **Hostname**: Select the hostname from the drop-down list.
    - **Private Certificate Thumbprint**: Select the uploaded certificate here.
    - **SSL Type**: Select **SNI SSLv**.
9. Then, click **Add Binding**, as follows:

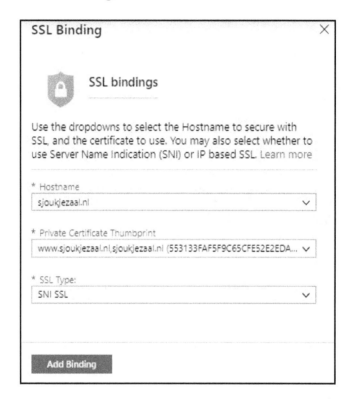

Add SSL binding

10. If you have a www hostname as well, you should repeat the previous step to bind the same certificate to this.
11. Lastly, we will set one of the protocol settings and switch the website to **HTTPS Only**. This way, the website can only be accessed using HTTPS and is not accessible using HTTP, as shown in the following screenshot:

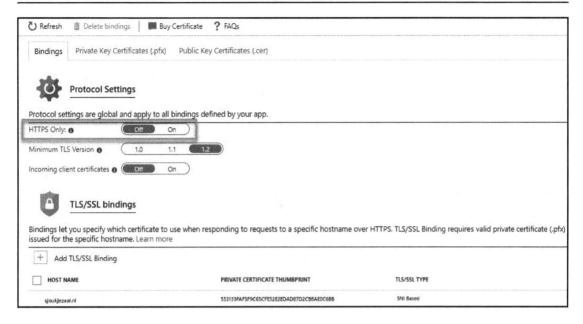

Add protocol setting

We have now covered how to assign an SSL certificate to your app. In the next section, we are going to cover OAuth2.

Understanding OAuth2 authentication in Azure AD

The Microsoft Identity platform supports industry-standard protocols such as OAuth 2.0 and OpenID Connect, as well as open-source libraries for different platforms. **Azure Active Directory** (**Azure AD**) uses OAuth 2.0 to enable you to authorize access to resources in your Azure AD tenant. OpenID Connect is then used in your custom applications as middleware to communicate with the OAuth 2.0 framework.

There are two primary use cases in the Microsoft identity platform programming model:

- During an OAuth 2.0 authorization grant flow—during this flow, a resource owner grants authorization to the client application. This will allow the client to access the resources from the resource owner.
- During resource access by the client—during this flow, the claim values present in the access token are used as a basis for making access control decisions. This is implemented by the resource server.

The OAuth 2.0 authorization code flow is used to perform authentication and authorization in most application types, including web apps and natively installed apps. At a high level, the entire authorization flow for an application looks like this:

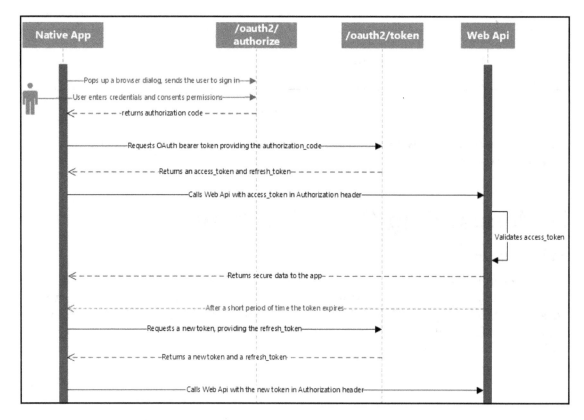

High-level OAuth 2.0 flow

In the next section, we are going to implement OAuth 2.0 authentication.

Implementing OAuth2 authentication

The first step to implement OAuth 2.0 authentication in Azure AD is by registering an application (service principal) in Azure AD. After registration, permissions can be set to the application, which gives access to various resources in Azure, such as the Microsoft Graph, and more.

Registering the application in Azure AD

In this demonstration, we are going to register an application in Azure AD (also called a service principal). We are going to give this service principal permission to access Azure resources. In this example, we are going to create a user in Azure AD using the Microsoft Graph.

We are going to use Postman as an API client to create the requests to the Graph. Under the *Technical requirements* section at the beginning of this chapter, you can click the link to install Postman.

For those who are unfamiliar with Postman, you can refer to the following website for more information, at `https://www.getpostman.com/product/api-client`.

To register the application in the Azure portal, we need to perform the following steps:

1. Navigate to the Azure portal by opening `https://portal.azure.com`.
2. In the left menu, select **Azure Active Directory**.

3. In the Azure Active Directory overview blade, click **App Registrations** and, then in the top menu, **+ New registration**:

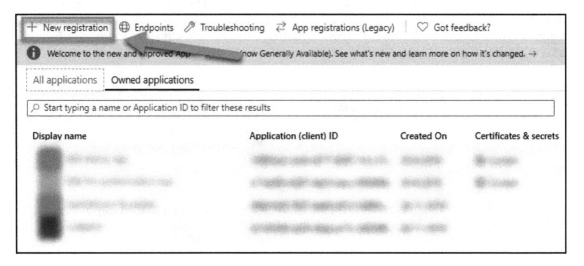

New app registration

4. In the **App registration** blade, add the following values:
   - **Name**: `PacktADApp`.
   - **Supported account types**: Accounts in this organizational directory only. There are three options here: the first will create a single-tenant app. This only has access to the Azure AD tenant where it is created. The second one, **Accounts in any organizational directory**, creates a multitenant app. You can access other Azure AD tenants with this registration as well. The last one creates a multi-tenant app as well, and besides work and school accounts, you can also log in with personal Microsoft accounts, such as outlook.com accounts.
   - **Redirect URI**: Here, you can fill in `https://localhost` because we don't actually have a real application where, after finishing the authentication process, the user needs to be redirected to:

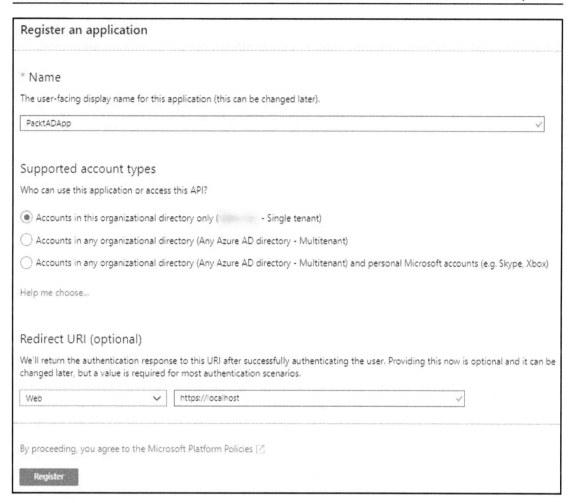

Register the application

Click **Register**.

5. During registration, Azure AD will assign your application a unique client identifier (the **Application ID**). You need this value in the next sections, so copy it from the application page.

6. Find your registered application in the Azure portal, click **App registrations** again, and then click **View all applications**.

7. The next step is to create an app secret. Therefore, from the application blade, on the left menu, click **Certificates & secrets**. In there, click **+ New client secret**:

Credentials enable applications to identify themselves to the authentication service when receiving tokens at a web addressable location (using an HTTPS scheme). For a higher level of assurance, we recommend using a certificate (instead of a client secret) as a credential.

Certificates

Certificates can be used as secrets to prove the application's identity when requesting a token. Also can be referred to as public keys.

⤒ Upload certificate

No certificates have been added for this application.

THUMBPRINT	START DATE	EXPIRES

Client secrets

A secret string that the application uses to prove its identity when requesting a token. Also can be referred to as application password.

+ New client secret

DESCRIPTION	EXPIRES	VALUE

No client secrets have been created for this application.

Create a new client secret

8. Add the following values:
   - **Description:** `Key1`.
   - **Expires: In 1 year**. You can also choose: **In 2 years or never**.

9. Click **Add**.

10. Then, copy the client secret, because it's only displayed once:

Credentials enable applications to identify themselves to the authentication service when receiving tokens at a web addressable location (using an HTTPS scheme). For a higher level of assurance, we recommend using a certificate (instead of a client secret) as a credential.

Certificates

Certificates can be used as secrets to prove the application's identity when requesting a token. Also can be referred to as public keys.

⬆ Upload certificate

No certificates have been added for this application.

THUMBPRINT	START DATE	EXPIRES

Client secrets

A secret string that the application uses to prove its identity when requesting a token. Also can be referred to as application password.

＋ New client secret

DESCRIPTION	EXPIRES	VALUE	
Key1	10/9/2020	qka0NDH6yUBTqay3@9SqkCbBCUBjw:]. 🗐	🗑

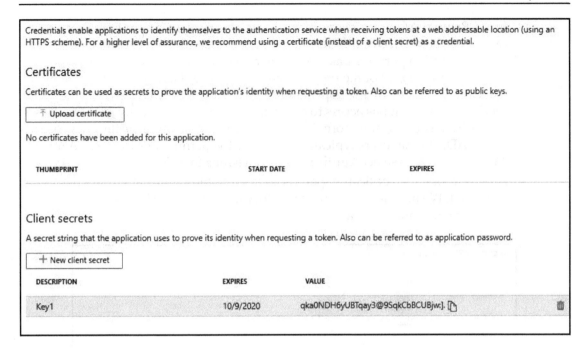

Client secret

11. Now that we have an application ID and a secret, we can set the appropriate permissions for the application. Therefore, in the left menu, select **API permissions**.

12. In the **API permissions** blade, you can see that one permission is already added: you are allowed to log in and read your own user profile. Click **+ Add a permission**:

Configured permissions

Applications are authorized to call APIs when they are granted permissions by users/admins as part of the consent process. The list of configured permissions should include all the permissions the application needs. Learn more about permissions and consent

＋ Add a permission	Grant admin consent for			
API / Permissions name	**Type**	**Description**	**Admin Consent Req...**	**Status**
⌄ Microsoft Graph (1)				•••
User.Read	Delegated	Sign in and read user profile	-	•••

Application permissions

13. In the Request API permissions blade, select the **Microsoft Graph.** In there, you can choose between two different types of permissions, **Delegated permissions** and **Application permissions**. The former gives you access to the API as the signed-in user. So, all of the permissions that the user has also apply to the data that can be accessed by the application. The latter basically creates a sort of service account that has access to all users in a tenant, all security groups, all Office 365 resources, and more. For this example, we want to create a new user in Azure AD. Normal users typically don't have the permissions to access Azure AD, so we have to select **Application permissions** for this.

14. After selecting the application permissions, all of the available permissions are displayed. We need to unfold the **Directory** item and then choose `Directory.ReadWrite.All`:

Select the appropriate permissions

15. Click **Add permissions.**

16. Because we are using application permissions, an administrator needs to grant admin consent as well. Therefore, you need to click the **Grant admin consent for...** and then, in the popup, log in with your administrator credentials and accept the license terms:

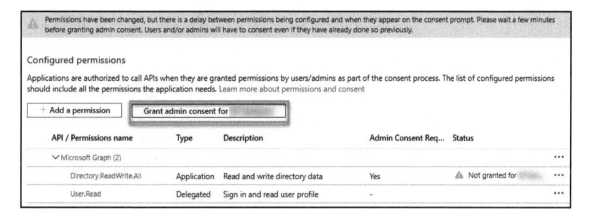

Grant admin consent

17. Now this application has the permissions to add a new user to the Azure Active Directory tenant:

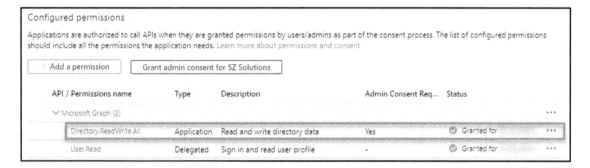

Admin consent granted

18. At last, select Azure Active Directory from the left menu again, and then under **Manage**, click **Properties**. In there, copy the Azure AD tenant ID. We need this to set up the request to Azure AD using the Microsoft Graph in the next section.

This concludes the first part of the demo. In the next section, we are going to implement tokens.

Implementing tokens

In this part of the demonstration, we are going to make some requests to Microsoft Graph to create a new user in Azure AD. The first part is creating a request to the login page of Microsoft and providing the Azure AD tenant ID, the application ID, and the secret. This will result in `access_token`, which we can use in the second request to create the actual user.

Therefore, we need to perform the following steps:

1. Open Postman and log in or create an account. For the request URL, add the following (make sure that you replace `{tenant_id}` in the request URL with the correct Azure AD tenant ID, which we copied in the previous step):

    ```
    POST
    https://login.microsoftonline.com/{tenant_id}/oauth2/token?api-
    version=1.0
    ```

2. Click **Body** in the top menu and add the following values:
    * **Key**: `grant_type`, **Value**: `client_credentials`
    * **Key**: `resource`, **Value**: `https://graph.microsoft.com`
    * **Key**: `client_id`, **Value**: `<replace-this-with-the-application-id>`
    * **Key**: `client_id`, **Value**: `<replace-this-with-the-application-secret>`

3. Then, click the **Send** button. In response, you will receive `access_token`. This token will be used to make the actual request to Graph to create the user:

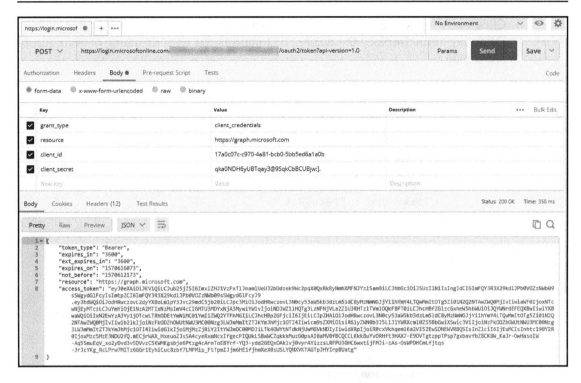

4. Open another tab in Postman and add the following in the request URL with the correct Azure AD tenant ID (which we copied in the previous step):

```
POST https://graph.microsoft.com/v1.0/users
```

5. Click **Headers** in the top menu and add the following values, **Key:**
Authorization, **Value:** `Bearer <access_token>`, as in the following screenshot:

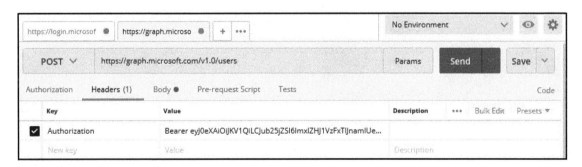

Add access_token

6. Click **Body** in the top menu and add select **raw** and **JSON**. Then, add the following value (replace the Azure AD tenant name with the name of your Azure AD tenant):

```
{
  "accountEnabled": true,
  "displayName": "PacktUser",
  "mailNickname": "PacktUser",
  "userPrincipalName": "PacktUser@<azure-ad-tenant-
name>.onmicrosoft.com",
  "passwordProfile" : {
    "forceChangePasswordNextSignIn": true,
    "password": "P@ss@Word"
  }
}
```

7. The output will be as follows:

```
{
    "@odata.context":
"https://graph.microsoft.com/v1.0/$metadata#users/$entity",
    "id": "82decd46-8f51-4b01-8824-ac24e0cf9fa4",
    "businessPhones": [],
    "displayName": "PacktUser",
    "givenName": null,
    "jobTitle": null,
    "mail": null,
    "mobilePhone": null,
    "officeLocation": null,
    "preferredLanguage": null,
    "surname": null,
    "userPrincipalName": "PacktUser@<azure-ad-tenant-
name>.onmicrosoft.com"
}
```

8. In Postman, this will look like the following screenshot:

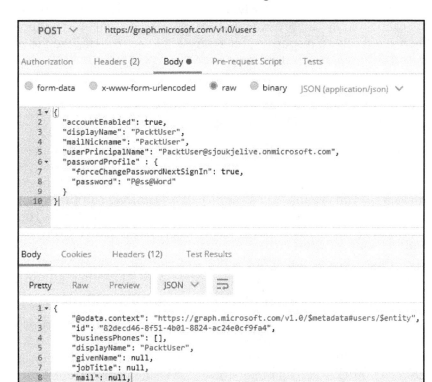

Graph request

Next, we will look at refreshing tokens.

Refreshing tokens

Access tokens are only valid for a short period of time. They must be refreshed to continue having access to the resources. You can refresh the access token by submitting another post to the token endpoint, as we did in the first step when we requested `access_token`. Refresh tokens are valid for all of the resources that we set consent to in Azure AD via the Azure portal.

Typically, the lifetimes of refresh tokens are relatively long. But in some cases, the tokens are revoked, expired, or lack sufficient privileges for the desired action. You must ensure that your application handles these errors that are returned by the token endpoint correctly. When you receive a response with a refresh token error, discard the current refresh token and request a new authorization code or access token.

Understanding managed identities

One of the challenges, when you build applications for the cloud, is how to manage the credentials in code for authentication. Keeping those credentials secure is key, so ideally these credentials will never appear on developer workstations and aren't checked into source control as well. You can use Azure Key Vault for securely storing credentials, keys, and secrets, but the application still needs to authenticate to Key Vault to retrieve them.

Managed identities solves this problem. It is a feature of Azure AD, which provides Azure services with an automatically managed identity in Azure AD. You can then use this identity to authenticate to every server that supports Azure AD authentication, including Key Vault, without any credentials in your code.

When you enable managed identities on your Azure resource, such as a virtual machine, Azure Function, or app, Azure will create a service principal and store the credentials of that service principal on the Azure resource itself. When it is time to authenticate, a **Managed Service Identity** (**MSI**) endpoint is called, passing your current Azure AD credentials and a reference to the specific resource.

Managed identities then retrieves the stored credentials from the Azure resource, passes it to Azure AD, and retrieves an access token that can be used to authenticate to the Azure resource or service.

You should note that the service principal is only known inside the boundaries of the specific Azure resource where it is stored. If it needs permissions for other resources as well, you should assign the appropriate role using **role-based access control** (**RBAC**) in Azure AD.

There are two types of managed identities:

- **System-assigned managed identity**: This identity is enabled directly on an Azure service instance. It is directly tied to the Azure service where it is created. It cannot be reused for other services. When the Azure service is deleted, the managed identity is deleted as well.

- **User-assigned managed identity**: This identity is created as a standalone Azure resource. After the identity is created, it can be assigned to one or more Azure service instances. Deleting the Azure service will not delete the managed identity.

In the next section, we are going to look at how to enable managed identities for a web app.

Implementing managed identities for Azure resources service principal authentication

You can enable MSI for your Azure resources in the Azure portal, PowerShell, or the CLI and by using ARM templates. In this demonstration, we are going to enable this in the Azure portal for the Azure web app that we created earlier in this chapter:

1. Navigate to the Azure portal by opening `https://portal.azure.com`.
2. Go to `PacktWebApp` that we created earlier.
3. From the overview blade of the web app, in the left menu under **Settings**, click **Identity**.
4. In the next blade, you can create a system-assigned or user-assigned managed identity. We are going to create a **System assigned** identity for this demo. Change the status to **On** and click **Save**:

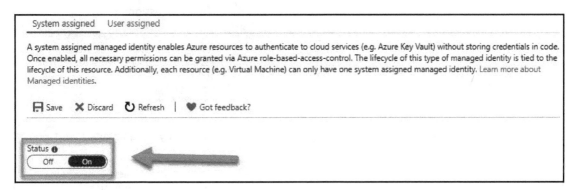

Managed identity settings

5. When the managed identity is created, we can assign permissions to it to access the Key Vault. Therefore, we first need to create the Key Vault. We will add the Key Vault to the same resource group that the web app is in. We will do this using the Azure CLI. Open Cloud Shell and add the following line of code:

```
az keyvault create --name WebAppEncryptionVault -g
"PacktAppServicePlan"
```

6. Once the Key Vault is created, navigate to it in the Azure portal. In the left menu, click **Access control (IAM)**. Then click **Add a role assignment**:

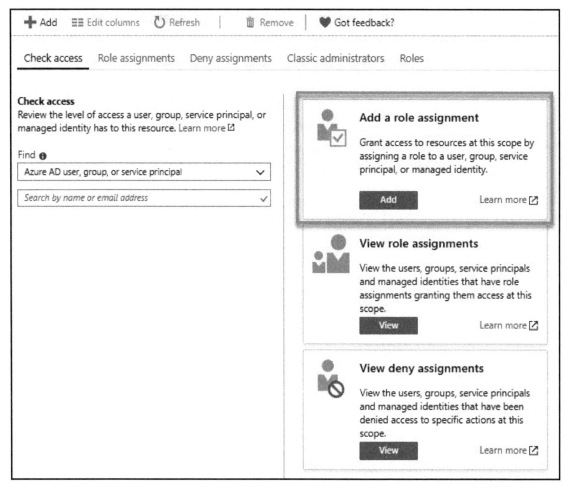

Add a role assignment

7. Then add the following values:
    - **Role**: **Key Vault Contributor**.
    - **Assign access to**: Under **System assigned managed identity**, select **App Service**.
    - **Subscription**: Pick the subscription in which the web app was created.
8. Then, you can select the managed identity that we created for the web app:

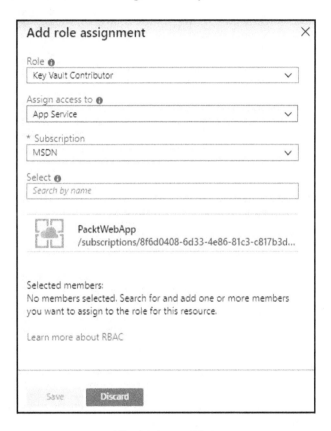

Add a role to the managed identity

9. Select the managed identity and click **Save**.
10. The managed identity now has access to the Key Vault.

From your custom code, you can call the MSI endpoint to get an access token to authenticate the Azure resource as well. For .NET applications, you can use the `Microsoft.Azure.Services.AppAuthentication` library to accomplish this. You can do this by calling the RESTful API as well, but then you have to create the request manually.

 For a sample application, you can refer to the page at `https://github.com/Azure-Samples/app-service-msi-keyvault-dotnet`.

Summary

In this chapter, we covered how to implement authentication. We covered how to implement this for Azure App Service and we covered the different authentication methods for Azure AD.

In the next chapter, we will continue with the *Implement Authentication and Secure Data* objective. We are going to cover how to implement secure data solutions.

Questions

Answer the following questions to test your knowledge of the information in this chapter. You can find the answers in the *Assessments* section at the end of this book:

1. Can authentication for App Service only be implemented from Azure AD?
    1. Yes
    2. No

2. If you want to secure your application using SSL certificates, you are required to buy that certificate from the Azure portal.
    1. Yes
    2. No

3. System-assigned managed identities can be used for multiple Azure resources.
    1. Yes
    2. No

Further reading

You can check the following links for more information about the topics that were covered in this chapter:

- **Authentication and authorization in Azure App Service**: `https://docs.microsoft.com/en-us/azure/app-service/overview-authentication-authorization`
- **Evolution of Microsoft identity platform**: `https://docs.microsoft.com/en-us/azure/active-directory/develop/about-microsoft-identity-platform`
- **Configurable token lifetimes in Azure Active Directory**: `https://docs.microsoft.com/en-us/azure/active-directory/develop/active-directory-configurable-token-lifetimes`
- **What is managed identities for Azure resources?**: `https://docs.microsoft.com/en-us/azure/active-directory/managed-identities-azure-resources/overview`

17
Implementing Secure Data Solutions

In the previous chapter, we covered the first part of the *Implement Authentication and Secure Data* objective by covering how to implement authentication for your web apps, APIs, and more.

In this chapter, we are going to cover how to implement secure data solutions. We are going to cover how to encrypt and decrypt data at rest and in transit, how to encrypt data with Always Encrypted, how to implement Azure confidential computing and SSL/TLS communications for your data, and how to create, read, update, and delete keys, secrets, and certificates by using the Key Vault API.

The following topics will be covered in this chapter:

- Understanding data security in Azure
- Encrypting and decrypting data at rest
- Encrypting and decrypting data in transit
- Encrypting data with Always Encrypted
- Understanding Azure confidential computing
- Creating, reading, updating, and deleting keys, secrets, and certificates by using the Key Vault API

Technical requirements

This chapter will use Azure PowerShell (`https://docs.microsoft.com/en-us/powershell/azure/install-az-ps?view=azps-1.8.0`), Visual Studio 2019 (`https://visualstudio.microsoft.com/vs/`), and Postman (`https://www.getpostman.com/`) for examples.

The source code for our sample application can be downloaded from `https://github.com/`
`PacktPublishing/Microsoft-Azure-Architect-Technologies-Exam-Guide-AZ-300/tree/`
`master/Chapter17`.

Understanding data security in Azure

These days, corporate data is stored, processed, and shared more than ever before. Organizations are migrating and storing more data in the cloud because they are looking for more efficient ways of doing business. This data is analyzed and used for prediction to innovate faster. To ensure that sensitive data isn't exposed to people that don't need access to it, putting security and controls in place is key.

To protect sensitive data, such as personally identifiable data, company financials, and intellectual property, Azure offers a set of features for data security and encryption. To protect your data, you need to know which state your data resides in and what controls are available for that state.

Protecting data

If you want to effectively protect your data in the cloud, you need to be aware of the different states in which data can occur, and what controls are available for that state. Azure data security encryption targets the following data states:

- **Data at rest**: This includes all containers, information storage objects, and types that exist statically on physical media, both magnetic and optical disk.
- **Data in transit**: Data is in transit when it is being transferred between programs, locations, or components. For instance, data can be transferred across a service bus, over the network (including hybrid connections, such as ExpressRoute), or during an input/output process.

Azure encryption models

Azure supports various encryption models, such as customer-managed keys in Key Vault, customer-managed keys on customer-controlled hardware, and server-side encryption using service-managed keys. You can also store and manage keys on-premises and in another secure location using client-side encryption.

Client-side encryption

Client-side encryption is performed outside of Azure; for example, data that is already encrypted when it is received in Azure, or data that is encrypted by a service application or an application that's running in the customer's data center.

By using client-side encryption, Azure doesn't have access to the encryption keys and cannot decrypt this data. This way, you maintain complete control over the keys.

Server-side encryption

Azure offers three server-side encryption models. These three models offer different key management characteristics, which can be chosen from according to the requirements of the solution:

- **Service-managed keys**: This gives low overhead because it provides a combination of controls and convenience.
- **Customer-managed keys**: Gives you control over the keys, including **Bring Your Own Keys** (**BYOK**) support, or allows you to generate new ones.
- **Service-managed keys in customer-controlled hardware**: This can be used to enable and manage keys in your own repository, outside of Microsoft control. This is also called **Host Your Own Key** (**HYOK**). However, configuration is complex, and most Azure services don't support this model.

In the next section, we are going to cover how to encrypt data at rest and in transit.

Encrypting and decrypting data at rest

Data at rest is information in any digital format that resides in persistent storage on physical media. This media also includes archived data, files on magnetic or optical media, and data backups. The variety of data storage solutions in Azure offers encryption for data at rest, such as table, blob, file, and disk storage. Azure also provides encryption to protect data in Azure SQL Database, Azure Data Lake, and Cosmos DB.

In the next section, we are going to cover data encryption and decryption at rest.

Encrypting and decrypting data at rest

Data encryption at rest is a mandatory step toward achieving data privacy and compliance. Data at rest is encrypted by default in Azure Storage and Azure SQL Database. Many other services offer default encryption as well. Azure Key Vault can be used to store the keys that access and encrypt the data. The following Azure services support one or more of the encryption-at-rest models.

Azure Disk Encryption

You can use Azure Disk Encryption to achieve encryption at rest for IaaS VMs and disks. It uses the BitLocker feature of Windows for Windows VMs, and the DM-Crypt feature of Linux for Linux VMs, to provide volume encryption for the OS and data disks of VMs in Azure.

Azure Disk Encryption is also integrated with Azure Key Vault to help control and manage disk encryption keys and secrets. It also ensures that all VM data that is stored on the VM disks is encrypted at reset while it is stored in Azure Storage. Azure Disk Encryption for Windows and Linux VMs is available for Standard VMs and VMs with Azure Premium Storage, and in all Azure public regions and government regions.

Azure Storage

All Azure Storage services (Table storage, Queue storage, Blob storage, and Azure Files) support server-side encryption at rest. All Azure Storage resources are encrypted, including blobs, disks, files, queues, and tables. All object metadata is also encrypted. Storage accounts are encrypted regardless of their performance tier (Standard or Premium) or deployment model (Azure Resource Manager or classic). All Azure Storage redundancy options support encryption, and all copies of a storage account are encrypted. Some services additionally have support for customer-managed keys and client-side encryption.

- **Server-side**: By default, service-managed keys are used by all Azure Storage services to support server-side encryption. Azure Blob storage and Azure Files also support RSA 2048-bit customer-managed keys in Azure Key Vault.
- **Client-side**: Client-side encryption is supported by Azure Blobs, Tables, and Queues. When using client-side encryption, key management is done by the customer. They also encrypt the data and upload the data as an encrypted blob.

Azure SQL Database

There is currently support for encryption at rest for Microsoft-managed server-side and client-side encryption scenarios.

- **Server-side**: This is currently provided through a feature called **Transparent Data Encryption** (**TDE**). Once TDE is enabled by the user, the TDE keys are automatically created and managed for them. TDE is enabled by default on newly created databases and stored on the physical disk in an encrypted state. It is transparent, which means that, for instance, when you create a select query, the data returns unencrypted. When you do an insert statement, the data is inserted unencrypted in the database as well. Once it is inserted, SQL Database will then encrypt the data automatically. TDE can be enabled at both the database and server level.
- **Client-side**: Client-side encryption is supported through the **Always Encrypted** feature. This uses a key that is created and stored by the user. The master key can be stored in Azure Key Vault, a Windows certificate store, or a local hardware security module. Using SQL Server Management Studio, SQL users can choose what key they would like to use to encrypt which column. Always Encrypted is covered in more detail later in this chapter.

In the next section, we are going to encrypt and decrypt blobs in Microsoft Azure Storage using Azure Key Vault.

Encrypting and decrypting blobs in Microsoft Azure Storage using Azure Key Vault

In this demonstration, we are going to encrypt and decrypt blobs in Microsoft Azure Storage using Azure Key Vault. We are going to use the Azure Storage client SDK for this. This will generate a **content encryption key** (**CEK**), which is a one-time-use symmetric key. The user can use this CEK to encrypt the data.

This CEK is then encrypted using the **key encryption key** (**KEK**). This KEK can then be managed locally, or you can store it in the Azure Key Vault. It is identified by a key identifier and can be an asymmetric key pair or a symmetric key. The storage client never has access to the KEK. The KEK will invoke a key wrapping algorithm that is provided by Azure Key Vault and the encrypted data will then be uploaded to the Azure Storage service.

The first step is to create the Key Vault. Therefore, we have to take the following steps.

Creating a storage account with a blob container

In this first step of the demonstration, we are going to create a storage account with a blob container in it. We are creating this using Azure CLI. Therefore, take the following steps:

1. Navigate to the Azure portal by opening `https://portal.azure.com/`.
2. Open **Azure Cloud Shell** and make sure that **Bash** is selected.
3. Add the following line of code to create a resource group:

   ```
   az group create --name "DataEncryptionResourceGroup" -l
   "EastUS"
   ```

4. Create a Blob storage account with a blob container (make sure that the name is unique and in lowercase):

   ```
   az storage account create \
       --name packtblobstorageaccount1 \
       --resource-group DataEncryptionResourceGroup \
       --location eastus \
       --sku Standard_LRS \
       --encryption blob
   ```

5. Display the storage account keys:

   ```
   az storage account keys list \
     --account-name packtblobstorageaccount1 \
     --resource-group DataEncryptionResourceGroup \
     --output table
   ```

6. Make note of the storage account name and the value. We are going to use this in the app settings of the application in the next section.

In the next section, we are going to create the Key Vault.

Creating an Azure Key Vault

In this first step of the demonstration, we are going to create an Azure Key Vault. We are also going to use Azure CLI for this:

1. Add the following line of code to create the Key Vault:

   ```
   az keyvault create --name PacktDataEncryptionVault -g
   "DataEncryptionResourceGroup"
   ```

We have now created the Key Vault. In the next section, we are going to create a service principal that has permission to access the Key Vault.

Creating a service principal

In the next part of this demo, we are going to create a console application to encrypt and decrypt the data. Authenticating a console application with Azure requires the use of a service principal and an access control policy.

The simplest way to authenticate any cloud-based .NET application is with a Managed Identity (see the previous chapter). However, for the sake of simplicity, this demonstration will use a console application. Authenticating a desktop application with Azure requires the use of a service principal and an access control policy.

We are going to create the service principal and the access control policy using Azure CLI in this example:

1. In Azure Cloud Shell, add the following line of code:

```
az ad sp create-for-rbac -n "http://PacktSP" --sdk-auth
```

2. The outcome will look like the following image:

```
sjoukje@Azure:~$ az ad sp create-for-rbac -n "http://PacktSP" --sdk-auth
Unable to load extension 'azure-batch-cli-extensions'. Use --debug for more information.
Creating a role assignment under the scope of "/subscriptions/8f6d0408-6d33-4e86-81c3-c817b3d7e060"
  Retrying role assignment creation: 1/36
{
  "clientId": "5aaa0b25-26e6-4466-b3dc-a0a0a1a6b7c8",
  "clientSecret": "6df4374a-a0b7-451a-a8a7-d3e2f8c4a262",
  "subscriptionId": "8f6d0408-6d33-4e86-81c3-c817b3d7e060",
  "tenantId": "233f4bcb-abf8-402b-989f-57d6500ed422",
  "activeDirectoryEndpointUrl": "https://login.microsoftonline.com",
  "resourceManagerEndpointUrl": "https://management.azure.com/",
  "activeDirectoryGraphResourceId": "https://graph.windows.net/",
  "sqlManagementEndpointUrl": "https://management.core.windows.net:8443/",
  "galleryEndpointUrl": "https://gallery.azure.com/",
  "managementEndpointUrl": "https://management.core.windows.net/"
}
sjoukje@Azure:~$ []
```

Service Principal values

3. Make a note of the `clientID` and the `clientSecret`. We are going to use this to authenticate to the Key Vault in the next step and in the final demo on using the Key Vault API.

4. Next, we need to create an access policy for your Key Vault that grants permission to your service principal. We will give the service principal get, list, and set permissions for both keys and secrets:

```
az keyvault set-policy \
 -n PacktDataEncryptionVault \
 --spn <clientId-of-your-service-principal> \
 --secret-permissions delete get list set \
 --key-permissions create decrypt delete encrypt get list
unwrapKey wrapKey
```

In this part of the demonstration, we created a service principal and created an access policy that granted the permissions to the service principal. In the next section, we are going to create a `SymmetricKey`, which is used to encrypt and decrypt the file.

Creating a SymmetricKey

In this step, we are going to create a `SymmetricKey`. The way to use a secret with client-side encryption is via the `SymmetricKey` class, because a secret is essentially a symmetric key. Therefore, we need to run a PowerShell script in Azure Cloud Shell:

```
$key = "qwertyuiopasdfgh"
$b = [System.Text.Encoding]::UTF8.GetBytes($key)
$enc = [System.Convert]::ToBase64String($b)
$secretvalue = ConvertTo-SecureString $enc -AsPlainText -Force

# Substitute the VaultName and Name in this command.
$secret = Set-AzureKeyVaultSecret -VaultName 'PacktDataEncryptionVault' -
Name 'Secret2' -SecretValue $secretvalue -ContentType "application/octet-
stream"
```

In this section, we created and stored a `SymmetricKey` key in Azure Key Vault. In the next section, we are going to create the console application.

Creating an application to encrypt and decrypt files

The Azure Key Vault client library for .NET allows you to manage keys and related assets such as certificates and secrets. The code samples next will show you how to retrieve the secret from Azure Key Vault. It then uses this secret to encrypt a file on the local system. This file will be uploaded to Azure Blob Storage, and then downloaded and decrypted as well:

1. Open Visual Studio and add a new project.
2. In the new project wizard, select **Console App (.NET Framework)** and click **Next**:

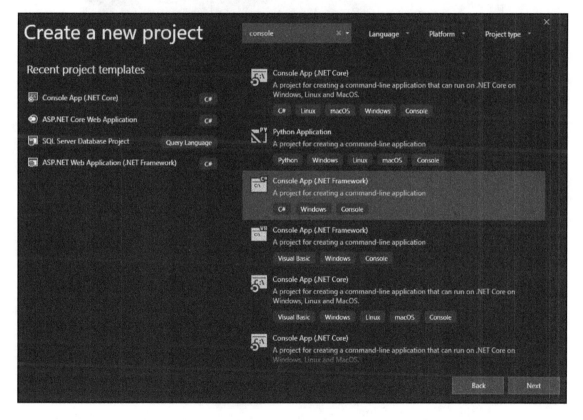

Creating a new console app

3. Add the following values and create a new project. Click **Next**:

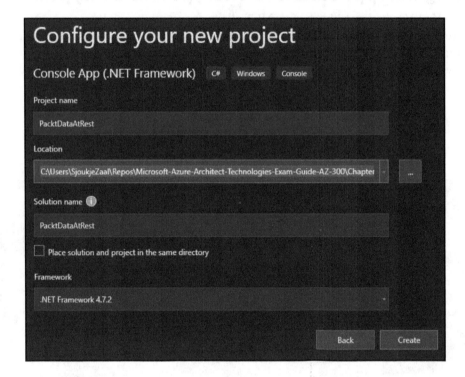

App values

4. Click **Create**.

5. The console application is now created. Open the NuGet Package Manager console and add the following packages:

```
Install-Package Microsoft.Azure.ConfigurationManager
Install-Package Microsoft.Azure.Storage.Common
Install-Package Microsoft.Azure.Storage.Blob
Install-Package Microsoft.IdentityModel.Clients.ActiveDirectory
Install-Package Microsoft.Azure.KeyVault
Install-Package Microsoft.Azure.KeyVault.Extensions
```

6. Add the following values to `App.config`:

```
<appSettings>
    <add key="accountName" value="<replace-this-with-the-
storage-account-name>"/>
    <add key="accountKey" value="<replace-this-with-the-key>"/>
    <add key="clientId" value="<replace-this-with-the-
```

```
application-id"/>
    <add key="clientSecret" value="<replace-this-with-the-
application-secret"/>
    <add key="container" value="packtcontainer"/>
</appSettings>
```

7. Replace the `accountName` value with the name of the Storage Account. Replace the `accountKey` with the key that you retrieved in the last step of the first section of this demo. Replace the `clientID` with the application ID that was registered in Azure AD and the `clientSecret` with the secret.

8. Open `Program.cs` and add the following `using` directives, and make sure to add a reference to `System.Configuration` to the project:

```csharp
using Microsoft.IdentityModel.Clients.ActiveDirectory;
using System.Configuration;
using Microsoft.Azure;
using Microsoft.Azure.Storage;
using Microsoft.Azure.Storage.Auth;
using Microsoft.Azure.Storage.Blob;
using Microsoft.Azure.KeyVault;
using System.Threading;
using System.IO;
```

9. Add a method to the `Program.cs` class to get a token to your console application. The following method is used by Key Vault classes that need to authenticate for access to your key vault:

```csharp
private async static Task<string> GetToken(string authority,
string resource, string scope)
        {
            var authContext = new
AuthenticationContext(authority);
            ClientCredential clientCred = new ClientCredential(
CloudConfigurationManager.GetSetting("clientId"),
CloudConfigurationManager.GetSetting("clientSecret"));
            AuthenticationResult result = await
authContext.AcquireTokenAsync(resource, clientCred);

            if (result == null)
                throw new InvalidOperationException("Failed to
obtain the JWT token");

            return result.AccessToken;
        }
```

10. In the `Main()` method, add the following code to interact with the blob container. If this container doesn't exist, it will get created. Then, use the `KeyVaultKeyResolver` to retrieve the token:

```
// This is standard code to interact with Blob storage.
StorageCredentials creds = new StorageCredentials(
      CloudConfigurationManager.GetSetting("accountName"),
      CloudConfigurationManager.GetSetting("accountKey")
      );
CloudStorageAccount account = new CloudStorageAccount(creds,
useHttps: true);
CloudBlobClient client = account.CreateCloudBlobClient();
CloudBlobContainer contain =
client.GetContainerReference(CloudConfigurationManager.GetSetti
ng("container"));
contain.CreateIfNotExists();

// The Resolver object is used to interact with Key Vault for
Azure Storage.
// This is where the GetToken method from above is used.
KeyVaultKeyResolver cloudResolver = new
KeyVaultKeyResolver(GetToken);
```

11. Now, create a `Temp` folder on your `C` drive and create a file with some text in it. Call this file `PacktFile.txt`.

12. Then below the previous code, add the following. This will retrieve the secret that we create in PowerShell in the previous section. Then, it will use this key to encrypt the file:

```
// Retrieve the secret that you created previously.
SymmetricKey sec =
(SymmetricKey)cloudResolver.ResolveKeyAsync(
"https://packtdataencryptionvault.vault.azure.net/secrets/Secre
t2/",
CancellationToken.None).GetAwaiter().GetResult();

// Now you simply use the SimmetricKey to encrypt by setting
it in the BlobEncryptionPolicy.
BlobEncryptionPolicy policy = new BlobEncryptionPolicy(sec,
null);
BlobRequestOptions options = new BlobRequestOptions() {
EncryptionPolicy = policy };

// Reference a block blob.
CloudBlockBlob blob =
contain.GetBlockBlobReference("PacktFile.txt");
```

```
//Upload using the UploadFromStream method.
using (var stream =
System.IO.File.OpenRead(@"C:\Temp\PacktFile.txt"))
        blob.UploadFromStream(stream, stream.Length, null,
options, null);
```

13. Last, we can decrypt the file, as well, by passing the resolver. Therefore, below
    the previous code, add the following:

```
BlobEncryptionPolicy policy1 = new BlobEncryptionPolicy(null,
cloudResolver);
BlobRequestOptions options1 = new BlobRequestOptions() {
EncryptionPolicy = policy1 };

using (var np = File.Open(@"C:\Temp\MyFileDecrypted.txt",
FileMode.Create))
        blob.DownloadToStream(np, null, options1, null);
```

We have now encrypted a text file and uploaded it to Azure Blob Storage, using a secret
that is stored in Azure Key Vault. We then downloaded and decrypted the file to our local
system.

We have now concluded this demo. In the next section, we are going to cover how to
encrypt and decrypt data in transit.

Encrypting and decrypting data in transit

Data that moves from one location to another is kept private by the different mechanisms
that Azure has to offer. The different mechanisms are described in the following sections.

TLS/SSL encryption in Azure

Data that is moving between cloud services and customers is protected by the **Transport
Layer Security** (**TLS**) protocol. TLS provides strong authentication, algorithm
flexibility, interoperability, message privacy, ease of deployment and use, and integrity
(enabling detection of message tampering, interception, and forgery).

Connections between customers' client systems and Microsoft cloud services are also protected by **Perfect Forward Secrecy** (**PFS**) using unique keys. PFS is an encryption style that produces temporary private key exchanges between clients and servers. For every individual session initiated by a user, a unique session key is generated. Connections also use RSA-based 2,048-bit encryption key lengths. This combination makes it difficult for someone to intercept and access data that is in transit.

Azure Storage transactions

All transactions with Azure Storage through the Azure portal take place over HTTPS. You can also use the storage REST API over HTTPS to interact with Azure Storage. When you call the REST API, you can enforce that the call is being made over HTTPS to access objects in storage accounts. To enforce this, you need to enable the secure transfer that's required for the storage account.

When you use shared access signatures to delegate access to Azure Storage objects, you can enable an option that only allows for the HTTPS protocol to be used when you use shared access signatures. This will ensure that links with SAS tokens use the proper protocol.

Azure Files uses **Server Message Block** (**SMB**) 3.0 encryption, which also supports encryption. It's available in Windows 8, Windows 8.1, Windows 10, and Windows Server 2012 R2. It allows cross-region access and even access on the desktop.

The data is encrypted by client-side encryption before it is transferred to the Azure Storage instance, so the data is encrypted as it travels across the network.

SMB encryption over Azure virtual networks

For VMs running on Windows Server 2012 and later, the SMB 3.0 protocol can be used. By encrypting data that is using SMB 3.0, data in transit over Azure Virtual Networks can be secured. This encryption can help protect against tampering and eavesdropping attacks. SMB encryption for specific shares or for the entire server can be enabled by administrators.

By default, after SMB encryption is turned on for a share or server, only SMB 3.0 clients are allowed to access the encrypted shares.

In-transit encryption in VMs

Depending on the nature of the connection, data in transit to, from, and between VMs that are running Windows is encrypted in a number of ways:

- **RDP sessions**: From a Windows client computer, you can connect and sign in to a VM using the **Remote Desktop Protocol** (**RDP**). From a Mac, you can connect with an RDP client installed. This can protect data in transit over the network using TLS. You can also use RDP to connect to a Linux VM in Azure.
- **Secure access to Linux VMs with SSH**: To manage Linux VMs in Azure, you can use the **Secure Shell** (**SSH**) for remote management. This is an encrypted protocol that allows secure logins over unsecured connections. SSH uses a public/private key pair (asymmetric encryption) for authentication, which eliminates the need for passwords to sign in.

Azure VPN encryption

To protect the privacy of the data that is being sent across the network, you can connect to Azure using a **virtual private network** (**VPN**). This VPN connection can create a private tunnel to access the data.

 Azure VPN is covered in more detail in `Chapter 11`, *Integrating On-Premises Networks with Azure Virtual Network*. So, this chapter will just briefly cover the different options.

- **Azure VPN gateways**: Azure VPN Gateway can be used to send encrypted traffic between virtual networks, and between virtual networks and on-premises locations across a public connection.
- **Site-to-site VPN**: A site-to-site VPN uses IPSec for transport encryption. By default, Azure VPN Gateway uses a set of default proposals. Azure VPN Gateway can also be configured to use a custom IPsec/IKE policy with specific cryptographic algorithms and key strengths.

    This can be used to connect your on-premises network to an Azure virtual network over an IPsec/IKE (IKEv1 or IKEv2) VPN tunnel. It is required for this type of connection to have an on-premises VPN device in place that has an external-facing public IP address assigned to it.

- **Point-to-site VPN**: By using a point-to-site VPN, individual client computers are allowed to access the Azure virtual network. The **Secure Socket Tunneling Protocol** (**SSTP**) is used to create the VPN tunnel. For connectivity, you can use your own internal **public key infrastructure** (**PKI**) root **certificate authority** (**CA**).
- **Data Lake**: The Data Lake Store encrypts the data in transit by default. Data in transit is secured by an HTTPS connection. This is the only protocol that is supported by the Data Lake Store REST interfaces.

This concludes this section. In the next section, we are going to cover how to encrypt data with Always Encrypted.

Encrypting data with Always Encrypted

Always Encrypted is a database encryption technology that can secure sensitive data stored in an Azure SQL Database and SQL Server on-premises, such as credit card numbers or national identification numbers (for example, U.S. social security numbers). It helps protect data at rest on the server, during movement between the client and the server. While this data is in use, it can ensure sensitive data never appears as plaintext inside the database system.

The client encrypts the data inside the application and the encryption keys are never revealed to the Database Engine (SQL Database or SQL Server). This results in Always Encrypted separating the data into who owns the data (and can view it), and who stores and manages the data (but should not have access to it). This way, organizations can confidently store sensitive data securely without having control over it, ensuring that on-premises database administrators, cloud database operators, and other unauthorized users cannot access the encrypted data.

An Always Encrypted-enabled driver needs to be installed on the client computer. The sensitive data is automatically encrypted and decrypted in the client application using this driver. The columns that have sensitive data stored in them will be encrypted before they are passed to the database engine. The driver will also rewrite the queries, and decrypt the data that is displayed in query results.

Always Encrypted is available in Azure SQL Database and SQL Server 2016 (13.x). Prior to SQL Server 2016 (13.x) SP1, Always Encrypted was limited to the Enterprise Edition.

For an example on how to configure Always Encrypted for your database, and creating an application that encrypts the data, you can refer to the following tutorial: `https://docs.microsoft.com/en-us/azure/sql-database/sql-database-always-encrypted`. I highly advise taking a good look at this tutorial, as it may be part of the exam.

In the next section, we are going to cover how to implement Azure confidential computing and SSL/TLS communications.

Understanding Azure confidential computing

In the previous sections, we covered how to secure data at rest and in transit, but you also need to protect data from threats as it's being processed. In many cases, poorly configured access control will result in breaches. However, most breaches can be traced to data that is accessed while it is in use. This can be done through administrative accounts and by using compromised keys to access the encrypted data. This is the main reason why customers are not willing to move their most sensitive data to the cloud.

Azure confidential computing offers protection for data in use. By using **Trusted Execution Environments (TEEs)** or encryption mechanisms to protect your data while in use, new data security capabilities are added by confidential computing. This means that data can be processed in the cloud with the assurance that it is always under customer control. A TEE can be implemented using hardware or software. The hardware secures a portion of the processor and memory by providing a protected container. Running and accessing data is only allowed by authorized code. This way, code and data are protected against viewing and modification from outside of the TEE.

Azure Confidential Computing works together with Intel SGX technology to address the following threads:

- Malicious insiders with administrative privilege or direct access to the hardware on which it is being processed.
- Hackers and malware that exploit bugs in the operating system, application, or hypervisor.
- Third parties accessing it without the owner's consent.

Azure offers the following hardware, software, and services that support confidential computing:

- **Hardware and Compute**: The DC-series of VMs enables the latest generation of Intel Xeon Processors with Intel SGX technology.
- **Development**: You can use the Open Enclave SDK, which provides an API around an enclaving abstraction, supporting portability across enclave types and flexibility in architecture. You can build C/C++ portable applications.
- **Attestation**: Verifying the identity of code running in TEEs is necessary to establish trust with that code to determine whether to release secrets to it.
- **Research**: Microsoft Research is actively researching advanced techniques to harden TEE application to prevent information leaks outside the TEE, both direct or indirect. This research will be brought to market in the form of tooling and runtimes for your use in developing confidential code.

In the next section, we are going to cover how you can use the Key Vault API to create, read, update, and delete keys and certificates.

Creating, reading, updating, and deleting keys, secrets, and certificates by using the Key Vault API

In the previous demo, we already created an application that uses the Key Vault SDK to retrieve keys from Azure Key Vault, and that can encrypt and decrypt data at rest. In this demonstration, we are going to create, read, update, and delete keys and certificates using the API. Therefore, we are going to use the service principal that we created in the previous demo to connect to the Key Vault. This service principal already has permissions to the Key Vault.

We are also going to use Postman as an API client to create requests to the API. Under the *Technical requirements* section, at the beginning of this chapter, you can click the link to install Postman.

 For those who are unfamiliar with Postman, you can refer to the following website for more information, at `https://www.getpostman.com/product/api-client`.

In this demonstration, I will create a couple of examples using the Azure Key Vault API. For more examples, you can refer to the Azure Key Vault REST API reference, available at `https://docs.microsoft.com/en-us/rest/api/keyvault/`.

1. Open Postman and log in or create an account. In **Request**, add the following (make sure that you replace the `{tenant_id}` in the request URL with the correct Azure AD tenant ID):

   ```
   POST
   https://login.microsoftonline.com/{tenant_id}/oauth2/token?api-
   version=1.0
   ```

2. Click **Body** in the top menu and add the following values:

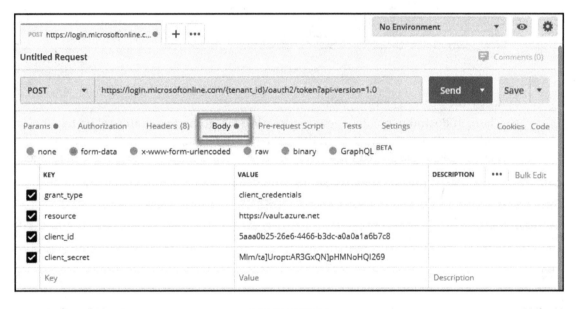

Requesting a bearer token

3. Click **Send**.

4. The output will look like the following:

Bearer token output

5. Copy the `access_token` value.

6. Then, in Postman, create a new request. We are going to use this token for authorization and pass it on in the request. Therefore, we need to create an **Authorization** key with the value: `Bearer <token>`, as in the following image:

Adding a token to the request

7. We now successfully authenticated to Azure Key Vault using the service principal credentials. We also added the `Bearer` token to the header of the request. Now, we can create some queries. First, let's start by retrieving secrets in Azure Key Vault. In Postman, add the following values and click **Send**:

- **Request Type and URL**: GET
  ```
  https://packtdataencryptionvault.vault.azure.net/secret
  s?api-version=7.0
  ```

8. This will result in an output displaying all the secrets that are in the vault:

```
Body   Cookies   Headers (15)   Test Results          Status: 200 OK   Time: 1016ms   Size: 1.39 KB   Save Response ▼

Pretty    Raw    Preview    Visualize BETA    JSON ▼    ⇥                                          ▣  Q

1   {
2       "value": [
3           {
4               "id": "https://packtdataencryptionvault.vault.azure.net/secrets/clientID",
5               "attributes": {
6                   "enabled": true,
7                   "created": 1570474741,
8                   "updated": 1570474741,
9                   "recoveryLevel": "Purgeable"
10              },
11              "tags": {
12                  "file-encoding": "utf-8"
13              }
14          },
15          {
16              "id": "https://packtdataencryptionvault.vault.azure.net/secrets/clientSecret",
17              "attributes": {
18                  "enabled": true,
19                  "created": 1570457772,
20                  "updated": 1570457772,
21                  "recoveryLevel": "Purgeable"
22              },
23              "tags": {
24                  "file-encoding": "utf-8"
25              }
26          },
```

Secrets in the vault

9. To create a secret, select **Body** from the top menu in Postman and make sure that **raw** and **JSON** is selected:

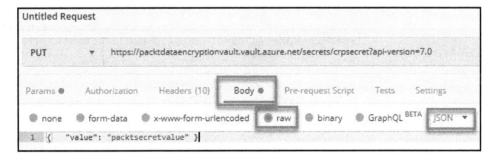

Postman settings

10. Then, add the following to create a secret:
    - HTTP:

    ```
    PUT {vaultBaseUrl}/secrets/crpsecret?api-version=7.0
    ```

    - Request Body:

    ```
    {   "value": "packtsecretvalue" }
    ```

    - Response:

    ```
    {
        "value": "packtsecretvalue",
        "id":
    "https://packtdataencryptionvault.vault.azure.net/secr
    ets/crpsecret/78508744072e4d1ea9c780fd9c31ecd0",
        "attributes": {
            "enabled": true,
            "created": 1570543118,
            "updated": 1570543118,
            "recoveryLevel": "Purgeable"
        }
    }
    ```

11. To delete the secret, add the following:
    - HTTP:

    ```
    DELETE {vaultBaseUrl}/secrets/crpsecret?api-
    version=7.0
    ```

    - Response:

    ```
    {
        "id":
    "https://packtdataencryptionvault.vault.azure.net/secr
    ets/crpsecret/41fa843e28104c9bbed7d6f89baf5390",
        "attributes": {
            "enabled": true,
            "created": 1570543575,
            "updated": 1570543575,
            "recoveryLevel": "Purgeable"
        }
    }
    ```

12. To create a key, add the following to Postman:
    - HTTP:

      ```
      POST {vaultBaseUrl}/keys/CreateSoftKeyTest/create?api-
      version=7.0
      ```

    - Request Body:

      ```
      {
        "kty": "RSA",
        "key_size": 2048,
        "key_ops": [
          "encrypt",
          "decrypt",
          "sign",
          "verify",
          "wrapKey",
          "unwrapKey"
        ],
        "attributes": {},
        "tags": {
          "purpose": "unit test",
          "test name ": "CreateGetDeleteKeyTest"
        }
      }
      ```

    - Response:

      ```
      {
          "key": {
              "kid":
      "https://packtdataencryptionvault.vault.azure.net/keys
      /CreateSoftKeyTest/66c103e3dd1c4cff8f86b9221c9c8419",
              "kty": "RSA",
              "key_ops": [
                  "encrypt",
                  "decrypt",
                  "sign",
                  "verify",
                  "wrapKey",
                  "unwrapKey"
              ],
              "n":
      "rJqJLUORU_jz1Yvt4CJt49VJ7VwIGcYQ5SF6ioegtUSZqX7thAKR-
      2e294tQPm68rtH1yxtzSinj2b6tJUtKWULOoxvh0FoV_ppR1PXEQck
      fy-Xlcd8M0AwjZ9xvHnsBv3DV2dyjf4z4aXmP2y7V7EGwJ__KtG-
      PDYPKS5sKTKmOkFTDLV8V0OJVQ0dNtuSstqIcTMiSEH27SWMKqwk0U
      ```

```
yodneMEOrYNNMC-
H5Jpm5mmexzi7j1w6jgjVGsJDrCGe6io1USzbLB7Y4NK1_kJ_OyV5d
5qxAOfGWtX6X1g6kJUWR8pc2Q0oaGhEpj5ksTIhIcDlJ2ZriaLyrI9
KemIyQ",
        "e": "AQAB"
    },
    "attributes": {
        "enabled": true,
        "created": 1570544847,
        "updated": 1570544847,
        "recoveryLevel": "Purgeable"
    },
    "tags": {
        "purpose": "unit test",
        "test name ": "CreateGetDeleteKeyTest"
    }
}
```

13. To delete a key, add the following to Postman:
    - HTTP:

    ```
    DELETE {vaultBaseUrl}/keys/CreateSoftKeyTest?api-
    version=7.0
    ```

    - Response:

```
{
    "key": {
        "kid":
"https://packtdataencryptionvault.vault.azure.net/keys
/CreateSoftKeyTest/e9d35e5432ad4da48239f725af90b733",
        "kty": "RSA",
        "key_ops": [
            "encrypt",
            "decrypt",
            "sign",
            "verify",
            "wrapKey",
            "unwrapKey"
        ],
        "n": "p8YP98mvABmPFEGwxLw-
WdyouR7DiG9prJ5t4KLLDEq9uXpRnZMmnq2zmN2-
XL333Hpj6wzJpmu5mM1LtgiUnAZMcYjx-
RSXyTk1ftdC50ahNrUwBIcqVG8M3hfrC-
JbVd2d0RCfusMHpcU1S8HgRe2cUZ-h4yeo5PVFy0MrkKXRtVVj-
qnKB1tMPbCDVxboTYEvMQxKP8YqHnxaMMDwySgFjLa3UCJMj1zyI5f
I-dCjLGYSSeeO_e19jn2DoWro83VQGOI-
K7uBj1qf82_D38xIIBc7qEFth_7dTj87hW0DkXnpa-63jycU69rSS5
```

```
PlsZXiUjfltwT8Y13yFFGqfQ",
            "e": "AQAB"
    },
    "attributes": {
        "enabled": true,
        "created": 1570545206,
        "updated": 1570545206,
        "recoveryLevel": "Purgeable"
    },
    "tags": {
        "purpose": "unit test",
        "test name ": "CreateGetDeleteKeyTest"
    }
}
```

14. To create a certificate, add the following:
    - HTTP:

    ```
    POST
    {vaultBaseUrl}/certificates/selfSignedCert01/create?api-version=7.0
    ```

    - Body:

    ```
    {
    "policy": {
    "key_props": {
    "exportable": true,
    "kty": "RSA",
    "key_size": 2048,
    "reuse_key": false
    },
    "secret_props": {
    "contentType": "application/x-pkcs12"
    },
    "x509_props": {
    "subject": "CN=*.sjoukjezaal.com",
    "sans": {
    "dns_names": [
    "test.sjoukjezaal.com",
    ]
    }
    },
    "issuer": {
    "name": "Self"
    }
    }
    }
    ```

- Response:

```
{
 "id":
 "https://packtdataencryptionvault.vault.azure.net/cert
 ificates/selfSignedCert01/pending",
 "issuer": {
 "name": "Self"
 },
 "csr":
 "MIICzTCCAbUCAQAwHDEaMBgGA1UEAwwRKi5zam91a2plemFhbC5jb
 20wggEiMA0GCSqGSIb3DQEBAQUAA4IBDwAwggEKAoIBAQCwQvaRmmI
 nr85fNLPoOU0wkbAhr2H/56h1g+zfXuILtUtQgG9OGXYPewWGYek7E
 j0KnGinuDT1E06q0RlmLlFs1CbeFWK1TJ8J1Vnv0kzZM71mBGf7fDe
 lBtvxpK2q1tCXWv3HokkMkhBJPZZWSd4cyGSGG9kNkcS2cmEHtIAlP
 90834URB0ZQI0ksFegxgeVulKP3umS//0SSWsfJVgkeaM5DRTujnTh
 UxkHXsJI9P9Wc8R6OoQxsnz8e2KQlFLamLM6iCz57F1winCbU9E5IZ
 p19N9WwpGxEiJS7Qj6Ib/8tt9+Vh+bnSzM6kOY3/xn3tVF8LvoCmIS
 728KZEjSPAgMBAAGgbDBqBgkqhkiG9w0BCQ4xXTBbMA4GA1UdDwEB/
 wQEAwIFoDAdBgNVHSUEFjAUBggrBgEFBQcDAQYIKwYBBQUHAwIwHwY
 DVR0RBBgwFoIUdGVzdC5zam91a2plemFhbC5jb20wCQYDVR0TBAIwA
 DANBgkqhkiG9w0BAQsFAAOCAQEAK2vrug9pjPmz94zRVc6eD9PNwUm
 DvnBoffuV17lKjIuqvuvaEeB40C3TmD38+0oHEVSoX0GEjJxt+NNly
 HP5wkkkb014otqAO5G15/euMTr1hwgJVPQojlEOP8uOf4kIDQp6sVD
 BwmMLnQrhWzrBAir1Rqcpeh/WB2Yt8E/VVsgLCnA9CwSmEwEX+HqJO
 m25KN28Bs9HiGk9NeQhUEWNfXNHRo46SF63K0/qfXgIZw/R191jhBo
 BOWjJ2/itAM1mqxfjO1N7Qf5pFhL0+ChD0/eFYiKX1r8Abem22ohvN
 D3Lc8IY2vH4LpZj7LjGk0IEO+Kog6A3JvC+bKi+nwiOCw==",
 "cancellation_requested": false,
 "status": "inProgress",
 "status_details": "Pending certificate created.
 Certificate request is in progress. This may take some
 time based on the issuer provider. Please check again
 later.",
 "request_id": "133c0973768b4fdda836b85b7d50cf41"
}
```

15. For this last request, I needed to add more permissions to the service principal in the Key Vault. Therefore, go to the Azure portal and navigate to the Key Vault overview blade. In the left menu, select **Access Policies**. There, you can add and remove the required permissions:

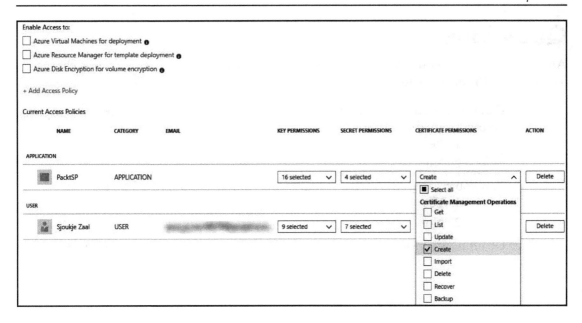

Changing the Service Principal permissions

In this demonstration, we covered how to use the Key Vault API to create, update, and delete keys, secrets, and more. This concludes this chapter.

Summary

In this chapter, we've covered how to implement secure data solutions. We covered how to encrypt data at rest and in transit. We also covered how to use the Key Vault API to create keys, secrets, and certificates.

In the next chapter, we will start with the last objective of this book: the *Developing for the Cloud and for Azure Storage* objective. We are going to cover how to develop solutions that use Cosmos DB storage.

Questions

Answer the following questions to test your knowledge of the information in this chapter. You can find the answers in the *Assessments* section at the end of this book:

1. Can you use Always Encrypted to encrypt data at rest using Azure Key Vault in your custom applications?
    1. Yes
    2. No
2. Can you create certificates in Azure Key Vault using the Key Vault API?
    1. Yes
    2. No
3. Do all Azure Storage services, except for Queue Storage, support server-side encryption at rest?
    1. Yes
    2. No

Further reading

You can check the following links for more information about the topics that are covered in this chapter:

- **Azure Disk Encryption overview**: https://docs.microsoft.com/en-us/azure/security/fundamentals/encryption-overview
- **Client-Side Encryption and Azure Key Vault for Microsoft Azure Storage**: https://docs.microsoft.com/en-us/azure/storage/common/storage-client-side-encryption
- **Always Encrypted (Database Engine)**: https://docs.microsoft.com/en-us/sql/relational-databases/security/encryption/always-encrypted-database-engine?redirectedfrom=MSDNamp;amp;view=sql-server-2017
- **Azure confidential computing**: https://azure.microsoft.com/en-us/blog/azure-confidential-computing/

Section 5: Developing for the Cloud and for Azure Storage

As this section's objective, you will learn how to develop for the cloud and create and deploy apps in Azure.

This section contains the following chapters:

- Chapter 18, *Developing Solutions That Use Cosmos DB Storage*
- Chapter 19, *Developing Solutions That Use a Relational Database*
- Chapter 20, *Message-Based Integration Architecture and Autoscaling*
- Chapter 21, *Mock Questions*
- Chapter 22, *Mock Answers*

18
Developing Solutions That Use Cosmos DB Storage

In the previous chapter, we covered the last part of the *Implementing Authentication and Secure data* objective by covering how to implement secure data solutions. We've covered how to encrypt and decrypt data at rest and in transit, Azure Confidential Compute, and more.

In this chapter, we are introducing the final objective: *Developing for the Cloud and for Azure Storage*. We are going to cover how to develop solutions that use Cosmos DB storage. We are going to cover how to create, read, update, and delete data by using appropriate APIs, how to set the appropriate consistency level for operations, and we will cover the different partition schemes.

The following topics will be covered in this chapter:

- Understanding Cosmos DB
- Create, read, update, and delete data by using appropriate APIs
- Understanding partitioning schemes
- Setting the appropriate consistency level for operations

Technical requirements

This chapter will use Visual Studio 2019 (`https://visualstudio.microsoft.com/vs/`) for examples.

The source code for our sample application can be downloaded from `https://github.com/PacktPublishing/Microsoft-Azure-Architect-Technologies-Exam-Guide-AZ-300/tree/master/Chapter18`.

Understanding Cosmos DB

Cosmos DB storage is the premium offering for Azure Table storage. It's a multimodel and globally distributed database service that is designed to horizontally scale and replicate your data to any number of Azure regions. By replicating and scaling the data, Cosmos DB can guarantee low latency, high availability, and high performance anywhere in the world. You can replicate or scale data easily inside the Azure portal by selecting the available regions on the map.

This high availability and low latency makes Cosmos DB most suitable for mobile applications, games, and applications that need to be globally distributed. The Azure portal also uses Cosmos DB for data storage. Cosmos DB is completely schemaless, and you can use a number of existing APIs with available SDKs to communicate with it. So, if you are using a specific API for your data and you want to move your data to Cosmos DB, all you need to do is change the connection string inside your application and the data is stored in Cosmos DB automatically.

Cosmos DB offers the following key benefits:

- **Turnkey global distribution**: With Cosmos DB, you can build highly responsive and highly available applications that scale globally. All data is transparently replicated to the regions where your users are, so they can interact with a replica of the data that is closest to them. Azure regions can easily be added and removed. Data will then seamlessly replicate to the selected regions without any downtime of the application.
- **Always on**: Cosmos DB provides an SLA with 99.99% high availability for both reads and writes. To ensure that your application is designed to fail over in case of regional disasters, Cosmos DB provides the ability to invoke regional failover using the Azure portal, or programmatically.
- **Worldwide elastic scalability of throughput and storage**: Elastic scalability to both reads and writes is offered by Cosmos DB. By a single API call, you can elastically scale up from thousands to hundreds of millions of requests per second around the globe, and you only pay for the throughput and storage you need.
- **No schema or index management**: With Cosmos DB, you don't have to deal with schema or index management, which is a painful process for globally distributed apps. Without schema and index management, there is also no downtime for applications while migrating schemas. Cosmos DB automatically indexes all data and serves queries fast.
- **Secured by default**: All data in Cosmos DB is encrypted at rest and in motion. Cosmos also provides row-level authorization.

Cosmos DB supports the following APIs for storing and interacting with your data:

- **SQL API**: With the SQL API, you can use SQL queries as a JSON query language against the dataset inside Cosmos DB. Because Cosmos DB is schemaless, it provides autoindexing of the JSON documents. Data is stored on SSD drives for low latency, and it is lock-free, so you can create real-time queries for your data. Cosmos DB also supports writing stored procedures, triggers, and **user-defined functions** (**UDFs**) in JavaScript, and it supports **ACID** (short for **Atomicity, Consistency, Isolation, Durability**) transactions inside a collection.

- **MongoDB API**: MongoDB is an open source document database that provides high performance, high availability, and automatic scaling by default. Using it inside Cosmos DB provides automatic sharding, indexing, replication, and encryption of your data on top of this. MongoDB also provides an aggregation pipeline that can be used to filter and transform the data in multiple stages. It also supports creating a full-text index, and you can integrate it easily with Azure Search and other Azure services as well.

- **Gremlin (Graph) API**: The Gremlin API is part of the Apache TinkerPop project, which is an open source graph computing framework. A graph is a way of storing objects (nodes) based on relationships. Each object can have multiple relations with other objects. You can interact with the data using JavaScript.

- **Table API**: The Azure Table API can be used for applications that are written for using Azure Table storage, but need the premium features, such as global distribution, automatic indexing, low latency, and high throughput.

- **Cassandra API**: The Cassandra API can be used for applications that are written for Apache Cassandra. Apache Cassandra is an open source distributed NoSQL database that offers scalability and high availability. Cosmos DB offers no operations management, SLA, and automatic indexing on top of this.

- **Etcd API (preview)**: The etcd API, allows you to use Azure Cosmos DB as the backend store for Azure Kubernetes. In Kubernetes, etcd is used to store the state and the configuration of the Kubernetes clusters. Azure Cosmos DB implements the etcd wired protocol. Developers can use this API to scale Kubernetes state management worldwide using Cosmos DB.

In the future, new APIs will be added to Cosmos DB as well.

In the next section, we are going to create, read, update, and delete data by using appropriate APIs.

Create, read, update, and delete data by using appropriate APIs

Before we can create, read, update, and delete data using the APIs, we first need to create a Cosmos DB in Azure. We will do this in the following subsection.

Creating a Cosmos DB

You can create a Cosmos DB using the Azure portal, PowerShell, CLI, and ARM templates. In this demonstration, we are going to create a Cosmos DB server, database, and container from the Azure portal. Therefore, you have to take the following steps:

1. Navigate to the Azure portal by opening `https://portal.azure.com`.
2. Click **Create a resource**, type `Azure Cosmos DB` in the search bar and create a new database server.
3. Add the following values:
   - **Subscription**: Pick a subscription.
   - **Resource group**: Create a new one and call it `PacktCosmosResourceGroup`.
   - **Account name**: `packtsqlapi`.
   - **API**: **Core (SQL)**.
   - **Location**: **East US**.
   - **Geo-Redundancy**: **Disable**.
   - **Multi-region Writes**: **Disable**.
   - **Availability Zones**: **Disable**.
4. Click **Review + create** and then **Create**.
5. When the deployment is finished, open the resource. The Quickstart is automatically opened, and there, you can let Azure automatically create a database and a container, and download a sample app in the language of your choice:

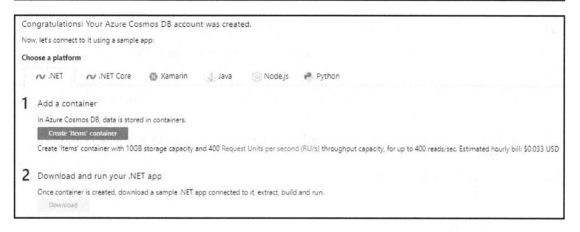

Create a sample application directly from the Azure portal

6. You can also create your database and container using the Data Explorer. Click **Data Explorer** in the left menu. In the top menu, click **New container**. In the **Add container** blade, add the following values:

- **Database id**: `PacktToDoList`
- **Throughput**: `400` (provisioning the throughput at the database level will be shared across unlimited containers)
- **Container id**: `Items`
- **Partition Key**: `/category`

7. Click **OK**.

In this demonstration, we created a database server, a database, and container from the Azure portal. In the next section, we are going to create an application that creates a database and container programmatically. Then we will create, read, update, and delete data using the APIs.

Creating the sample application

In this second part of the demonstration, we are going to create the sample application. For this, we are going to create a new console application in Visual Studio 2019. We will first connect to our Cosmos DB account.

Connecting to the Cosmos DB account

The first step is to connect to the Cosmos DB account that we already created in the previous exercise, as follows:

1. Open Visual Studio and create a new Console App (.NET) project.

2. Name the project `PacktCosmosApp`.

3. Right-click your project in the Solution Explorer and select **Manage NuGet packages**.

4. Select **Browse**, search for `Microsoft.Azure.Cosmos`, and install the package.

5. Open `Program.cs` and replace the references with the following:

```
using System;
using System.Threading.Tasks;
using System.Configuration;
using System.Collections.Generic;
using System.Net;
using Microsoft.Azure.Cosmos;
```

6. Add the following variables in the `Program.cs` method:

```
// Azure Cosmos DB endpoint.
        private static readonly string EndpointUri = "<your
endpoint here>";
        // Primary key for the Azure Cosmos account.
        private static readonly string PrimaryKey = "<your primary
key>";

        // The Cosmos client instance
        private CosmosClient cosmosClient;

        // The database we will create
        private Database database;

        // The container we will create.
        private Container container;

        // The name of the database and container we will create
        private string databaseId = "FamilyDatabase";
        private string containerId = "FamilyContainer";
```

7. Now, go back to the Azure portal. Navigate to the Cosmos DB that we created in the previous step and under **Settings**, select **Keys**. Copy both the keys:

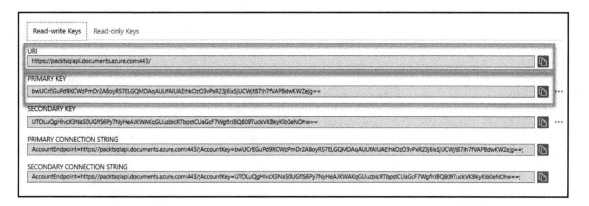

8. In `Program.cs`, replace `<your endpoint here>` with the URI that you've copied. Then, replace `<your primary key>` with the primary key you just copied.

   Replace the `Main()` method with the following:

   ```
   public static async Task Main(string[] args)
   {
   }
   ```

9. Below the `Main` method, add a new asynchronous task called `GetStartedDemoAsync`, which instantiates our new `CosmosClient`. We use `GetStartedDemoAsync` as the entry point that calls methods that operate on Azure Cosmos DB resources:

   ```
   public async Task GetStartedDemoAsync()
   {
       this.cosmosClient = new CosmosClient(EndpointUri, PrimaryKey);
   }
   ```

10. Add the following code to run the `GetStartedDemoAsync` synchronous task from your `Main` method:

    ```
    public static async Task Main(string[] args)
            {
                try
                {
                    Console.WriteLine("Beginning operations...\n");
                    Program p = new Program();
    ```

```
                       await p.GetStartedDemoAsync();

               }
               catch (CosmosException de)
               {
                   Exception baseException = de.GetBaseException();
                   Console.WriteLine("{0} error occurred: {1}",
       de.StatusCode, de);
               }
               catch (Exception e)
               {
                   Console.WriteLine("Error: {0}", e);
               }
               finally
               {
                   Console.WriteLine("End of demo, press any key to
       exit.");
                   Console.ReadKey();
               }
           }
```

If you now run the application, the console will display the message: **End of demo, press any key to exit**. This means that the application successfully connected to the Cosmos DB account.

Now that we've successfully connected to the Cosmos DB account, we can create a new database.

Creating a new database

To create a new database, take the following steps:

1. Now, we can create a database. Copy and paste the CreateDatabaseAsync method below your GetStartedDemoAsync method:

```
   private async Task CreateDatabaseAsync()
       {
           // Create a new database
           this.database = await
   this.cosmosClient.CreateDatabaseIfNotExistsAsync(databaseId);
           Console.WriteLine("Created Database: {0}\n",
   this.database.Id);
       }
```

2. In the `GetStartedDemoAsync` method, you should now add the line of code to call the `CreateDatabaseAsync` method. The method will now look like the following:

```
public async Task GetStartedDemoAsync()
        {
                // Create a new instance of the Cosmos Client
                this.cosmosClient = new CosmosClient(EndpointUri,
PrimaryKey);

                //ADD THIS PART TO YOUR CODE
                await this.CreateDatabaseAsync();
        }
```

3. Run the application. You will now see that the database is created. In the next part, we will create the container.

Creating a container

To create the container, add the following:

1. Copy and paste the `CreateContainerAsync` method below your `CreateDatabaseAsync` method. `CreateContainerAsync` creates a new container with the `FamilyContainer` ID, if it doesn't already exist, by using the ID specified from the `containerId` field partitioned by the `LastName` property:

```
    private async Task CreateContainerAsync()
        {
                // Create a new container
                this.container = await
    this.database.CreateContainerIfNotExistsAsync(containerId,
    "/LastName");
                Console.WriteLine("Created Container: {0}\n",
    this.container.Id);
        }
```

2. In the `GetStartedDemoAsync` method, you should now add the line of code to call the `CreateContainerAsync` method. The method will now look like the following:

```
public async Task GetStartedDemoAsync()
        {
                // Create a new instance of the Cosmos Client
                this.cosmosClient = new CosmosClient(EndpointUri,
PrimaryKey);
                await this.CreateDatabaseAsync();

                //ADD THIS PART TO YOUR CODE
                await this.CreateContainerAsync();
        }
```

3. You can now run the application again, and you will see that the container is created.

In the next section, we are going to add items to the container.

Adding items to the container

In this part, we are going to add items to the container using the API. First, we need to create a `Family` class that represents the objects that we are going to store in the container. You can create an item using the `CreateItemAsync` method. When you use the SQL API, items are created and stored as documents. These documents are user-defined arbitrary JSON content. You can then insert an item into your Azure Cosmos container.

Besides the `Family` class, we will also add some subclasses, such as `Parent`, `Child`, `Pet`, and `Address`, which are used in the `Family` class. Therefore, we have to take the following steps:

1. Add a new class to the project and call it `Family.cs`:

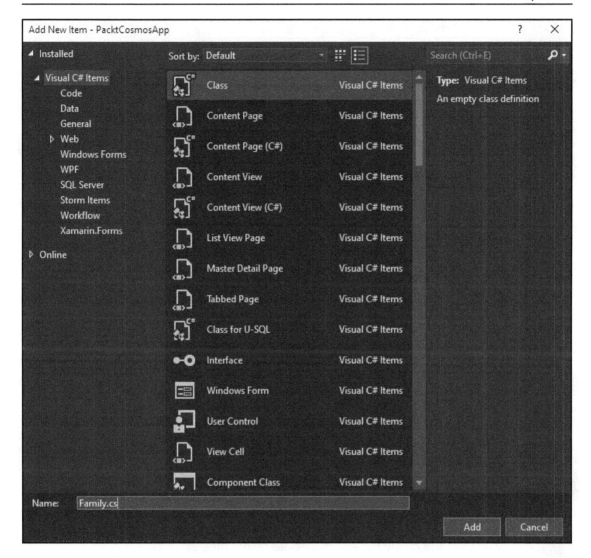

Creating a new class

2. Click **Add**.

3. Replace the references with the following (you should be prompted to install the NuGet package for this; if not, open the NuGet package manager and add it manually):

```
using Newtonsoft.Json;
```

4. Then add the following code to create the `Family` class:

```
public class Family
    {
        [JsonProperty(PropertyName = "id")]
        public string Id { get; set; }
        public string LastName { get; set; }
        public Parent[] Parents { get; set; }
        public Child[] Children { get; set; }
        public Address Address { get; set; }
        public bool IsRegistered { get; set; }
        public override string ToString()
        {
            return JsonConvert.SerializeObject(this);
        }
    }
```

5. Then we can create the `Child` class below the `Family` class:

```
public class Parent
    {
        public string FamilyName { get; set; }
        public string FirstName { get; set; }
    }
```

6. Next, we will create the `Pet` class below the `Child` class:

```
public class Child
    {
    public string FamilyName { get; set; }
    public string FirstName { get; set; }
    public string Gender { get; set; }
    public int Grade { get; set; }
    public Pet[] Pets { get; set; }
    }
```

7. Lastly, we will create the `Address` class below the `Pet` class:

```
public class Address
    {
        public string State { get; set; }
        public string County { get; set; }
        public string City { get; set; }
    }
```

8. In `Program.cs`, add the `AddItemsToContainerAsync` method after your `CreateContainerAsync` method and create the first `Family` item:

```
private async Task AddItemsToContainerAsync()
{
    Family ZaalFamily = new Family
    {
        Id = "Zaal.1",
        LastName = "Zaal",
        Parents = new Parent[]
        {
    new Parent { FirstName = "Thomas" },
    new Parent { FirstName = "Sjoukje" }
        },
        Children = new Child[]
        {
    new Child
    {
        FirstName = "Molly",
        Gender = "female",
        Grade = 5,
        Pets = new Pet[]
        {
            new Pet { GivenName = "Fluffy" }
        }
    }
        },
        Address = new Address { State = "WA", County =
"King", City = "Seattle" },
        IsRegistered = false
    };
```

9. Then, below `item`, add the code to add `item` to `container`:

```
    try
    {
        // Read the item to see if it exists.
        ItemResponse<Family> zaalFamilyResponse = await
this.container.ReadItemAsync<Family>(ZaalFamily.Id, new
PartitionKey(ZaalFamily.LastName));
        Console.WriteLine("Item in database with id: {0}
already exists\n", zaalFamilyResponse.Resource.Id);
    }
    catch (CosmosException ex) when (ex.StatusCode ==
HttpStatusCode.NotFound)
    {
        // Create an item in the container representing the
Zaal family. Note we provide the value of the partition key for
```

```
this item, which is "Zaal"
                ItemResponse<Family> zaalFamilyResponse = await
this.container.CreateItemAsync<Family>(ZaalFamily, new
PartitionKey(ZaalFamily.LastName));

                // Note that after creating the item, we can access
the body of the item with the Resource property off the
ItemResponse. We can also access the RequestCharge property to see
the amount of RUs consumed on this request.
                Console.WriteLine("Created item in database with
id: {0} Operation consumed {1} RUs.\n",
zaalFamilyResponse.Resource.Id, zaalFamilyResponse.RequestCharge);
            }
```

10. For the second `Family` item, right underneath the previous code (in the same method), add the following:

```
// Create a family object for the PacktPub family
        Family PacktPubFamily = new Family
        {
            Id = "PacktPub.1",
            LastName = "PacktPub",
            Parents = new Parent[]
            {
        new Parent { FamilyName = "PacktPub", FirstName =
"Robin" },
        new Parent { FamilyName = "Zaal", FirstName = "Sjoukje"
        }
            },
```

11. Add `children` to `Family`:

```
    Children = new Child[]
    {
            new Child
            {
                FamilyName = "Merriam",
                FirstName = "Jesse",
                Gender = "female",
                Grade = 8,
                Pets = new Pet[]
                {
                    new Pet { GivenName = "Goofy" },
                    new Pet { GivenName = "Shadow" }
                }
            },
            new Child
            {
```

```
                    FamilyName = "Miller",
                    FirstName = "Lisa",
                    Gender = "female",
                    Grade = 1
                }
            },
            Address = new Address { State = "NY", County =
"Manhattan", City = "NY" },
            IsRegistered = true
        };
```

12. Then, below `item`, add the code to add `item` to `container` again:

```
    try
    {
        // Read the item to see if it exists
        ItemResponse<Family> packtPubFamilyResponse = await
this.container.ReadItemAsync<Family> (PacktPubFamily.Id, new
PartitionKey(PacktPubFamily.LastName));
        Console.WriteLine("Item in database with id: {0} already
exists\n", packtPubFamilyResponse.Resource.Id);
    }
    catch (CosmosException ex) when (ex.StatusCode ==
HttpStatusCode.NotFound)
    {
        // Create an item in the container representing the Wakefield
family. Note we provide the        value of the partition key for
this item, which is "PacktPub"
        ItemResponse<Family> packtPubFamilyResponse = await
this.container.CreateItemAsync<Family>(PacktPubFamily, new
PartitionKey(PacktPubFamily.LastName));

        // Note that after creating the item, we can access the body of
the item with the Resource property off the ItemResponse. We can
also access the RequestCharge property to see the amount of RUs
consumed on this request.
        Console.WriteLine("Created item in database with id: {0}
Operation consumed {1} RUs.\n", packtPubFamilyResponse.Resource.Id,
packtPubFamilyResponse.RequestCharge);
    }
}
```

13. Finally, we need to call `AddItemsToContainerAsync` in the `GetStartedDemoAsync` method again:

```
public async Task GetStartedDemoAsync()
{
    // Create a new instance of the Cosmos Client
    this.cosmosClient = new CosmosClient(EndpointUri, PrimaryKey);
    await this.CreateDatabaseAsync();
    await this.CreateContainerAsync();

    //ADD THIS PART TO YOUR CODE
    await this.AddItemsToContainerAsync();
}
```

14. Now, run the application again. The items will be added to the container.

In this part, we have added some items to the container. In the next part, we will query the resources.

Querying Azure Cosmos DB resources

In this part of the demonstration, we are going to query the resources. Azure Cosmos DB supports rich queries against JSON documents stored in each container. The following code will show you how to run a query against the items that we stored in the container in the previous step:

Therefore, we need to take the following steps:

1. Copy and paste the `QueryItemsAsync` method after your `AddItemsToContainerAsync` method:

```
private async Task QueryItemsAsync()
{
    var sqlQueryText = "SELECT * FROM c WHERE c.LastName = 'Zaal'";

    Console.WriteLine("Running query: {0}\n", sqlQueryText);

    QueryDefinition queryDefinition = new
QueryDefinition(sqlQueryText);
    FeedIterator<Family> queryResultSetIterator =
this.container.GetItemQueryIterator<Family>  (queryDefinition);

    List<Family> families = new List<Family>();

    while (queryResultSetIterator.HasMoreResults)
```

```
    {
        FeedResponse<Family> currentResultSet = await
queryResultSetIterator.ReadNextAsync();
        foreach (Family family in currentResultSet)
        {
            families.Add(family);
            Console.WriteLine("\tRead {0}\n", family);
        }
    }
}
```

2. Add a call to `QueryItemsAsync` in the `GetStartedDemoAsync` method:

```
public async Task GetStartedDemoAsync()
    {
        // Create a new instance of the Cosmos Client
        this.cosmosClient = new CosmosClient(EndpointUri, PrimaryKey);
        await this.CreateDatabaseAsync();
        await this.CreateContainerAsync();
        await this.AddItemsToContainerAsync();

        //ADD THIS PART TO YOUR CODE
        await this.QueryItemsAsync();
    }
```

3. Run the application, and you will see the query results displayed in the console.

We have now created a query to retrieve the data from the container. In the next section, we are going to update a `Family` item.

Updating a JSON item

In this part of the demo, we are going to update a `Family` item. Therefore, add the following code:

1. Copy and paste the `ReplaceFamilyItemAsync` method after your `QueryItemsAsync` method:

```
    private async Task ReplaceFamilyItemAsync()
        {
            ItemResponse<Family> PacktPubFamilyResponse = await
this.container.ReadItemAsync<Family>("PacktPub.1", new
PartitionKey("PacktPub"));
            var itemBody = PacktPubFamilyResponse.Resource;
```

```
            // update registration status from false to true
            itemBody.IsRegistered = true;
            // update grade of child
            itemBody.Children[0].Grade = 6;

            // replace the item with the updated content
            PacktPubFamilyResponse = await
this.container.ReplaceItemAsync<Family>(itemBody, itemBody.Id, new
PartitionKey(itemBody.LastName));
            Console.WriteLine("Updated Family [{0},{1}].\n \tBody
is now: {2}\n", itemBody.LastName, itemBody.Id,
PacktPubFamilyResponse.Resource);
        }
```

2. Then, add a call to
   ReplaceFamilyItemAsync in the GetStartedDemoAsync method:

```
public async Task GetStartedDemoAsync()
    {
        // Create a new instance of the Cosmos Client
        this.cosmosClient = new CosmosClient(EndpointUri,
PrimaryKey);
        await this.CreateDatabaseAsync();
        await this.CreateContainerAsync();
        await this.AddItemsToContainerAsync();
        await this.QueryItemsAsync();

        //ADD THIS PART TO YOUR CODE
        await this.ReplaceFamilyItemAsync();
    }
```

3. Run the application, and you will see that the Family item is being updated.

In this part of the demonstration, we updated an item in the container. In the next part, we
will delete an item from the container.

Deleting an item

To delete a Family item, take the following steps:

1. Add the DeleteFamilyItemAsync method after your
   ReplaceFamilyItemAsync method:

```
private async Task DeleteFamilyItemAsync()
    {
        var partitionKeyValue = "Zaal";
```

```
                var familyId = "Zaal.1";

                // Delete an item. Note we must provide the partition
        key value and id of the item to delete
                _ = await
        this.container.DeleteItemAsync<Family>(familyId, new
        PartitionKey(partitionKeyValue));
                Console.WriteLine("Deleted Family [{0},{1}]\n",
        partitionKeyValue, familyId);
            }
```

2. Then, add a call to `DeleteFamilyItemAsync` in the `GetStartedDemoAsync` method:

```
    public async Task GetStartedDemoAsync()
        {
            // Create a new instance of the Cosmos Client
            this.cosmosClient = new CosmosClient(EndpointUri,
    PrimaryKey);
            await this.CreateDatabaseAsync();
            await this.CreateContainerAsync();
            await this.AddItemsToContainerAsync();
            await this.QueryItemsAsync();
            await this.ReplaceFamilyItemAsync();

            //ADD THIS PART TO YOUR CODE
            await this.DeleteFamilyItemAsync();
        }
```

3. Run the application, and you will see that the item is deleted.

In this demo, we created a Cosmos DB server, database, and container. We also added data to the container, ran a query on the data, updated the data, and lastly, we deleted the data.

In the next section, we are going to cover partitioning schemes.

Understanding partitioning schemes

To meet the performance needs of your application, Azure Cosmos DB uses partitioning to scale individual containers in a database. Cosmos DB partitions in a way that the items are divided into distinct subsets called **logical partitions**. These are formed based on the value of the partition key that is added to each item in the container. All of the items that are in a logical partition have the same partition key. Each item in a container has an **item ID** (which is unique within the logical partition). To create the item's index, the partition key and the item ID are combined. This uniquely identifies the item.

If you look at our sample application from the previous section, you will see that the partition key and item ID are combined.

Besides logical partitions, Azure Cosmos DB also has physical partitions:

- **Logical partitions**: A set of items that have the same partition key are called a logical partition. For instance, if you have a container that stores items that all contain a `Product` property, you can use this as the partition key. Logical partitions are then formed by groups that have the same values, such as `Books`, `Videos`, `Movies`, and `Music`. Containers are the fundamental units of scalability in Azure Cosmos DB. Data that is added to the container, together with the throughput (see next section) that is provisioned on the container, are automatically (horizontally) partitioned across a set of logical partitions based on the partition key.
- **Physical partitions**: Internally, one or more logical partitions are mapped to a physical partition. This partition consists of a set of replicas, also called a replica set. Each replica set is hosting an instance of the Azure Cosmos database engine. It makes the data that is stored inside the physical partition highly available, consistent, and durable. The maximum amount of **request units** (**RUs**) and storage are supported by the physical partition.

The following chart shows how logical partitions are mapped to physical partitions that are distributed globally over multiple regions:

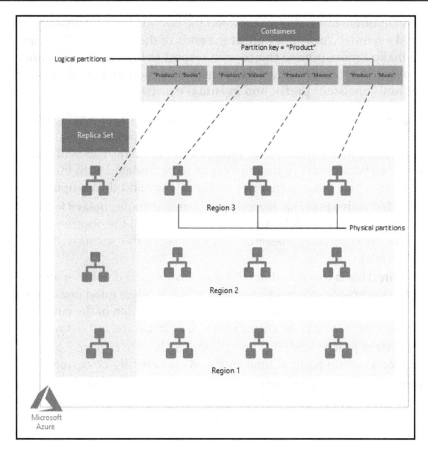

Partitioning in Azure Cosmos DB

In the next section, we are going to cover how to set the appropriate consistency level for operations.

Setting the appropriate consistency level for operations

When you use distributed databases that rely on high availability and low latency, you can choose between two different extreme consistency models: **strong** consistency and **eventual** consistency. The former is the standard of data programmability, but this will result in reduced availability during failures and higher latency. The latter offers higher availability and better performance, but makes it much harder to program applications.

Azure Cosmos DB offers more choices between the two extreme consistency models. Strong consistency and eventual consistency are at the ends of the spectrum. This can help developers to make a more precise choice with respect to high availability and performance. Azure Cosmos DB offers five consistency models, including **strong**, **bounded staleness**, **session**, **consistent prefix**, and **eventual** consistency:

- **Strong**: Strong consistency is the easiest model to understand. The most recent committed version of an item is returned when the data is read. A partial or uncommitted write is never returned to the client. This will give a lot of overhead because every instance needs to be updated with the latest version of the data, which has a huge price on the latency and throughput of the data.
- **Bounded staleness**: This is a compromise that trades delays for strong consistency. This model doesn't guarantee that all the observers have the same data at the same time. Instead, it allows a lag of five seconds' delay (100 operations).
- **Session**: This is the default level for newly created databases and collections. It is half as expensive as strong consistency and it offers good performance and availability. It ensures that everything that is written in the current session is also available for reading. Anything else will be accurate, but delayed.
- **Consistent prefix**: With this level, updates that are returned contain accurate data for a certain point in time, but won't necessarily be current.
- **Eventual**: There's no ordering guarantee of how long it will take (like consistent prefix) and the updates aren't guaranteed to come in order. When there are no further writes, the replicas will eventually be updated.

For more information on how to choose the right consistency level for the different APIs that Azure Cosmos DB has to offer, you can refer to the article at `https://docs.microsoft.com/en-us/azure/cosmos-db/consistency-levels-choosing`.

Summary

In this chapter, we've covered how to develop solutions that use Cosmos DB storage. We covered how to use the different APIs from Visual Studio to create databases, containers, data, and more. We also covered the partition schemes and the different consistency levels that are provided for Azure Cosmos DB.

In the next chapter, we will continue with this objective. We are going to cover how to develop solutions that use a relational database.

Questions

Answer the following questions to test your knowledge of the information in this chapter. You can find the answers in the *Assessments* section at the end of this book:

1. You can only create a Cosmos DB using the Azure portal, PowerShell or CLI.
    1. Yes
    2. No

2. Azure Cosmos DB offers two different consistency models.
    1. Yes
    2. No

3. A horizontal partition is used to distribute the data over different Azure Cosmos DB instances.
    1. Yes
    2. No

Further reading

You can check the following links for more information about the topics that are covered in this chapter:

- **Azure Cosmos DB documentation**: https://docs.microsoft.com/en-us/azure/cosmos-db/
- **Getting started with SQL queries**: https://docs.microsoft.com/en-us/azure/cosmos-db/sql-query-getting-started
- **Request Units in Azure Cosmos DB**: https://docs.microsoft.com/en-us/azure/cosmos-db/request-units
- **Getting Behind the 9-Ball: Cosmos DB Consistency Levels Explained**: https://blog.jeremylikness.com/blog/2018-03-23_getting-behind-the-9ball-cosmosdb-consistency-levels/

19
Developing Solutions That Use a Relational Database

In the previous chapter, we covered the first part of the *Developing for the Cloud and for Azure Storage* objective, by covering how to develop solutions that use Cosmos DB storage. We've covered how to create, read, update, and delete data by using appropriate APIs, and more.

In this chapter, we are continuing with this objective. We are going to cover how to develop solutions that use a relational database. We are going to cover how to provision and configure relational databases, how to configure elastic pools for Azure SQL Database, and how to create, read, update, and delete data tables by using code.

The following topics will be covered in this chapter:

- Understanding Azure SQL Database
- Provisioning and configuring an Azure SQL database
- Creating, reading, updating, and deleting data tables by using code
- Configuring elastic pools for Azure SQL Database
- Understanding Azure SQL Database managed instances

Technical requirements

This chapter will use Visual Studio 2019 (`https://visualstudio.microsoft.com/vs/`) for its examples.

The source code for our sample application can be downloaded from `https://github.com/PacktPublishing/Microsoft-Azure-Architect-Technologies-Exam-Guide-AZ-300/tree/master/Chapter19`.

Understanding Azure SQL Database

Azure SQL Database offers a relational database in the cloud. It uses the last stable SQL Server on-premises database engine. Azure SQL Database can be used for a variety of applications, because it enables you to process both relational data and non-relational structures, such as graphs, JSON, spatial, and XML.

Azure SQL Database offers scalability, without causing any downtime for your databases. It offers column-based indexes, which make your queries perform much more quickly. There is built-in monitoring for your databases and built-in intelligence for increasing the performance of your database automatically, and it provides high availability, by providing automatic backups and point-in-time restores. You can also use active geo-replication, for global applications.

Azure SQL Database offers the following tiers for your databases:

- **Elastic database pool**: Elastic pools are a feature that helps in managing and scaling databases that have unpredictable usage demands. All databases in an elastic pool are deployed on the same database server and share the same resources. By managing the pool of databases and not the individual databases, they can share performance and scaling. The performance of this tier is expressed in **elastic Database Transaction Units** (**eDTUs**).
- **Single database**: This is a good fit if you have a database with predictable performance. Scaling is done for each database separately. The performance of this tier is expressed in **Database Transaction Units** (**DTUs**).
- **Managed instance**: This is a fully managed instance of the last stable SQL Server on-premises database engine. This option is most suitable for migrating on-premises SQL databases as-is to the cloud. It offers 100% compatibility with the latest SQL Server on-premises (Enterprise edition) database engine.

SQL Server Stretch Database

SQL Server Stretch Database was introduced in SQL Server 2016 and is a feature that can move or archive your cold data from your on-premises SQL Server to Azure SQL Database. This results in better performance for your on-premises server, and the stretched data resides in the cloud, where it is easily accessible for other applications. Inside SQL Server, you can mark a table as a stretch candidate, and SQL Server will move the data to Azure SQL Database transparently. Large transactional tables with lots of historical data can benefit from enabling for Stretch. These are mostly massive tables with hundreds, or millions, of rows in them, which don't have to be queried frequently.

High availability

Even when your databases are hosted in Azure, there is still a chance that failures and outages will occur. In the case of an outage (such as a total regional failure, which can be caused by a natural disaster, an act of terrorism, war, a government action, or a network or device failure external to the data centers of Microsoft), your data still needs to be accessible.

To create highly available SQL Server databases on Azure, you can use failover groups and active geo-replication, described in the following list:

- **Active geo-replication**: Geo-replication is a business continuity feature that allows you to replicate the primary database and up to four read-only secondary databases, in the same or different Azure regions. You can use the secondary databases to query data, or for failover scenarios when there is a data center outage. Active geo-replication has to be set up by the user or the application manually.

- **Failover groups**: Failover groups are a feature that automatically manages the failover for the database. They automatically manage the geo-replication relationship between the databases, the failover at scale, and the connectivity. To use failover groups, the primary and the secondary databases need to be created inside of the same Azure subscription.

In the next section, we are going to cover how to provision and configure an Azure SQL database.

Provisioning and configuring an Azure SQL database

In this demonstration, we are going to create and configure an Azure SQL database. You can create the database from the Azure portal, PowerShell, CLI, and ARM templates, and by using the .NET libraries. In this demonstration, we are going to create a single database in the Azure portal. Therefore, we need to take the following steps:

1. Navigate to the Azure portal by opening `https://portal.azure.com`.
2. Click **Create a resource**, type **SQL Database** in the search bar, and create a new database server.

3. Add the following values:
   1. **Subscription**: Pick a subscription.
   2. **Resource group**: Create a new one, and call it `PacktSQLResourceGroup`.
   3. **Database name**: `PacktSql`.
   4. **Server**: Create a new one, and add the following values:
      1. **Server name**: `packtsqlserver`
      2. **Server admin login**: `PacktAdmin`
      3. **Password**: `P@ss@word123`
      4. **Location**: **East US**
   5. **Want to use SQL elastic pool**: No, we are going to use a single database.
   6. **Compute + storage**: Keep the default setting here.
4. Click **Review + create**, and then **Create**.
5. The database is now being created.

Now that we have created the database, we can configure a server-level firewall rule.

Creating a server-level firewall rule

When you want to connect to the database from on-premises or remote tools, we need to configure a server-level firewall rule for the database. The firewall is created at the database server level for single and pooled databases. This prevents a client application from connecting to the server of any of its single or pooled databases.

To connect to the server from an IP address outside Azure, you need to create a firewall rule for a specific IP address or range of addresses.

To create a firewall rule, we have to take the following steps:

1. When the deployment is finished, open the resource. The overview blade is automatically displayed. In the top menu, select **Set server firewall**, as shown in the following screenshot:

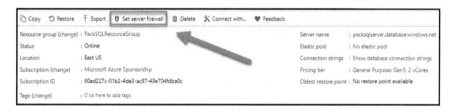

Overview blade of the database

2. In the **Firewall settings** page, you can add your current client IP address, by clicking the **+ Add client IP** button in the top menu. This IP address will then automatically be added to the rules, as can be seen in the following screenshot:

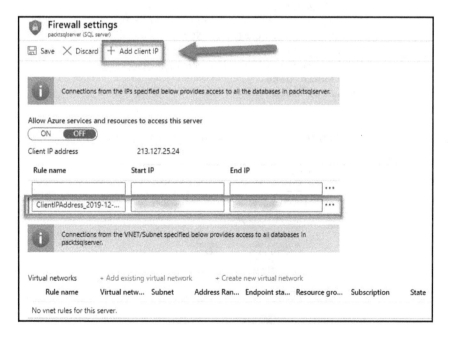

Adding a client IP address

3. Click **Save**.

4. We can now connect from outside of Azure to the database.

In the next section, we are going to create a new table in the database, using the Query Editor.

Creating a table in the database

In this part of the demonstration, we are going to create a new table in the database to store employees. We are going to use the Query Editor for this, which is available in the Azure portal.

Therefore, we need to take the following steps:

1. In the settings of Azure SQL Database in the Azure portal (created previously), in the left-hand menu, click **Query editor (preview)**. Log in to the SQL server, using the username and password (PacktAdmin and P@ss@word123).

2. In the **Query** screen, add the following line of SQL code, to create a new table with the appropriate columns in it:

```
CREATE TABLE Employee (
    Employeeid int IDENTITY(1,1) PRIMARY KEY,
    FirstName varchar(255) NOT NULL,
    LastName varchar(255) NOT NULL,
    Title varchar(255) NOT NULL,
    BirthDate date,
    HireDate date
);
```

3. In the Query Editor, this will look like the following screenshot:

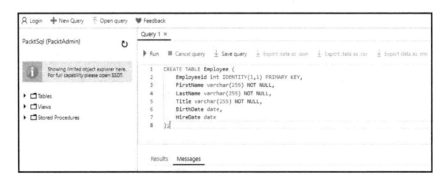

Query Editor in the Azure portal

4. Run the query, and the table will be created.

We have created and configured our database, and have created a table with columns. In the next section, we are going to create a console application that creates, reads, updates, and deletes data tables programmatically.

Creating, reading, updating, and deleting data tables by using code

In this demonstration, we are going to create the sample application. For this, we are going to create a new console application in Visual Studio 2019. We will first connect to our Azure SQL Database account.

Connecting to the Azure SQL database

1. Open Visual Studio, and create a new console app (.NET) project.
2. Name the project `PacktSQLApp`.
3. Right-click on your project in the Solution Explorer, and select **Manage NuGet Packages**.
4. Select **Browse**, search for `System.Data.SqlClient`, and install the package.
5. Open `Program.cs`, and replace the references with the following:

```
using System;
using System.Data.SqlClient;
```

6. Add the following variable in the `Program.cs` method:

```
static string connectionstring;
```

7. Now, go back to the Azure portal. Navigate to the Azure SQL database that we created in the previous section. Under **Settings**, select **Connection strings**. Copy the connection string, as follows:

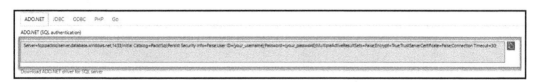

SQL database connection string

8. Below the `Main` method, add a new asynchronous task called `GetStartedDemoAsync`, which instantiates our new `SqlConnection`. We use `GetStartedDemoAsync` as the entry point that calls methods operating on Azure Cosmos DB resources. In the method, replace `<replace-with-your-connectionstring>` with the connection string that you copied. Also, in the connection string, replace `{your-username}` with the username you specified when you created the database, and replace `{your-password}` with the password you provided, as follows:

```
static void GetStartedDemo()
    {
        connectionstring = "<replace-with-your-
connectionstring";
    }
```

9. Add the following code, to run the `GetStartedDemo` synchronous task from your `Main` method:

```
static void Main(string[] args)
    {
        try
        {
            Console.WriteLine("Beginning operations...\n");
            GetStartedDemo();

        }
        catch (SqlException de)
        {
            Exception baseException =
de.GetBaseException();
            Console.WriteLine("{0} error occurred: {1}",
de.Message, de);
        }
        catch (Exception e)
        {
            Console.WriteLine("Error: {0}", e);
        }
        finally
        {
            Console.WriteLine("End of demo, press any key
to exit.");
            Console.ReadKey();
        }
    }
```

Now that we have successfully added the connection string to the Azure SQL database, we can create some data in the new database.

Adding items to the database

In this part of the demonstration, we are going to add an employee to the database. First, we need to create an `Employee` class that represents the objects we are going to store in the container. You can create an item using the `CreateItem` method, as follows:

1. Add a new class to the project, and call it `Employee.cs`.
2. Replace the references with the following (you should be prompted to install the NuGet package for this; if not, open the NuGet package manager and add it manually):

```
using Newtonsoft.Json;
using System;
```

3. Then, add the following code, to create the `Employee` class:

```
public class Employee
{
    public int EmployeeID { get; set; }
    public string LastName { get; set; }
    public string FirstName { get; set; }
    public string Title { get; set; }
    public DateTime? BirthDate { get; set; }
    public DateTime? HireDate { get; set; }
}
```

4. In `Program.cs`, add the following code, to create a new employee object before the `Main` method:

```
static Employee NewEmployee = new Employee
    {
        FirstName = "Sjoukje",
        LastName = "Zaal",
        Title = "Mrs",
        BirthDate = new DateTime(1979, 7, 7),
        HireDate = new DateTime(2020, 1, 1)
    };
```

5. In `Program.cs`, add the `AddItemsToDatabase` method after your
   `GetStartedDemo` method. Then, add the following code, to add the new
   employee to the database. First, create the connection, and create the query, as
   follows:

```
static void AddItemsToDatabase()
    {
        connection = new SqlConnection(connectionstring);

        using (connection)
        {
            try
            {
                Console.WriteLine("\nCreate a new
employee:");
Console.WriteLine("========================================\n"
);

                var cmd = new SqlCommand("Insert Employee
(FirstName, LastName, Title, BirthDate, HireDate) values
(@FirstName, @LastName, @Title, @BirthDate, @HireDate)",
connection);
                cmd.Parameters.AddWithValue("@FirstName",
NewEmployee.FirstName);
                cmd.Parameters.AddWithValue("@LastName",
NewEmployee.LastName);
                cmd.Parameters.AddWithValue("@Title",
NewEmployee.Title);
                cmd.Parameters.AddWithValue("@BirthDate",
NewEmployee.BirthDate);
                cmd.Parameters.AddWithValue("@HireDate",
NewEmployee.HireDate);
```

6. Then, open the connection, execute the query, and close the connection, as
   follows:

```
                connection.Open();
                cmd.ExecuteNonQuery();
                connection.Close();

                Console.WriteLine("\nFinsihed Creating a
new employee:");
Console.WriteLine("========================================\n"
);
            }
            catch (SqlException e)
            {
```

```
                        Console.WriteLine(e.ToString());
                }
            }
    }
```

7. Finally, we need to call `AddItemsToDatabase` in the `GetStartedDemo` method again, as follows:

```
static void GetStartedDemo()
    {
            connectionstring = "<replace-with-your-
connectionstring>";

            //ADD THIS PART TO YOUR CODE
            AddItemsToDatabase();
    }
```

In this part of the demonstration, we have added some items to the database. In the next part, we will query the database.

Querying Azure SQL Database items

In this part of the demonstration, we are going to query the database. The following code will show you how to run a query against the items that we stored in the database in the previous step.

Therefore, we need to take the following steps:

1. Copy and paste the `QueryItems` method after your `AddItemsToDatabase` method. Create the connection again, and create the query, as follows:

```
static void QueryItems()
    {
            connection = new SqlConnection(connectionstring);

            using (connection)
            {
                try
                {
                        Console.WriteLine("\nQuerying database:");
Console.WriteLine("=======================================\n"
);

                        var cmd = new SqlCommand("SELECT * FROM
Employee WHERE LastName = @LastName", connection);
```

```
                                cmd.Parameters.AddWithValue("@LastName",
        NewEmployee.LastName);
```

2. Then, open the connection, execute the query, and close the connection. Write some values to the console app, as follows:

```
                        connection.Open();
                        cmd.ExecuteNonQuery();

                        using (SqlDataReader reader =
        cmd.ExecuteReader())
                        {
                            while (reader.Read())
                            {
                                for (int i = 0; i <
        reader.FieldCount; i++)
                                {
        Console.WriteLine(reader.GetValue(i));
                                }
                            }
                            connection.Close();
                        }
                        Console.WriteLine("\nFinsihed querying
        database:");
        Console.WriteLine("===========================================\n"
        );
                    }
                    catch (SqlException e)
                    {
                        Console.WriteLine(e.ToString());
                    }
                }
            }
```

3. Then, we need to call `QueryItems` in the `GetStartedDemo` method again, as follows:

```
        static void GetStartedDemo()
            {
                connectionstring = "<replace-with-your-
        connectionstring>";
                connection = new SqlConnection(connectionstring);

                AddItemsToDatabase();

                //ADD THIS PART TO YOUR CODE
                QueryItems();
            }
```

4. Run the application, and you will see the query results displayed in the console.

We have now created a query to retrieve the data from the database. In the next section, we are going to update the Employee item.

Updating an Azure SQL Database row

In this part of the demonstration, we are going to update the Employee item. Therefore, add the following code:

1. Copy and paste the UpdateEmployeeItem method after your QueryItems method. Create the connection again, and the query, as follows:

```
static void UpdateEmployeeItem()
{
    connection = new SqlConnection(connectionstring);

    using (connection)
    {
        try
        {
            Console.WriteLine("\nUpdating employee:");
            Console.WriteLine("=========================================\n"
);

            var cmd = new SqlCommand(" UPDATE Employee
SET FirstName = 'Molly' WHERE Employeeid = 1", connection);
```

2. Execute it, as follows:

```
            connection.Open();
            cmd.ExecuteNonQuery();
            connection.Close();

            Console.WriteLine("\nFinished updating
employee");
            Console.WriteLine("=========================================\n"
);
        }
        catch (SqlException e)
        {
            Console.WriteLine(e.ToString());
        }
    }
}
```

3. Then, we need to call `UpdateEmployeeItem` in the `GetStartedDemo` method again, as follows:

```
static void GetStartedDemo()
    {
        connectionstring = "<replace-with-your-
connectionstring>";
        connection = new SqlConnection(connectionstring);

        AddItemsToDatabase();
        QueryItems();

        //ADD THIS PART TO YOUR CODE
        UpdateEmployeeItem();
    }
```

In this part of the demonstration, we updated a row in the database. In the next part, we will delete the employee from the database.

Deleting an item

To delete a `Family` item, take the following steps:

1. Add the `DeleteEmployeeItem` method after your `UpdateEmployeeItem` method. Create the connection, and a query, as follows:

```
static void DeleteEmployeeItem()
    {
        connection = new SqlConnection(connectionstring);

        using (connection)
        {
            try
            {
                Console.WriteLine("\nDeleting employee:");
Console.WriteLine("=========================================\n"
);

                var cmd = new SqlCommand(" Delete FROM
dbo.Employee where Employeeid = 1", connection);
```

2. Then, open the connection and execute the query. Write some details to the console app, as follows:

```
connection.Open();
cmd.ExecuteNonQuery();
connection.Close();
Console.WriteLine("\nFinished deleting
employee");
Console.WriteLine("=========================================\n"
);
                }
                catch (SqlException e)
                {
                    Console.WriteLine(e.ToString());
                }
            }
        }
```

3. Next, we need to call `UpdateEmployeeItem` in the `GetStartedDemo` method again, as follows:

```
static void GetStartedDemo()
        {
            connectionstring = "<replace-with-your-
connectionstring>";
            connection = new SqlConnection(connectionstring);

            AddItemsToDatabase();
            QueryItems();
            UpdateEmployeeItem();

            //ADD THIS PART TO YOUR CODE
            DeleteEmployeeItem();
        }
```

4. If you now run the application, the console will create a new employee, then query the database. Next, it will update the employee, and finally, it will delete the employee from the database.

We have now created an application that can create, read, update, and delete items from an Azure SQL database. In the next section, we are going to configure elastic pools for the database.

Configuring elastic pools for Azure SQL Database

When the usage demands for an Azure SQL Database server are unpredictable during creation, SQL Database elastic pools are a simple, cost-effective solution for managing and scaling multiple databases. The databases, in an elastic pool, share a set of resources at a set price.

You can configure elastic pools for an Azure SQL database in two different ways. The first is to enable it during the creation of the database server and database. The other option is to enable this on an existing database. In this demonstration, we are going to enable this on the database that we created in the first demonstration of this chapter. Therefore, we need to take the following steps:

1. Navigate to the Azure portal, by opening `https://portal.azure.com`.
2. Navigate to the overview blade of the Azure SQL database that we created in the first demonstration of this chapter. In the top menu, click on the link that is displayed next to **Elastic pool**, as shown in the following screenshot:

Elastic pool settings

3. You will now be redirected to the Azure SQL Database Server settings. In the overview blade, in the top menu, select **+ New pool**, as shown in the following screenshot:

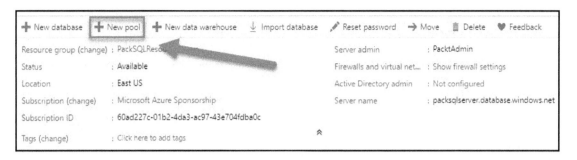

Adding a new pool

4. In the Elastic pool blade, add the following values:
    1. **Name:** `PacktElasticPool`.
    2. **Configure pool:** Here, you can select the pool's service tier. This determines the features available to the elastics in the pool. It also determines the maximum amount of resources available for each database, as shown in the following screenshot:

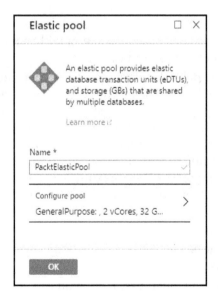

Configuring the elastic pool

5. Click **OK** to create the pool.

6. When the pool is created, in the left-hand menu, under **Settings**, select **SQL elastic pools**. In there, you can see the newly created pool, as follows:

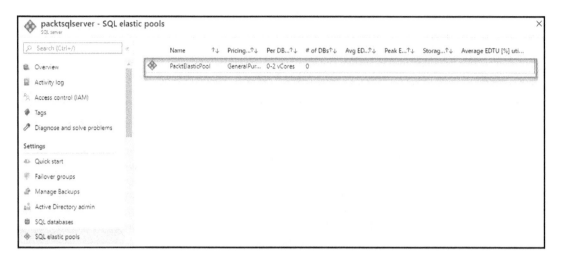

Overview of elastic pools

7. By clicking on the newly created pool, you will be redirected to the settings of the pool. Here, you can monitor and configure it.
8. On the overview blade of the elastic pool, you can monitor the utilization of the pool and its databases. The monitoring includes recent alerts and recommendations (if available) for the elastic pool, and monitoring charts, showing resource usage of the elastic pool. If you want more information about the pool, you can click on the available information in this overview. Clicking on the available notifications will take you to a blade that shows the full detail of the notification. Clicking on the **Resource utilization** chart will take you to the Azure Monitoring view, where you can customize the metrics and time window shown in the chart.
9. If you would like to monitor the databases inside your pool, you can click on **Database Resource Utilization** in the **Monitoring** section on the left-hand side of the resource menu.
10. Under **Settings**, select **Configure**. Here, you can make any combination of the following changes to the pool: add or remove databases to and from the pool, change the service tier of the pool, scale the performance (DTU or vCore) and storage up or down, review the cost summary to view any changes to your bill as a result of your new selections, and set a min (guaranteed) and max performance limit for the databases in the pools, as shown in the following screenshot:

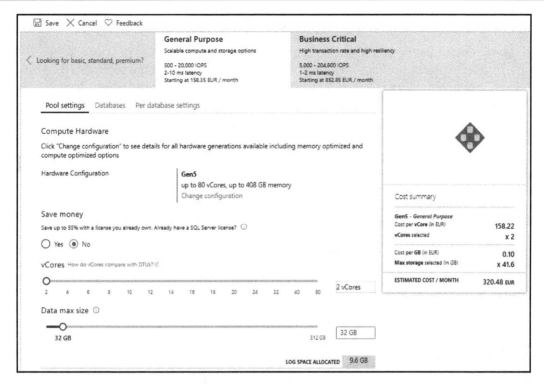

Configuring the elastic pools

In this section, we have covered how to create elastic pools. In the next section, we are going to cover Azure SQL Database managed instance.

Understanding Azure SQL Database managed instances

Azure SQL Database managed instance provides a near-100% compatibility with the latest SQL Server on-premises (Enterprise edition) database engine. Azure will then handle all the updates and patches for your databases, like when using PaaS services. It also provides a native **virtual network** (**VNet**) implementation that addresses common security concerns.

This allows customers to easily lift and shift their on-premises SQL databases to Azure, with minimal database and application changes. Databases can be migrated using the **Database Migration Service** (**DMS**) in Azure to a completely isolated instance, with native VNet support. Because of the isolation, this instance offers high security for your databases.

A managed instance is available in two service tiers:

- **General purpose**: This tier offers normal performance and I/O latency for applications. It offers high-performance Azure Blob storage (up to 8 TB). The high availability is based on Azure Service Fabric and Azure Blob storage.
- **Business critical**: This tier is designed for applications with low I/O latency requirements. It also offers the minimal impact of underlying maintenance operations on the workload. It comes with SSD local storage e (up to 1 TB on Gen4, and up to 4 TB on Gen5). High availability is based on Azure Service Fabric and Always On availability groups. For read-only workloads and reporting, it also offers built-in additional read-only database replicas. For workloads with high-performance requirements, in-memory OLTP is used.

 Azure SQL Database managed instance is quite expensive to implement compared to Azure SQL Database. For more information about the pricing, you can refer to the following website: `https://azure.` `microsoft.com/en-us/pricing/details/sql-database/managed/`.

Summary

In this chapter, we've covered how to develop solutions that use a relational database. We've covered how to create an Azure SQL database, how to add, remove, update, and query data from a custom application, how to enable elastic pools, and more.

In the next chapter, we will continue with the last chapter of this book. We are going to cover how to configure a message-based integration architecture, and how to develop for autoscaling.

Questions

Answer the following questions, to test your knowledge of the information in this chapter. You can find the answers in the *Assessments* section at the end of this book:

1. An elastic pool can only be created during the creation of the Azure SQL database.
    1. Yes
    2. No

2. Azure SQL Database managed instance is based on the last stable SQL Server on-premises database engine.
    1. Yes
    2. No

3. Failover groups automatically manage the geo-replication relationship between the databases, the failover at scale, and the connectivity.
    1. Yes
    2. No

Further reading

You can check the following links for more information about the topics that are covered in this chapter:

- **What is the Azure SQL Database service?**: https://docs.microsoft.com/en-us/azure/sql-database/sql-database-technical-overview
- **Azure SQL Database service tiers**: https://docs.microsoft.com/en-us/azure/sql-database/sql-database-service-tiers-general-purpose-business-critical
- **Elastic pools help you manage and scale multiple Azure SQL databases**: https://docs.microsoft.com/en-us/azure/sql-database/sql-database-elastic-pool
- **What is Azure SQL Database managed instance?**: https://docs.microsoft.com/en-us/azure/sql-database/sql-database-managed-instance

20
Message-Based Integration Architecture and Autoscaling

In the previous chapter, we covered the second part of the *Developing for the Cloud and for Azure Storage* objective by covering how to develop solutions that use a relational database. We've covered how to provision and configure relational databases, how to configure elastic pools for Azure SQL Database, how to create, read, update, and delete data tables by using code, and more.

In this chapter, we are going to cover how to configure a message-based integration architecture and how to develop for autoscaling. We are going to cover how to configure an app or service that can send emails, and how to create and configure the Notification hub, Event Hubs, and Service Bus. We also are going to look at how to implement autoscaling rules and patterns, and how to implement code that addresses the transient state.

The following topics will be covered in this chapter:

- Understanding Azure Integration Services
- Routing events using Azure Event Grid
- Designing an effective messaging architecture
- Implement autoscaling rules and patterns

Technical requirements

This chapter uses Azure PowerShell (`https://docs.microsoft.com/en-us/powershell/azure/install-az-ps?view=azps-1.8.0`) for its examples.

The source code for our sample application can be downloaded from `https://github.com/PacktPublishing/Microsoft-Azure-Architect-Technologies-Exam-Guide-AZ-300/tree/master/Chapter20`.

Understanding Azure Integration Services

Azure offers a variety of integration services, all serving different needs. In the next section, we are going to cover different services. This also includes the different IoT services, because some of these services have an overlap with other messaging services.

 `Chapter 9`, *Configuring Serverless Computing*, covers Azure Service Bus and Event Grid.

We will start with the Azure Relay service.

Azure Relay service

With Azure Relay, you can connect your on-premises application with a gateway in Azure, without having to open a firewall connection or make any other big adjustments to your on-premises network.

You can create an Azure Relay service in the Azure portal. Inside the Azure Relay service, a secure connection is created by using an outbound port and a bi-directional connection to your on-premises application. This connection is dedicated to one client and encrypted using **Transport Layer Security** (**TLS**). The on-premises application imports the Azure Relay namespace and makes a call to the Azure Relay service in the Azure portal using access keys for authentication:

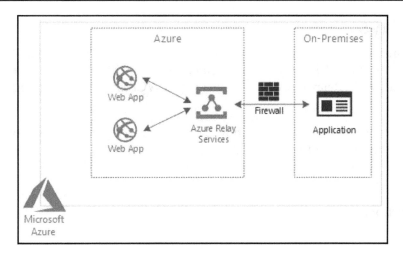

Azure Relay services

Azure Relay services support peer-to-peer traffic, one-way, request/response traffic, publish/subscribe scenarios, and bi-directional socket communication for increased point-to-point efficiency.

The difference between using Azure Relay services instead of using a VPN to create a hybrid connection is that the Azure Relay service can be scoped to one application on a single machine instead of using one connection for all sorts of connection types. Azure Relay services offer two features, a hybrid connection and WCF relays, that are different implementations, but both share the same gateway.

Hybrid connections

With hybrid connections, a rendezvous point is established in the cloud. An application can then connect to this using HTTP and web sockets. You can use all programming languages that support web sockets, such as .NET Core, JavaScript, and Node.js, as well as multiple remote procedure models.

For more information about the Azure Relay hybrid connections protocol, you can refer to the following website: `https://docs.microsoft.com/en-us/azure/service-bus-relay/relay-hybrid-connections-protocol`.

For more information on how to get started with relay hybrid connections, you can refer to the following tutorial: `https://docs.microsoft.com/en-us/azure/service-bus-relay/relay-hybrid-connections-dotnet-get-started`.

WCF Relays

Windows Communication Foundation (**WCF**) relays (formerly Service Bus Relays) uses .NET Framework and WCF to establish a connection and send a message. The on-premises application uses WCF Relay bindings, which creates WCF channels that integrate with the Azure Service Bus.

 For more information on how to use Azure Relay WCF relays with .NET, you can refer to the following article: `https://docs.microsoft.com/en-us/azure/service-bus-relay/service-bus-relay-tutorial`.

In the next section, we are going to cover Azure Notification Hubs.

Azure Notification Hubs

Notification Hubs in Azure offers a push notification service to send notifications from backends to mobile devices. Push notifications on mobile devices are usually displayed to a user in a pop-up or dialog box. Users can then decide whether they want to view or dismiss the message. You can use push notifications for various scenarios, such as sending codes for MFA, sending notifications from social media, and sending news. Notification Hubs offers cross-platform notifications by offering a set of SDKs and APIs for iOS, Android, and Windows devices. Normally, applications will use **Platform Notification Systems** (**PNSes**), which are dedicated infrastructure platforms. Apple has the Apple Push Notification service, and Windows has the Windows Notification service, for instance.

Notification Hubs removes all the complexity that comes with calling the different PNSes manually in your applications because it offers platform independence by offering a single API, massive scaling, a variety of delivery patterns, rich telemetry, and more.

In the next section, we are going to cover Azure IoT Hub.

Azure IoT Hub

In an **Internet of Things** (**IoT**) solution, devices send massive amounts of data to Azure for further processing. The IoT Hub is used to connect these devices securely and route the messages from those devices to different resources in Azure for further processing. The IoT Hub offers the following capabilities:

- **Bi-directional communication**: It provides bi-directional communication between devices and Azure, such as one-way messaging, file transfer, and request-reply messaging. Devices can send data to Azure IoT Hub, but the IoT Hub can send data to the devices as well. It supports various communication protocols, such as HTTPS, AMQP, and MQTT. It provides built-in declarative message routing to other Azure services.

- **Secure connectivity**: Communication between devices and the IoT Hub can be secured using per-device security keys or X.509 certificates. Azure IoT Hub does not open any connections; only connected devices initiate all the connections. Azure IoT Hub stores the messages inside a per-device queue for 2 days and waits for the device to connect. It uses Azure AD for user authentication and authorization.

- **Scaling**: The IoT Hub offers massive scaling because it can scale up to millions of simultaneously connected devices and millions of events per second.

- **Monitoring**: This offers a monitoring solution in Azure. The IoT Hub is integrated with Azure Monitor, which gives you detailed information about device management operations and connectivity events.

Azure IoT Hub offers the Azure IoT SDK, which consists of device SDKs and can be used to create apps that run on IoT devices and can send data to the IoT Hub. The SDK also offers service SDKs, which can be used to manage the IoT Hub.

Next to the IoT Hub, Azure offers Azure Event Hubs. Azure Event Hubs offers similar capabilities to the Azure IoT Hub, except that the IoT Hub offers more advanced capabilities. If your architecture demands cloud-to-device communication or per-device security and performance management, the IoT Hub is the best solution. The Event Hubs is covered in more detail in the following section:

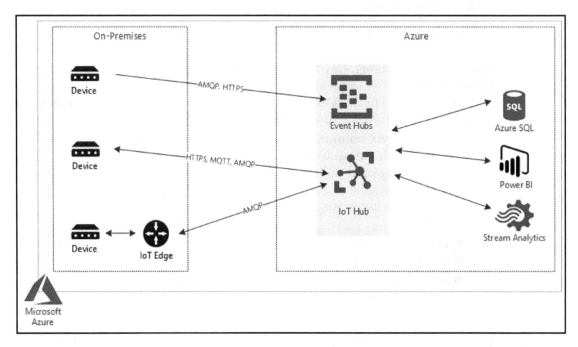

IoT Hub

In the next section, we are going to cover Azure Event Hubs.

Azure Event Hubs

Azure Event Hubs is designed for the high-throughput ingress of data streams generated by devices and services. It provides a telemetry ingestion service that can collect, transform, and store millions of events. It offers similar capabilities to the IoT Hub, but there are differences as well. When to use which solutions depends on the scenario. If your solution demands high-throughput data ingestion only, Azure Event Hubs is a more cost-effective solution than the IoT Hub. However, if your solution requires bi-directional communication, such as communicating from the cloud to your devices, the IoT Hub is a better solution.

To make the correct decision on which solution to use for your IoT architecture, you can look at the following differences:

- **Device protocol support**: Azure Event Hubs supports HTTPS and AMQP, whereas the IoT Hub supports MQTT, MQTT over WebSockets, AMQP, AMQP over WebSockets, and HTTPS. The IoT Hub supports file upload.
- **Communication patterns**: The Event Hubs only supports event ingress where the IoT Hub supports device-to-cloud communications and cloud-to-device communications as well.
- **Security**: The Event Hubs supports Shared Access Policies, where the IoT Hub supports per-device identity and revocable access control.
- **Monitoring**: The IoT Hub offers a complete set of monitoring capabilities, where the Event Hubs only offers aggregate metrics.
- **Scale**: The IoT Hub can scale up to millions of simultaneously connected devices and millions of events per second, whereas the Event Hubs can scale up to 5,000 AMQP connections per namespace.
- **SDKs**: The Event Hubs supports .NET Core, .NET Framework, Java, Python, Node.js, Go, C (send only), and Apache Storm (receive only), whereas the IoT Hub supports .NET, C, Node.js, Java, and Python.

For a complete overview of the differences between the Event Hubs and the IoT Hub, you can refer to `https://docs.microsoft.com/en-us/azure/iot-hub/iot-hub-compare-event-hubs`.

In the next section, we are going to cover Azure Event Grid, by explaining how to route events with Azure Event Grid to an Azure function.

Routing events using Event Grid

In this example, we are going to route events from Event Grid to an Azure function. First, we need to create a new Event Grid Topic in Azure. To create this, follow these steps:

Azure Event Grid is also covered in `Chapter 9`, *Configuring Serverless Computing*.

1. Navigate to the Azure portal by opening `https://portal.azure.com`.
2. Click **Create a resource**, type `Event Grid Topic` in the search bar, and create a new Event Grid Topic.
3. Add the following values:
    1. **Name**: `PacktEventGridTopic`.
    2. **Subscription**: Pick a subscription.
    3. **Resource group:** Create a new one and call it `PacktEventGridResourceGroup`.
    4. **Location**: **East US**.
    5. **Event Schema:** Event Grid Schema.
4. Click **Create**.
5. Next, we are going to create a new Azure function.
6. Click **Create a resource**, type `Function App` in the search bar, and create a new function app.
7. Add the following values:
    1. **Subscription:** Pick a subscription.
    2. **Resource group:** Select `PacktEventGridResourceGroup`.
    3. **Function App Name:** `PacktEventGridFunction`.
    4. **Publish:** Code.
    5. **Runtime Stack:** .NET Core.
    6. **Region: East US**.
8. Click **Review + create** and then **create.**
9. When the function app is created, navigate to the settings and click on the function app:

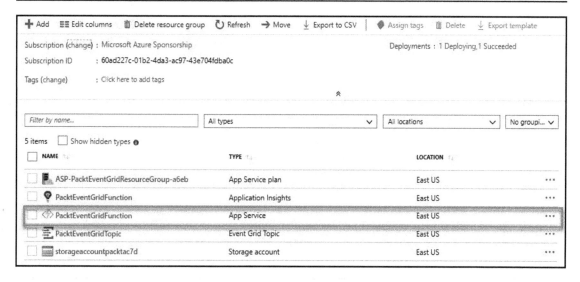

Selecting the Azure function app

10. Click the **+**, on the right-hand side of **Functions**. Then, select **in-portal** to create the function app in the Azure portal:

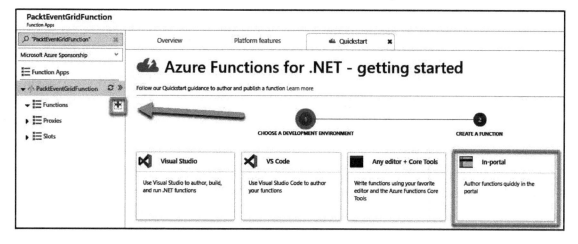

Creating a function in the portal

11. Click **Continue**.

12. Then, click **More templates...** and then **Finish and view templates**. In the next screen of the wizard, scroll down a bit and select **Azure Event Grid trigger**:

Selecting the Azure Event Grid trigger

13. If you get a notification that `Microsoft.Azure.WebJobs.Extensions.EventGrid` is not installed, then install it.

14. Keep the default settings, and then click **Create**:

Creating a new trigger

15. When the trigger is created, the `run.csx` file is opened by default. Click on the **Add Event Grid subscription** link in the top menu:

Selecting Event Grid subscription

16. Add the following values:
    1. **Name:** `PacktEventSubscription`.
    2. **Event Schema**: Event Grid Schema.
    3. **Topic Types**: Event Grid Topics.
    4. **Subscription**: Pick a subscription.
    5. **Resource group**: Select `PackEventGridResourceGroup`.

6. **Resource**: `PacktEventGridTopic`:

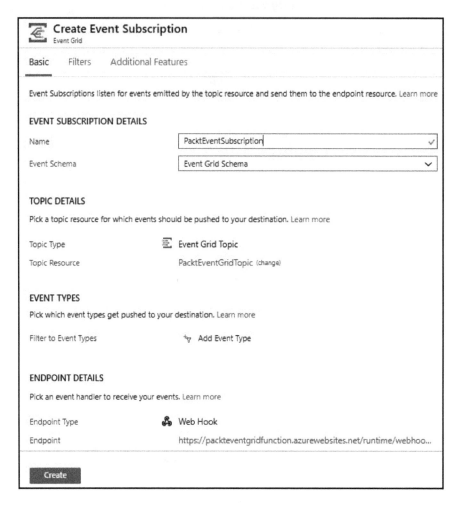

Creating the event subscription

17. Click **Create**. This will create a new event subscription that subscribes to the **Event Grid Topic**.

18. Now, open PowerShell, and run the following commands.

19. First, we need to log in to the Azure account:

```
Connect-AzAccount
```

20. If necessary, select the correct subscription:

```
Select-AzSubscription -SubscriptionId "********-****-****-
****-***********"
```

21. Get a reference to the endpoint and the key:

```
$endpoint = (Get-AzEventGridTopic `
            -ResourceGroupName PacktEventGridResourceGroup `
            -Name PacktEventGridTopic).Endpoint

$keys = Get-AzEventGridTopicKey `
        -ResourceGroupName PacktEventGridResourceGroup `
        -Name PacktEventGridTopic
```

22. Create a random event ID and sort the date and time:

```
$eventID = Get-Random 99999
$eventDate = Get-Date -Format s
```

23. Construct the body using a hash table:

```
$htbody = @{
    id= $eventID
    eventType="recordInserted"
    subject="myapp/packtpub/books"
    eventTime= $eventDate
    data= @{
        title="Microsoft Azure Architect Technologies"
        eventtype="Ebook"
}
dataVersion="1.0"
```

24. Use `ConvertTo-Json` to convert the event body from the hash table to a JSON object. Append square brackets to the converted JSON payload, since they are expected in the event's JSON payload syntax:

```
$body = "["+(ConvertTo-Json $htbody)+"]"
Invoke-WebRequest -Uri $endpoint -Method POST -Body $body -
Headers
@{"aeg-sas-key" = $keys.Key1}
```

25. This will create a custom event. You can now check the Azure Function logs for the result (the Azure Function logs have a delay of 5 minutes).

In this demonstration, we've routed an event from Azure Event Grid to an Azure function. In the next section, we are going to cover how to design an effective messaging architecture.

Designing an effective messaging architecture

Azure offers various features and capabilities in order to design and implement messaging solutions. In order to create successful applications and solution architectures on the Azure platform, an effective messaging architecture is key. This will result in robust solutions and applications that can fully benefit from the scaling capabilities that Azure has to offer. It will also result in high performance for your applications and decoupled applications.

Throughout this book, multiple Azure resources are described and you should know by now what each resource is capable of. In the following section, some of them will be covered again from a messaging and integration perspective. This will give an overview and help you make the right decision when designing your messaging and IoT solutions on the Azure platform:

- **Azure Functions versus Logic Apps**: You can think of logic apps as workflows that are triggered by an event, and Azure Functions as code that is triggered by an event. So, when your solution requires custom code or custom transformations, choose Azure Functions. Use Logic Apps when your solution needs to connect to other SaaS solutions, such as Office 365, Azure Storage, and SalesForce. It offers a huge amount of connectors to connect using HTTPS out of the box. Also, when a graphical editor is required, choose Logic Apps.

- **Azure IoT Hub versus Azure Event Hubs**: Azure IoT Hub offers two-way communication, from devices to Azure and from Azure to devices. It can process millions of events per second and supports multiple device protocols, such as MQTT, MQTT over WebSockets, AMQP, AMQP over WebSockets, HTTPS, and file upload. So, if your solution requires massive event processing and bi-directional communication, choose Azure IoT Hub. Event Hubs only allows one-way communication from devices to Azure. So, when your solution requires only data ingest, Event Hubs can be a more appropriate and cost-effective solution.

- **Azure Functions versus Web Jobs**: Like Azure Functions, Web Jobs with the WebJobs SDK is a code-first integration service. The Web Jobs feature of the app service can be used to run a script or code in the context of an App Service web app. The WebJobs SDK simplifies the code you write to respond to events in Azure services. Azure Functions is built on the WebJobs SDK, so it shares many of the same event triggers and connections to other Azure services. Web Jobs supports C#, Java, JavaScript, Bash, .cmd, .bat, PowerShell, PHP, TypeScript, Python, and more (a WebJob can run any program or script that can run in the App Service sandbox). Functions supports C#, F#, JavaScript, Java, and Python. Also, if you need a serverless app model with automatic scaling, want to develop and test your code in the browser, make use of the pay-per-use pricing, and require integration with Logic Apps, you should choose Functions over Web Jobs.

We have now covered how to design an effective messaging architecture. In the next section, we are going to look at implementing autoscaling rules and patterns.

Implementing autoscaling rules and patterns

Autoscaling offers a solution to match performance requirements and meet SLAs for Azure resources and applications. It can add additional resources, such as adding VMs and CPUs to VMs and other Azure resources, and when those resources are no longer needed, they can be removed to minimize costs.

Autoscaling is one of the key benefits of cloud technologies because you add and remove additional resources easily and even automatically without the need to manage those resources. Autoscaling can be done in the following two different ways:

- **Vertical scaling**: This is also called scaling up and down. You can move applications to a different VM size. By changing the VM size, applications become unavailable for a short period of time, so this type of scaling is normally not executed automatically.
- **Horizontal scaling**: This is also referred to as scaling in and out. You scale horizontally when you add additional resources, such as adding or removing containers to Azure Container Services for instance. This type of scaling is mostly done automatically because it doesn't require resources to become unavailable.

To design an effective autoscaling strategy, you can use the following approaches and services:

- **Monitoring and alerting**: Use the monitoring and alerting capabilities that are available from the different monitoring solutions in Azure. Next to the monitoring solutions, different Azure resources offer autoscaling as well, such as virtual machines, Azure Service Fabric, Azure Functions, Azure App Service, and other cloud services. These resources can be configured from the setting pages in the Azure portal.
- **Decision-making logic**: Make use of decision-making logic that helps to decide whether a resource needs to be scaled. This can be done dynamically inside Azure Logic Apps by calling automation runbooks or by using predefined schedules at times where the system is heavily used.
- **Azure monitoring scale**: This is a service integrated in Azure Monitor that offers autoscaling for VMs, VM scale sets, Azure App Services, and Azure Cloud Services. You can use this to schedule instances, scale-out when a certain CPU usage is met, and when a certain number of messages are added to a queue. Azure Monitor is covered in more detail in the next section.
- **Application architectures**: Architect custom applications accordingly, so that they can be scaled horizontally. This applies to Azure Service Fabric applications, applications that run inside containers, applications that run on Kubernetes clusters, or batch applications. For this, the throttling pattern and the competing consumers pattern can be used. Code that addresses singleton application instances can be used for this as well. Application design considerations are covered in more detail later in this chapter.

In the next section, we are going to cover Azure Monitor autoscaling.

Azure Monitor autoscaling

Azure Monitor offers a set of functionalities for autoscaling. There are features for VM scale sets, Azure Cloud Services, and Azure App Services. You can scale the resources based on a runtime metric, such as CPU or memory usage, or on a schedule.

The following points need to be considered when using autoscale:

- If you use the SDK for autoscaling instead of the Azure portal, you can create your own metrics and use these in your autoscaling rules or specify a more detailed schedule.
- If you can't predict the load on the application accurately enough, it is better to use reactive autoscaling based on runtime metrics, followed by scheduled autoscaling. You can also combine these two approaches.
- Autoscaling rules based on a measured trigger attribute (such as CPU usage or queue length) use an aggregated value over time. This prevents the system from reacting too quickly, and allows time for new instances that are automatically started to settle into running mode.
- When you use autoscale in an App Service environment, any worker pool or frontend metrics can be used to define the autoscale rules.
- When you set up autoscaling for Azure Service Fabric, you need to set up autoscale rules for each node type. The node types in an Azure Service Fabric cluster consist of virtual machine scale sets at the backend. The number of nodes that must be present must be taken in to account before you set up autoscaling. The minimum number of nodes is driven by the reliability level that is chosen.
- Multiple rules and policies may conflict with one another. The following conflict resolution is used by autoscale:
  - Scale-out operations are executed over scale-in operations.
  - When scale-out operations conflict, the rule that initiates the largest increase in the number of instances is executed first.
  - When scale-in operations conflict, the rule that initiates the smallest decrease in the number of instances is executed first.

Autoscaling can be configured in the Azure portal, PowerShell, CLI, and ARM templates, and by using the autoscaling SDK. If you want more detailed control over autoscaling, you can use the Azure resource manager, REST API. For custom applications, you can use the Azure Monitoring Service Management Library, and the Microsoft Insights Library.

In this section, we have covered Azure Monitor autoscaling. In the next section, we are going to look at the different design considerations for applications.

Application design considerations

There is more to designing an autoscaling strategy than only adding resources to a system or running more instances of the system. You should consider the following point when designing an autoscaling strategy from an application perspective:

- If your application or system implements a long-running task, the task needs to be designed for both scaling in and scaling out. Without this, the task can lose data if it is forcibly terminated, or the task can prevent an instance of a process from being shut down. The best approach is to break up the task into smaller pieces, so that it can be picked up by other instances easily.

- The application or system must be designed to scale horizontally. Do not design solutions that require that the code is always running in a specific instance of a process. For web apps, don't assume that all web requests are made to the same instance. Design stateless services whenever possible. You can implement a checkpoint mechanism that records state information at regular intervals. This state can then be saved into durable storage, which can then be accessed from all the instances.

- The length of a queue that is used for communication from the UI with the backend of the application is a good criterion for your autoscaling strategy. This is the best indicator of an imbalance between the current load and the load capacity.

- Autoscaling is not always the best mechanism for handling more requests on the system. It takes some time before it is provisioned and before new instances are started. And the peak moment may have passed by before all the resources are added. In this case, throttling is a better approach.

- Consider limiting the maximum number of instances that can automatically be added in order to prevent that excessive scale. Most autoscaling mechanisms allow you to specify the minimum and a maximum number of instances for a rule.

- Monitor the autoscaling process, and log the details of each autoscaling event (what triggered it, what resources were added or removed, and when this happened).

The following patterns may be relevant for the scenario where you want to implement autoscaling:

- **Pipes and filters pattern**: This pattern describes how you can decompose a task that performs complex processing into a series of separate elements that can be reused. This allows task elements to be deployed and scaled independently.

- **Competing consumers pattern**: This pattern describes how a pool of service instances can be implemented that can handle messages from any application instance.
- **Throttling pattern**: Throttling can be used together with autoscaling to prevent an application or system from being overburdened. This pattern describes how an application can continue to execute and meet SLAs when an increase in demand places an extreme load on the resources.

If you want more information about cloud patterns, you can refer to the following website: `https://docs.microsoft.com/en-us/azure/architecture/patterns/`. The URLs to the preceding patterns can be found in the *Further reading* section at the end of this chapter.

Summary

In this chapter, we've covered the last chapter of this objective and this book. We covered how to configure a message-based integration architecture and how to develop for autoscaling. We covered the different messaging solutions that Azure has to offer, how to design an effective messaging strategy, how to implement different scaling patterns and rules, and more.

With the knowledge gained throughout these chapters, you should be able to pass the AZ-300 exam. Don't forget to look at the *Further reading* sections at the end of each chapter, because there is a lot of extra information there that could be covered in the exam as well.

Questions

Answer the following questions to test your knowledge of the information in this chapter. You can find the answers in the *Assessments* section at the end of this book:

1. You are designing a serverless solution for your organization and need to call an external SDK in your solution for image processing. Is Azure Logic Apps the appropriate solution for this?
    1. Yes
    2. No

2. You are designing a messaging solution for your organization and have a requirement for messages that are approximately 1 MB in size. Should you use Azure Storage Queue?
    1. Yes
    2. No

3. One of the approaches to designing an effective autoscaling strategy is to architect applications accordingly.
    1. Yes
    2. No

Further reading

You can check the following links for more information about the topics that are covered in this chapter:

- **Getting started with Azure Storage Queue using .NET**: `https://docs.microsoft.com/en-us/azure/storage/queues/storage-dotnet-how-to-use-queues`
- **Adding push notifications to your Android app**: `https://docs.microsoft.com/en-us/azure/app-service-mobile/app-service-mobile-android-get-started-push`
- **Adding push notifications to your iOS app**: `https://docs.microsoft.com/en-us/azure/app-service-mobile/app-service-mobile-ios-get-started-push`
- **Autoscaling**: `https://docs.microsoft.com/en-us/azure/architecture/best-practices/auto-scaling`
- **Throttling pattern**: `https://docs.microsoft.com/en-us/azure/architecture/patterns/throttling`
- **Competing Consumers pattern**: `https://docs.microsoft.com/en-us/azure/architecture/patterns/competing-consumers`
- **Pipes and Filters pattern**: `https://docs.microsoft.com/en-us/azure/architecture/patterns/pipes-and-filters`

21
Mock Questions

1. You have an Azure subscription that has eight VMs deployed in it. You need to configure monitoring for this, and want to receive a notification when the **Central Processing Unit** (**CPU**) or available memory reaches a certain threshold value. The notification needs to be sent using an email and needs to create a new issue in the corporate issue tracker. What is the minimum number of action groups and alerts that you need to create to meet these requirements?
   1. Eight alerts and one action group
   2. Two alerts and two action groups
   3. One alert and two action groups
   4. One alert and one action group

2. You have a Windows Server 2016 machine deployed inside an availability set. You need to change the availability set assignment for the VM. What will you do?
   1. Migrate the VM to another Azure region.
   2. Assign the VM to a new availability set.
   3. Redeploy the VM from a recovery point.
   4. Move the VM to a different availability set.

3. You have an Azure Application Gateway deployed that currently load balances all traffic on port 80 to a single backend pool. You now have a requirement to load balance all traffic that includes /Video/* in the path to be forwarded to a different backend pool. What should you do?
   1. Create a new backend pool, and then create a new basic rule and include the /Video/* path and the new backend pool.
   2. Create a new backend pool, and then create a new path-based rule and include the /Video/* path and the new backend pool.

3. Create a new Application Gateway and traffic manager and load balance all requests that contain the `/Video/*` path to the correct target.

4. Add the `/Video/*` path to the default rule.

4. You have an application that uses Azure Service Bus, Azure Functions, and Azure Logic Apps. The Service Bus is deployed on the basic tier. You want to protect the Service Bus namespace from an outage in one data center. What should you do first?

   1. Change the pricing tier to Standard.

   2. Create a Service Bus namespace in another data center.

   3. Pair the namespace with another namespace in a different data center.

   4. Geo-replicate the relay endpoints to another data center.

5. You are developing a workflow solution using Azure technologies. Which solution is the best fit if you want to debug the solution using Visual Studio?

   1. Durable functions only

   2. Logic Apps only

   3. Durable functions and Logic Apps

6. You are developing a workflow solution using Azure technologies. Which solution is the best fit if you want to deploy the solution using Azure DevOps?

   1. Durable functions only

   2. Logic Apps only

   3. Durable functions and Logic Apps

7. You have an Azure subscription that contains 10 VMs. You need to ensure that you receive an email when any VM is powered off, restarted, or deallocated. What is the minimum number of rules and action groups that you need to create?

   1. Three rules and three action groups

   2. One rule and one action groups

   3. Three rules and one action group

   4. One rule and three action groups

8. Your company wants to deploy a storage account. You need to ensure that the data is available in the case of the failure of an entire data center. The solution must be the most cost-effective. What should you do?

   1. Configure geo-redundant storage.

   2. Configure local redundant storage.

   3. Configure read-access geo-redundant storage.

   4. Configure zone-redundant storage.

9. You need to assign a static IPv4 address for a Windows Server VM
named `PacktVM1` running in a VNet named `PacktVNet1`. What should you do?
    1. Modify the IP configuration of the VNet interface associated with
    the `PacktVM1` VM.
    2. Edit the address range of the `PacktVNet1` VNet.
    3. Connect to the `PacktVM1` VM by using WinRM and run the `Set-NetIPAddress` cmdlet.
    4. Connect to the `PacktVM1` VM by using Remote Desktop Protocol and
    edit the VM's virtual network connection properties.

10. You need to add another administrator who will be responsible for managing
all **Infrastructure-as-a-Service (IaaS)** deployments in your Azure subscription.
You create a new account in Azure AD for the user. You need to configure the
user account to meet the following requirements: read and write access to all
Azure IaaS deployments, read-only access to Azure AD, and no access to Azure
subscription metadata. The solution must also minimize your access maintenance
in the future. What should you do?
    1. Assign the owner role at the resource level to the user account.
    2. Assign the global administrator directory role to the user account.
    3. Assign the virtual machine operator role at the subscription level to the
    user account.
    4. Assign the contributor role at the resource group level to the user
    account.

11. Your company wants to enable all user accounts to use SSO to log in to
applications and Office 365. The company has an on-premises AD and uses
smartcard authentication. Which solution do you need to deploy to allow users
to log in without providing a password?
    1. Azure AD Connect with pass-through authentication and SSO
    2. Azure AD Connect with pass hash synchronization and SSO
    3. Azure AD Connect with pass hash synchronization
    4. Active Directory Federation Services

12. You have Azure Site Recovery configured for failover protection for seven on-
premises machines to Azure in case of an accident. You want to ensure that only
10 minutes of data is lost when an outage occurs. Which PowerShell cmdlet
should you use for this?
    1. `Edit-AzureRmSiteRecoveryRecoveryPlan`
    2. `Get-AzureRmSiteRecoveryPolicy`

3. `Get-AzureRmSiteRecoveryRecoveryPlan`
4. `Update-AzureRmSiteRecoveryPolicy`

13. Your organization has Azure resources deployed in the West US, West Europe, and East Australia regions. The company has four offices located in these regions. You need to provide connectivity between all the on-premises networks and all the resources in Azure using a private channel. You configure a VPN gateway for each Azure region and configure a site-to-site VPN for each office and connect to the nearest VPN gateway. You then configure virtual network peering. You need to ensure that users have the lowest traffic latency. Does this solution meet your goal?
    1. Yes
    2. No

14. Your company has an Azure AD tenant and an on-premises AD that are synced using Azure AD Connect. The security department notices a high number of logins from various public IP addresses. What should you do to reduce these logins?
    1. Enable Azure AD smart lockout.
    2. Add all the public IP addresses to conditional access and use location blocking to deny all login attempts.
    3. Create a conditional access rule to require MFA for all risky logins labeled medium risk and above.
    4. Turn on Azure MFA fraud alerts.

15. You have an Azure App Service API that allows users to upload documents to the cloud with a mobile device. A mobile app connects to the service by using REST API calls. When a document is uploaded to the service, the service extracts the document metadata. Usage statistics for the app show a significant increase in app usage. The extraction process is very CPU-intensive. You plan to modify the API to use a queue. You need to ensure that the solution scales, handles request spikes, and reduces costs between the spikes. What should you do?
    1. Configure a CPU-optimized VM and install the Web App service on the new instance.
    2. Configure a series of CPU-optimized VMs and install the extraction logic for the app to process a queue.
    3. Move the extraction logic to an Azure function. Create a queue-triggered function to process the queue.
    4. Configure Azure Container Instances to retrieve the items from the queue and run the extraction logic across a pool of VM nodes.

16. You want to create a group of resource group managers in the Azure portal. Which RBAC role do you need to assign to them to manage all the resource groups in the Azure subscription?
    1. Contributor
    2. Reader
    3. Owner
    4. Monitoring reader

17. Your company has an application that requires data from a blob storage to be moved from the hot access tier to the archive access tier to reduce costs. Which type of storage account do you need to create?
    1. General Purpose V2 storage account
    2. General Purpose V1 storage account
    3. Azure File storage
    4. Azure Blob storage

18. You are planning data security for your Azure resources. The confidentially of code on your VMs must be protected while the code is being processed. Which feature should you use for this?
    1. Azure Batch
    2. Azure Confidential Compute
    3. Azure Container Instances
    4. Azure Disk Encryption

19. You have two Azure resource groups, named `ResourceGroup1` and `ResourceGroup2`. The `ResourceGroup1` resource group contains 20 Windows Server VMs and all the VMs are connected to an Azure Log Analytics workspace named `Workspace1`. You need to write a log search query that collects all security events with the following properties: all security levels other than 8 and with the Event ID 4672. How should you write your query?
    1. `SecurityEvent | where Level == 8 | and EventID == 4672`
    2. `SecurityEvent | where Level <> 8 | where EventID == 4672`
    3. `SecurityEvent | where Level == 8 | summarize EventID == 4672`
    4. `SecurityEvent | where Level <> 8 | and EventID == 4672`

20. You are using an Azure Logic App to integrate SharePoint Online, Dynamics, and an on-premises Oracle database. You are informed that the Logic App access key has been compromised. What should you do?

    1. Delete the Logic App and redeploy it.

    2. Only allow internal IP addresses to access the Logic App.

    3. Add a resource lock.

    4. Regenerate the access key.

21. You have two subscriptions named subscription 1 and subscription 2. Each subscription is associated with a different Azure AD tenant. Subscription 1 contains a virtual network named VNet 1. VNet 1 contains an Azure VM named VM1 and has an IP address space of `10.0.0.0/16`. Subscription 2 contains a virtual network named VNet 2. VNet 2 contains an Azure VM named VM2 and has an IP address space of `10.0.0.0/24`. You need to connect VNet1 to VNet 2. What should you do first?

    1. Move VM2 to subscription 1.

    2. Provision virtual network gateways.

    3. Move VNet 1 to subscription 2.

    4. Modify the IP address range of VNet 2.

22. Your company has a VM that is stored inside a resource group. You need to deploy additional VMs in the same resource group. You are planning to deploy them using an ARM template. You need to create a template from the original VM using PowerShell. Which cmdlet should you use?

    1. Use the `Export-AzResourceGroup`

    2. Use the `Get-AzResourceGroupDeployment`

    3. Use the `Get-AzResourceGroupDeploymentOperation`

    4. Use the `Get-AzResourceGroupDeploymentTemplate`

23. You are developing an app that references data that is shared across multiple Azure SQL databases. The app must guarantee transactional consistency for changes across several sharding key values. You need to manage the transactions. What should you implement?

    1. Elastic database transactions with horizontal partitioning

    2. Distributed transactions coordinated by **Microsoft Distributed Transaction Coordinator (MSDTC)**

    3. Server-coordinated transactions from a .NET application

    4. Elastic database transactions with vertical partitioning

24. You create a VM called VM1 with a Premium SSD operating system disk. You enable Azure Disk Encryption for the VM and then you add a Premium SSD data disk. Is the data disk automatically encrypted?
    1. Yes
    2. No

25. Your company has an application that uses an Azure SQL Database to store information. The company has also deployed System Center Service Manager. You need to configure an alert when the database reaches 80% of CPU usage. When this alert rises, you want your administrator to be notified using email and SMS. You also need to create a ticket in the corporate issue tracker automatically when the alert arises. Which two actions should you perform?
    1. Configure System Center Service Manager with Azure Automation.
    2. Configure one action group with three actions: one for email, one for SMS, and one for creating the ticket.
    3. Configure an IT Service Management Connector.
    4. Configure two actions groups: one for email and SMS, and one for creating the ticket.

26. A VM named `PacktVM1` is deployed in a resource group named `PacktResourceGroup1`. The VM is connected to a VNet named `PacktVNet1`. You plan to connect the `PacktVM1` VM to an additional VNet named `PacktVNet2`. You need to create an additional **network interface** on the `PacktVM1` VM and connect it to the `PacktVNet2` VNet. Which two Azure **Command-line Interface** (CLI) commands should you use?
    1. `az vm nic add`
    2. `am vm nic create`
    3. `az network update`
    4. `az network nic create`

27. You need to grant access to an external consultant to some resources inside your Azure subscription. You plan to add this external user using PowerShell. Which cmdlet should you use?
    1. New-AzADUser
    2. New-AzureADMSInvitation
    3. Get-AzADUser
    4. Get-AzureADMSInvitation

28. You are planning to migrate your on-premises environment to Azure using Azure Site Recovery. You have already created a storage account, a virtual network, a Recovery Services vault, and a resource group in the Azure portal. You now need to grant the cloud engineer the requisite privileges to perform the migration. Which two built-in roles should you use, using the principle of least privilege?

    1. Site Recovery Contributor
    2. Network Contributor
    3. Reader
    4. Virtual Machine Contributor

29. You use Azure AD Connect to synchronize all AD domain users and groups with Azure AD. As a result, all users can use **Single Sign-on** (**SSO**) to access applications. You should reconfigure the directory synchronization to exclude domain services accounts and user accounts that shouldn't have access to the application. What should you do?

    1. Rerun Azure AD Connect.
    2. Stop the synchronization service.
    3. Remove the domain services and user accounts manually.
    4. Configure conditional access rules in Azure AD.

30. You configure Azure Application Gateway to host multiple websites on a single instance of the Application Gateway. You create two backend server pools, named `PacktPool1` and `PackPool2`. Requests for `http://Packt1.info` should be routed to `PacktPool1`, and requests for `http://Packt2.info` should be routed to `PacktPool2`. Users only see the content of `PacktPool2`, regardless of the URL they use. You need to identify which component is configured incorrectly. What should you check?

    1. CName resource record
    2. Backend port settings
    3. Routing rule
    4. SSL certificate

31. Your company is developing a .NET application that stores information in an Azure storage account. You need to ensure that the information is stored in a secure way. You ask the developers to use a **shared access signature** (**SAS**) when accessing the information. You need to make the required configurations on the storage account to follow security best practices. Which statement is true?

    1. You need to configure a stored access policy.
    2. To revoke an SAS, you can delete the stored access policy.
    3. You should set the SAS start time to now.

32. You have an application running on an Azure VM. Your on-premises network connects to the Azure Virtual Network using an Azure VPN Gateway. The application cannot be exposed directly to the internet due to security requirements. Users of the marketing department should be able to access the application when they are traveling and are using their company laptop. Which kind of connection should you configure?
    1. ExpressRoute
    2. Point-to-site
    3. Site-to-site
    4. VNet-to-VNet

33. You are asked to create a new set of Azure **Active Directory (AD)** security groups that represent the entire hierarchy of a manager's team. This includes people who are managed by the manager. You need to implement the request using the least amount of administrative effort. What should you do?
    1. Create new groups using the Direct Reports rule.
    2. Create new Azure AD groups for each manager and use a custom script to detect the `ManagerID` attribute changes and modify the group membership when needed.
    3. Create dynamic groups and Azure AD using a ruleset, including the `ManagerID` attribute.
    4. Create multiple Azure AD groups and add the members with the same `ManagerID` attribute value to each group.

34. Your company has an Azure AD tenant and an on-premises AD that are synced using Azure AD Connect. You have one subscription called `Packt_Main`. The helpdesk administrators are members of the `Packt_HD` group. You need to grant the helpdesk group the permissions to reset user passwords using the Azure portal, while using the least amount of permissions. What should you do?
    1. Grant the `Packt_HD` group the password administrator role in Azure administrator.
    2. Delegate password reset privileges to the `Packt_HD` group on the user's **Organizational Unit (OU)** in Azure Directory users and computers.
    3. Add the `Packt_HD` group to the domain admins user group.
    4. Grant the `Packt_HD` group the ownership role on the `Packt_Main` subscription.

35. You need to use an Azure logic app to receive a notification when an administrator modifies the settings of a virtual machine in a resource group, `ResourceGroup1`. Which three components should you create next in the Logic Apps Designer? Pick the three components and set them in the correct order.
    1. An action
    2. An Azure Event Grid trigger
    3. A condition control
    4. A variable

36. Your company has an Azure AD tenant and an on-premises AD that are synced using Azure AD Connect. Your on-premises environment is running a mix of Windows Server 2012 and Windows Server 2016 servers. You use Azure MFA for multi-factor authentication. Users report that they are required to use MFA while using company devices. You need to turn MFA off for domain-joined devices. What should you do?
    1. Enable SSO on Azure AD Connect.
    2. Create a conditional access rule to allow users to use either MFA or a domain-joined device when accessing applications.
    3. Configure Windows Hello for Business on all domain-joined devices.
    4. Add the company external IP address to the Azure MFA Trusted IPs list.

37. You maintain an existing Azure SQL Database instance. Management of the database is performed by an external party. All cryptographic keys are stored in Azure Key Vault. You must ensure that the external party cannot access the data in the SSN column of the Person table. What should you do?
    1. Enable AlwayOn encryption.
    2. Set the column encryption setting to disabled.
    3. Assign users to the public fixed database role.
    4. Store the column encryption keys in the system catalog view in the database.

38. You have an Azure resource group named `PacktResourceGroup1` that contains a Linux VM named `PacktVM1`. You need to automate the deployment of 30 additional Linux machines. The VMs should be based on the configuration of the `PacktVM1` VM. Which of the following solutions will meet the goal?
    1. From the VM Automation's script blade, you click **Deploy**.
    2. From the **Templates** blade, you click **Add.**
    3. From the resource group's policy blade, you click **Assign policy.**

39. You have an Azure subscription that contains two different VNets. You want the VNets to communicate through the Azure backbone. Which solution should you choose?
    1. VNet peering
    2. Site-to-site VPN
    3. Point-to-site VPN
    4. Azure Expressroute

40. You are using Azure Application Gateway to manage traffic for your corporate website. The Application Gateway uses the standard tier with an instance size of medium. You are asked to implement WAF to guard the website against SQL injection attacks and other vulnerabilities. To configure WAF, which two actions should you perform?
    1. Enable WAF in detection mode.
    2. Change the Azure Application Gateway to an instance size of large.
    3. Enable WAF in prevention mode.
    4. Change the Azure Application Gateway tier.

41. Your company has two **Virtual Networks** (**VNets**) deployed, VNet1 and VNet2. You need to connect both VNets together. What is the most cost-effective solution?
    1. VNet-to-VNet
    2. Site-to-site
    3. User-defined routes
    4. VNet peering

42. You have VMs deployed inside a Hyper-V infrastructure and you are planning to move those VMs to Azure using Azure Site Recovery. You have the following types of machines. Can all these types of machines be moved using Azure Site Recovery?:
    - Windows VMs Generation 2
    - Linux VMs Generation 2
    - Windows VMs with BitLocker installed on it

43. You have a web app named `PacktApp`. You are developing a triggered App Service background task using the WebJobs SDK. This task will automatically invoke a function in code whenever any new data is received in the queue. Which service should you use when you want to manage all code segments from the same Azure DevOps environment?
    1. Logic Apps
    2. A custom web app

3. Web Jobs
4. Functions

44. You are managing the network of your organization. The on-premises infrastructure consists of multiple subnets. A new branch office was recently added. The network devices in the new office are assigned to a `192.168.22.0/24` subnet. You need to configure the Azure VPN Gateway to make sure that all the network devices in the branch office are accessible from the Azure network as well. Which PowerShell cmdlet should you use?
    1. `Add-AzureRmVirtualNetworkSubnetConfig`
    2. `Set-AzureRmLocalNetworkGateway`
    3. `Set-AzureRmNetworkInterface`
    4. `Add-AzureRmNetworkInterfaceIpConfig`

45. You are developing a workflow solution using Azure technologies. Which solution is the best fit if you want to use a collection of ready-made actions?
    1. Durable functions only
    2. Logic Apps only
    3. Durable functions and Logic Apps

46. You are asked to configure a solution that allows users to log into Office 365 applications without providing their passwords. Your company also wants to deploy cloud-based, two-factor authentication for some user profiles. What should you do?
    1. Enable password hash synchronization.
    2. Enable pass-through authentication.
    3. Install Azure AD Connect.
    4. Enable Azure Multi-Factor authentication.

47. You are creating a new Azure Function app to run a serverless C# application. This function has an execution duration of one second and a memory consumption of 256 MB, and executes up to 1 million times during the month. Which plan should you use?
    1. Linux App Service plan
    2. Windows Consumption plan
    3. Windows App Service plan
    4. Kubernetes App Service plan

48. You need to delegate some of the global administrator privileges to a new cloud engineer in your office. You decide to create a custom role using a JSON file and the following PowerShell cmdlet to add the custom role: `New-AzureRmRoleDefinition -InputFile "C:\ARM_templates/customrole.json"`. Is this correct?

    1. Yes
    2. No

49. You deploy **Multi-Factor Authentication** (**MFA**) in your Azure AD tenant. You don't want your users to be required to enter any additional passwords or code in the browser when using MFA. Which two methods should you make available?

    1. Call to phone
    2. Text message to phone
    3. Notification through the mobile app
    4. Verification code from hardware token

50. You plan to create a Docker image that runs on an ASP.NET Core application named `PacktApp`. You have a setup script named `setupScrip.ps1` and a series of application files including `PacktApp`. You need to create a Dockerfile document that calls the setup script when the container is built and runs the app when the container starts. The Dockerfile must be created in the same folder where `PacktApp.dll` and `setupScrip.ps1` are stored. In which order do the following four commands need to be executed?

    1. `Copy ./.`
    2. `WORKDIR /apps/PacktApp`
    3. `FROM microsoft/aspnetcore:2.0`
    4. `RUN powershell ./setupScript.ps1 CMD ["dotnet", "PacktApp.dll"]`

51. You have a web app named PacktApp. You are developing a triggered App Service background task using the WebJobs SDK. This task will automatically invoke a function in code whenever any new data is received in the queue. Which service should you use to process a queue data item?

    1. Logic Apps
    2. A custom web app
    3. Web Jobs
    4. Functions

52. You are migrating an existing on-premises, third-party website to Azure. The website is stateless. You don't have access to the source code of the website and you don't have the original installer. The number of visitors to the website varies throughout the year. The on-premises infrastructure was resized to accommodate peaks, but the extra capacity was not used. You need to implement a VM scale set instance. What should you do?

   1. Use an autoscale setting to scale instances vertically.
   2. Create 100 autoscale settings per resource.
   3. Use an autoscale setting with an unlimited maximum number of instances.
   4. Use Azure Monitor to create autoscale settings using custom metrics.

53. You have two Azure Active Directory tenants. You have a Microsoft account that can be used to sign into both accounts. You need to configure the default sign-in tenant for the Azure portal. What should you do?

   1. From Azure Cloud Shell, run `Set-AzContext`.
   2. From Azure Cloud Shell, run `Set-AzSubscription`.
   3. From the Azure portal, change the directory.
   4. From the Azure portal, configure the portal settings.

22
Mock Answers

1. **4**—You should create one alert and one action group for this. One alert can contain multiple metrics-based conditions and a single action group can contain more than one notification or remediation step, so you can create the metrics for both the CPU and memory in one alert. You can use one action group for sending out the email and creating an issue in the corporate issue tracker.

2. **3**—You should redeploy the VM from a recovery point. VMs can only be assigned to an availability set during initial deployment.

3. **2**—You should create a path-based rule for this.

4. **2**—You should create a new service bus namespace in another data center first before you replicate the endpoints and pair the namespace with another namespace in a different data center.

5. **1**—You should use durable functions only.

6. **1**—You should use durable functions only.

7. **3**—Three rules and one action group is the minimum here.

8. **4**—You should configure a storage account with **zone-redundant storage (ZRS)** replication. This makes a synchronous copy of the data between three different zones in the same region.

9. **1**—You should modify the IP configuration of the virtual network interface associated with `PacktVM1`.

10. **4**—You should assign the Contributor role at the resource group level to the user account. This provides the user with full read/write access at the resource group level, but doesn't grant the user any permissions in the subscription or Azure AD levels.

11. **4**—You should deploy ADFS. Using this solution, users can log in using SSO and use smartcard authentication. Smartcard authentication is not supported for Azure AD Connect.

12. **4**—You should use the `Update-AzureRmSiteRecoveryPolicy` cmdlet. This has the recovery points method in it, which you can set to specify the maximum amount of time that data will be lost for.

13. **1**—Yes: because you configure a VPN gateway for each region, this solution meets the goals. This will result in the lowest traffic latency for your users.

14. **3**—You should create a conditional access rule to require MFA authentication for all risky logins labeled medium-risk and above. Azure AD can apply risk levels to all sign-in attempts using a selection of parameters. You can use conditional access to enforce sign-in requirements based on those levels.

15. **3**—You should move the extraction logic to an Azure function. This is the most scalable and cost-effective solution.

16. **3**—You should assign the Owner role to the group of resource group managers.

17. **1**—You need to configure a general-purpose V2 storage account to move data between different access tiers.

18. **3**—You should use Azure Confidential Compute for this requirement.

19. **2**—The right query should be `SecurityEvent | where Level <> 8 | where EventID == 4672`.

20. **4**—You should regenerate the access key. This will automatically make the old access key invalid.

21. **2**—You need virtual network gateways to connect VNets that are associated with different Azure AD instances.

22. **1**—You should use the `Export-AzResourceGroup` cmdlet. This captures the specified resource group as a template and saves it to a JSON file.

23. **1**—You should implement Elastic database transactions with horizontal partitioning.

24. **1**—The data disk is automatically encrypted using the Premium disks.

25. **2 and 3**—You need to create one action group and you need to configure the **IT Service Management Connector (ITSMC)**. This connector connects the System Center Service Manager with Azure.

26. **1 and 4**—You should use `az vm nic add` to create a new NIC. Then you should use `az network nic create` to attach the NIC to `PacktVM1`.

27. **2**—You should use the `New-AzureADMSInvitation` cmdlet to add an external user to your Azure AD tenant using PowerShell.

28. **1** and **4**—You need to grant the cloud engineer the Virtual Machine Contributor role to enable the replication of a new VM. You do this by creating a new VM inside the Azure portal. You should also grant the Site Recovery Contributor role to the engineer. This way, the engineer has permission to manage the site recovery vault without permission to create new vaults or assign permissions to other users.

29. **1**—You should rerun Azure AD Connect. This will perform OU filtering and refresh the directory schema.

30. **2**—You should check the routing rule; backend port settings is configured incorrectly.

31. **1**—True: you need to configure a stored access policy. **2**—True: to revoke an SAS, you can delete the stored access policy. **3**—False: when you set the timer to now, there can be differences in the clock of the servers hosting your storage account. This can lead to access problems for a short period of time.

32. **2**—You should configure an Azure VPN gateway to accept point-to-site VPN connections from users' laptops.

33. **1**—You should create new groups using the Direct Reports rule. This will create a dynamic group that includes all members who have the same `ManagerID` attribute. This will also handle updates to the group accordingly.

34. **1**—You should grant the `Packt_HD` group the Password Administrator role in Azure AD. This role grants the right to reset nonadmin passwords, which are the minimal permissions that are required.

35. **2**, **3** and **1**—You should set them in the following order:
    1. An Azure Event Grid trigger
    2. A condition control
    3. An action

36. **2**—You should create a conditional access rule to allow users to use either MFA or a domain-joined device when accessing applications. The rule will not force MFA when using a domain-joined device.

37. **3**—You should enable AlwaysOn encryption.

38. **1** and **2**—You can deploy the ARM template of the virtual machine from the virtual machine's **Automation script** blade and you can deploy the template from the **Templates** blade in the Azure portal.

39. **1**—VNet peering is the only solution that makes it possible to communicate directly through the Azure backbone.

40. **3** and **4**—You should enable WAF in prevention mode and change the application gateway tier. The Standard tier doesn't support the ability to configure WAF. Prevention mode actively blocks SQL-injection attacks.

41. **4**—VNet peering is the most cost-effective solution for connecting different VNets.

42. **2**—No: you can only use Azure Site Recovery for the Windows VMs Generation 2 machines that you have installed inside your Hyper-V environment. The rest are not supported.

43. **3**—You should use Web Jobs to manage all the code segments from the same DevOps environment.

44. **2**—You should use the `Set-AzureRmLocalNetworkGateway` cmdlet. You need to reconfigure the local network gateway for this.

45. **2**—You should use Logic Apps only.

46. **2**—You should enable pass-through authentication. This enables SSO for users and allows the company to implement two-factor authentication using Azure MFA.

47. **2**—You should use the Windows Consumption plan. This plan supports per-second resource consumption and execution.

48. **1**—Yes: this is the right way to create a custom role using PowerShell.

49. **1** and **3**—Both calls to a phone and notification via mobile apps don't require the user to enter a code in a browser.

50. **3, 2, 1**, and **4**—The script should look like the following:
    1. `FROM microsoft/aspnetcore:2.0`
    2. `WORKDIR /apps/PacktApp`
    3. `Copy ./.`
    4. `RUN powershell ./setupScript.ps1 CMD ["dotnet", "PacktApp.dll"]`

51. **3**—You should use Web Jobs to process the queue item.

52. **4**—You should use an autoscale setting with an unlimited maximum number of instances.

53. **3**—You should change the directory from the Azure portal.

Assessments

Chapter 1: Analyzing Resource Utilization and Consumption

1. Yes—Log Analytics is integrated in Azure Monitor. However, the data is still stored inside the Log Analytics Workspace.
2. No—you can't use SQL. You need to use the Kusto Query Language to query the data.
3. No—Action Groups are unique sets of recipients and actions that can be shared across multiple alert rules.

Chapter 2: Creating and Configuring Storage Accounts

1. No—you can also download the Azure Storage Explorer for Linux and macOS.
2. No—you can also configure storage accounts to be accessed from on-premises networks as well.
3. No—you can change the replication type of your storage account later as well, from the Azure portal, PowerShell, or CLI.

Chapter 3: Implementing and Managing Virtual Machines

1. Yes—you use VM Scale Sets to automate the deployment of multiple VMs.
2. Yes—by using Availability Sets, you can spread VMs across different fault and update domains.
3. Yes—you use resource providers to deploy different artifacts in Azure using ARM templates.

Chapter 4: Implementing and Managing Virtual Networking

1. No—there is a maximum of 60 dynamic public IP addresses and 20 static public IP addresses per subscription.
2. Yes—by defining user-defined routes, you can adjust the routing between the different resources in your VNet, according to your needs.
3. No—you can only assign IPv6 addresses to external load balancers.

Chapter 5: Creating Connectivity between Virtual Networks

1. No—VNet peering uses the backbone infrastructure of Azure; there is no need to create gateways.
2. No—VNet-to-VNet uses a virtual network gateway, which is set up with a public IP address.
3. Yes—VNet peering doesn't use a virtual network gateway, so it doesn't have any bandwidth limitations. Those limitations typically belong to the gateway.

Chapter 6: Managing Azure Active Directory (Azure AD)

1. Yes—you need to use `New-AzureADMSInvitation` to add a guest user to your Azure AD tenant.
2. No—Azure AD Join can be used without connecting an on-premises Active Directory to Azure AD.
3. Yes—when you add a custom domain to Azure AD, you need to verify it by adding a TXT record to the DNS settings of your domain registrar. After adding this record, you can verify the domain in the Azure portal.

Chapter 7: Implementing and Managing Hybrid Identities

1. No—password hash synchronization is enabled by default if you use the Express settings during the Azure AD Connect installation.
2. No—password sync needs to be enabled on the on-premises domain controller and in the Azure portal.
3. No—you can install Azure AD Connect when the on-premises forest name doesn't match one of the Azure AD custom domain names, but you will receive a warning during installation that SSO is not enabled for your users.

Chapter 8: Migrating Servers to Azure

1. Yes—Azure Migrate can be used for migrating web applications using the Web Application Migration Assistant.
2. Yes—the Azure Migrate Assessment tools are capable of visualizing server dependencies.
3. No—you can also use Azure Migrate to migrate physical machines.

Chapter 9: Configuring Serverless Computing

1. No—for executing small tasks, such as image processing, Azure Functions is the most suitable option.
2. No—the alias is created automatically when you pair the primary and the secondary namespaces.
3. Yes—you can access on-premises data from your Logic App using the on-premises data gateway.

Chapter 10: Implementing Application Load Balancing

1. Yes—the Azure Application Gateway can be used as a load balancer as well as a **web application firewall (WAF)**.

2. Yes—you can route traffic based on specific URLs using Azure Application Gateway. This is called URL-based routing.

3. No—frontend IP configurations are mandatory for the Azure Application Gateway to function properly. This is the incoming URL from where the traffic is routed according to the specified rules.

Chapter 11: Integrating On-Premises Networks with Azure Virtual Networks

1. No—traffic over an ExpressRoute circuit is not encrypted by default. However, you can create a solution that encrypts the traffic that goes over the ExpressRoute circuit.

2. Yes—a point-to-site VPN connection is designed to create a secure connection between an individual client and your virtual network over the internet. This connection type is most suitable for employees who work from other locations.

3. Yes—it is not allowed to host the server behind a NAT.

Chapter 12: Managing Role-Based Access Control (RBAC)

1. No—to assign permissions to users, you need to use role-based access control.

2. Yes—you can use the Azure policy to check whether all of the virtual machines inside your Azure subscription use managed disks.

3. No—custom policies are created in JSON.

Chapter 13: Implementing Multi-Factor Authentication (MFA)

1. Yes—trusted IP addresses are meant for bypassing **multi-factor authentication (MFA)** for certain IPs. This way, you can disable MFA for users who log in from the company intranet, for instance.
2. No—you can use conditional access policies to enable MFA for users and applications.
3. Yes—fraud alerts can only be enabled for MFA Server deployments.

Chapter 14: Creating Web Apps by Using PaaS

1. No—developers don't have to add additional code to log information to the different web server logs. This only needs to be done for application logs.
2. No—WebJobs are not yet supported on Linux.
3. No—you can also pull containers from a private Azure container registry.

Chapter 15: Designing and Developing Apps That Run in Containers

1. No—Azure Kubernetes Service allows you to have more control over the containers than Azure Container Instances.
2. No—you can view them from the Azure portal.
3. Yes—Docker files can be created directly in Visual Studio.

Chapter 16: Implementing Authentication

1. No—you can set this directly from App Services.
2. No—you can attach all kinds of SSL certificates to Azure App Services, regardless of where they come from.
3. No—system-assigned managed identities can only be assigned to the scope of the Azure resource where they are created.

Chapter 17: Implementing Secure Data Solutions

1. No—Always Encrypted is a feature of Azure SQL Database and SQL Server, which encrypts data that is stored in a database table.
2. Yes—you can use the Key Vault API to create a self-signed certificate.
3. No—all Azure storage services support server-side encryption at rest. This also includes Queue Storage.

Chapter 18: Developing Solutions That Use Cosmos DB Storage

1. No—you can also use the APIs to create a database and container in Cosmos DB.
2. No—Azure Cosmos DB offers five different consistency models: strong, bounded staleness, session, consistent prefix, and eventual consistency.
3. Yes—horizontal partitioning is used to distribute the data over different Azure Cosmos DB instances.

Chapter 19: Developing Solutions That Use a Relational Database

1. No—an Elastic pool can also be configured for databases that already exist.
2. Yes—Azure SQL Database Managed Instances are based on the last stable SQL Server on-premises database engine.
3. Yes—failover groups automatically manage the geo-replication relationship between the databases, the failover at scale, and the connectivity.

Chapter 20: Message-Based Integration Architecture and Autoscaling

1. No—Azure Logic Apps doesn't provide a solution for calling external SDKs. Azure Functions does, so this is the best solution.
2. No—Azure Queue Storage can only handle messages with sizes of up to 64 KB. You should use Azure Service Bus queues for this.
3. Yes—one of the approaches to designing an effective autoscaling strategy is to architect applications accordingly.

Another Book You May Enjoy

If you enjoyed this book, you may be interested in this other book by Packt:

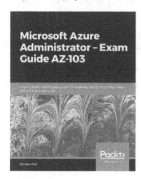

Microsoft Azure Administrator – Exam Guide AZ-103
Sjoukje Zaal

ISBN: 978-1-83882-902-5

- Configure Azure subscription policies and manage resource groups
- Monitor activity log by using Log Analytics
- Modify and deploy Azure Resource Manager (ARM) templates
- Protect your data with Azure Site Recovery
- Learn how to manage identities in Azure
- Monitor and troubleshoot virtual network connectivity
- Manage Azure Active Directory Connect, password sync, and password writeback

Leave a review - let other readers know what you think

Please share your thoughts on this book with others by leaving a review on the site that you bought it from. If you purchased the book from Amazon, please leave us an honest review on this book's Amazon page. This is vital so that other potential readers can see and use your unbiased opinion to make purchasing decisions, we can understand what our customers think about our products, and our authors can see your feedback on the title that they have worked with Packt to create. It will only take a few minutes of your time, but is valuable to other potential customers, our authors, and Packt. Thank you!

Index

www.ingramcontent.com/pod-product-compliance
Lightning Source LLC
Chambersburg PA
CBHW060639060326
40690CB00020B/4447